THE FIFTH
RECORD

THE FIFTH RECORD

Understanding the Last Jewish Exodus

LEO PEVSNER

The Fifth Record
Copyright © 2019 by Leo Pevsner. All rights reserved.

No part of this publication may be reproduced, stored in a retrieval system or transmitted in any way by any means, electronic, mechanical, photocopy, recording or otherwise without the prior permission of the author except as provided by USA copyright law.

The opinions expressed by the author are not necessarily those of URLink Print and Media.

1603 Capitol Ave., Suite 310 Cheyenne, Wyoming USA 82001
1-888-980-6523 | admin@urlinkpublishing.com

URLink Print and Media is committed to excellence in the publishing industry.

Book design copyright © 2019 by URLink Print and Media. All rights reserved.

Published in the United States of America

ISBN 978-1-64367-687-6 (Paperback)
ISBN 978-1-64367-686-9 (Digital)

31.07.19

Contents

Foreword 7
Introduction 11

1. **THE UNCOMMON CIVILIZATION** 17
2. **TRIBAL HISTORY** 41
   Starodub's Pale Of Settlement and Pogroms..........41
   Catastrophe 51
   The American Kinfolk..55
   Generation Of "Rootless Cosmopolitans"............63
   Generations X and Millenials 75
3. **IN THE LAND OF EXODUS**............................84
   Same But Different 86
   Russian Arguments Of The Past Century 99
   Beyond The Iron Curtain 116
   Portraits Of The Real Socialism 126
   Perestroikas 146
   Post-Soviet Russia In Search Of The
   National Idea 167
4. **THE FIFTH RECORD AND THE
   COMMON ANTI-SEMITISM** 175
   The State's Anti-Semitism 176
   The Grassroots' Anti-Semitism 188
5. **EXODUS OF THE 20TH CENTURY** 202
6. **IN THE LAND OF OPPORTUNITY** 216
   Jews and America 216
   The Ideal Immigrant 228

  Soviet Brighton Beach 240
  Challenges Of The New American 248
  September 11, 2001, New York.........................263
  Former Russians, Not Yet Americans..................267
  The Country I Do Not Want To Lose 278

7. JEWISH IDENTITY AND LOYALTY 290
  Identity Crisis..291
  Jewish Loyalty 305

In Place of the Epilogue..315

Foreword

The mandatory *fifth record* in a passport was pure Soviet invention to disclose if a citizen is of the "right" or "wrong" nationality. Jews suffered the most from this revelation. That was like the yellow Star of David that Jews had to expose on their suits in Nazi Germany in 1930s-1940s. The oppressions and discriminations of Jews under the communist dominance were comprehensive but not new - it took place in the ancient and medieval worlds as well as in the contemporary times. Therefore, the concept of Exodus is essential in Jewish history. Hundreds of thousands of modern-day Jews emigrated in 1970s – 1990s from Russia and other former Soviet republics and now live in Israel, United States, and elsewhere. By 2000, almost three quarters of former Soviet Jews dispersed throughout the world as ancient Jews did many centuries ago.

Exodus has always been the last resort in these people's history. Assyrian and Babylonian exiles in eighth – seventh centuries B.C., fleeing from Judea, dissipation of Jews in the first centuries A.D. with Roman conquest and Judean War, their expulsion from many countries of the medieval Europe, ending up with massive immigration waves at the end of nineteenth – beginning of twentieth centuries and finally, Jewish repatriation to Israel and immigration to other countries at the end of the twentieth century. Have any other people such a long history of exile and migration? During European enlightenment, the figure of a wandering Jew was associated initially with negative image and then with the struggle for Jewish emancipation in Europe. In the modern world, the Jewish communities emancipated but still hated by many. Russian and former Soviet Jews are the distinctive part of world's Jewry searching for a better destiny.

Jewish escape from the tsarist Russia and then from the Soviet Union transpired in waves occurred at the time of unfavorable treatment of Jews and lessening limitation for emigration by the government. By the number of Jews fled Russia through the years, two big waves of migration observed: first at the beginning and the last one at the end of the twentieth century. Millions left their country for good. We do not enlighten the Jewish fortunes and characters – every individual and family have a unique success or failure. This book expresses the author's views on political and social events led to the new exodus at the end of the twentieth century. It discloses the attributes of specifically Russian anti-Semitism the way it occurred, also what the modern-day wandering Jews renounced in their former country and found in the new one.

Many books on the Soviet Jews published in the United States depict Jewish emigration on the background of their troubled life. That dramatic aspect of the Jewish past has been well elucidated. My interest in the subject related to the role and place of the former Soviet and Russian Jews, challenges of the last exodus and puzzle of their new identity. Predominantly from Russia, Ukraine and other republics of the former Soviet Union, they were the unwanted people in the country with limited opportunities for career, for certain job categories, promotions, cultural expressions, etc. Apart from the middle age, the modern-day Jews were not expelled but maltreated by the communist regime. As immigrants, these modern-day Russian Jews are mostly secular, educated, conservatives by the political expression, ambitious, and capable to adjust to the intellectual jobs market, which makes them valuable part of the western society. Under the name Russian Jews, I of course meant all Jews lived in the former Soviet Union.

Most of them chose exodus from their homeland to not tolerate the alternately inflamed, then fading and again aggravated explicit anti-Semitism. Our story is about the character of the contemporary wandering Jews, their meanings, aims, and values, and understanding their reasons.

New Jersey
February 2019

Introduction

I think it was 1997. The crew on the remediation site in one of the New York City boroughs included Poles, Yugoslavians, and the Latino American workers. I was the only one from Russia. I remember lunch breaks when workers chatted about when each of them was going back to their home countries. Some intended to return after earning their American pensions. Others wanted to save enough money to buy a property and return home for good. Everyone was thinking of returning eventually. When it was my turn to share the vision of my future, I said I had no plans to return to Russia. I remember they were astounded. Although that did not mean they would return, in their minds, they had another home… the real one… and they all dreamed of going there. I did not tell them that I am Jewish. For them, if I am from Russia, I am Russian, no matter who my parents are. Your nation is what your mother tongue is. That is a common understanding of people from many countries, apart from Russia. Despite this, ethnicity matters there, and the Jews are not seen as Russians.

Soviet Union was the state that treated peoples selectively upon their ethnicity and provided advantages to one over another. And there were the multi-ethnical people, which also paid attention on what your ethnicity is, although it did not go too far beyond calling you out for your nationality or not too often fights. Were all these enough for hundreds of thousands of Jews to leave the country of birth and again (which time in history!) dissipate throughout the world? And finally, what we, the modern-time wandering Jews lost and what found in far edge?

After two hundred years together, the greater part of Jews left Russia and moved to Israel, America, Canada, Australia, Germany, and elsewhere. Was Russia a motherland or a stepmother for these people? Which country are they loyal to? What memories do Russian Jews keep of their country of origin and of new places? Why do people who used to be Jews in Russia became Russians in America, and what is their identity? In addition, who is the Russian Jew in America? Many questions but fewer answers.

Another Jewish exodus came about at the end of the twentieth century. Many talented people emigrated. The children they took to new countries, or who were born there, grew up and now lead in technology, industries, medicine, and arts, far from the land native to their parents. Russia has lost them eternally.

Historically, an exodus has been the last resort for the Jewish community to survive the hardship of persecution. Every time was thought to be the last one. Yet, after a few decades or centuries, they must move with a hope for a better destiny. With migration and new settlement, this nation has had to adjust to new restrictions and even absorb the traits of the local people. Although they remained Jewish, the cross current traditions and religion affected their culture.

After receiving his Nobel Prize, a journalist asked Joseph Brodsky, an ingenious poet exiled from Russia: "You are an American citizen who is receiving the Prize for Russian-language poetry. Who are you, an American or a Russian?" "I am Jewish… a Russian poet… and an English essayist," he responded. The response shows poet's identity confusion as being Russian, Jewish and English simultaneously. Still the confusion exists among the community members about who the Russian Jewish Americans are. Three entirely different cultures input into this new commonness. This observable fact has predetermined the plot of the book.

After much hesitation, I made up my mind with the contemplation that someone bearing this triple identity should attempt to understand who we are. At the outset, I started with my personal story but later redefined it to make a step toward generalization. It was essential to understand how strong our bonds are with Russia, the country where we grew up; about the Jewish heritage that has never been an important part of our Russian life; and how effectively we can adjust to the lifestyle and work ethics of the new home country. This book is about common fortune and identity riddle of the Russian-speaking Jews who used to live in Russia but now live in America. It takes in notes and reflections of a man who has lived in two diverse societies at the time when these two countries – Russia and America – experienced immense social and political transformations.

In a way, America and Russia are antipodes. My criticisms of Russia are natural. It is a country where I was born, lived through different political times, and still root for anything occurring there. I can understand people's motivations behind social and political changes, although often irrational. In America, it is a different game play, too rational for the Russian soul.

The Russian community is doomed to disappear in a few decades. Mere knowledge of the Russian and Jewish roots will live in our descendants. They will become part of the American mainstream, the same as it was with the immigration wave at the beginning of the twentieth century. The last Jewish migration from the Soviet Union and then Russia lasted about thirty years, from the beginning of 1970s until the end of the 1990s – I find both the likenesses and differences in these two waves, but the differences are deeper. To realize who the Russian Jews are culturally, their ethnic and social roots need to be understood. The cultural basis, life style, social being, customs and features are described here as episodes of the Soviet civilization that formed the Russian Jewish identity. I depicted them in the first face on the backdrop of political and social events in the Soviet Union of the 1960s to the beginning of 1990s.

One of the serious reasons for Jewish emigration was anti-Semitism, the inherent policy of the totalitarian government and the unfortunate prejudice of different strata of the society. In the Soviet Union, it was most cynical. The so-called "fifth record" was a nationality (ethnicity) in the passport. The exposed *fifth record* was a black mark for the Jews, symbolizing the government supported anti-Semitism. Soviet Jews felt and suffered it mostly after the World War II (WWII) until the USSR collapsed in 1991. The question of Jewish disloyalty to a country of living has always been a milestone in the relations of Jews with other peoples. In different countries where they lived, Jews were blamed for not fully absorbing the values of the root nation, in other words for being disloyal. I considered this problem from the opposite side of coin. Based on the historical instances, Jews have always been loyal to the countries where they had an equal opportunity and no persecution; they were disloyal to those who oppressed them.

This book is also about the principled fiber of the people who left Russia and went through challenges of immigration and the identity puzzlement. Some of these people kept their cultural fit, while others altered. Many of them watched the decisive events of recent history both in Russia and in the US at their grave moments. As one of them, I will never forget the spirit of freedom in Russia in August 1991 that I watched in Leningrad, nor will I forget the American tragedy of September 11, 2001 that I witnessed in downtown

Manhattan. Events like these are the milestones of a history and affect people's national moral.

One more subject I would like to bring up at the beginning: Russian is my first language and a few people with whom I shared my thoughts to write the book asked why I do not write it in Russian, my natural language. My answer is associated with the potential readers. Even if my grandchildren speak some Russian, they would not be able to enjoy reading a Russian book because that language for them will have become like what Yiddish was for my generation – barely understood but not used or neither understood, nor used, like it is for me. The book is not edited. I think a not edited text may give reader a better representation of author's real thoughts and sentiments.

In addition, I would like that the cultural and national experience collected by the Russian migrants was thought over by various strata of American society, including mainstream and immigrant groups. It is to look for anything in common within our diverse society. To reach out these readers, I thought it was better if the book written in the common language of this country. I, therefore, apologize for my Russian accent.

Few books on the Russian (Soviet) Jewish history of immigration have been published in the US. The topic has thoroughly explored. None of the books have written by a community member. This book is an insider's view and an attempt to understand what we as the people are.

Most of the Soviet Jews left Russia with mixed and even bitter feelings about their country of birth. The enmity toward the Jews has always existed but why did Jew-hatred grasp Russia so strappingly in the twentieth century? The view on the accusations ascribed to Jews here is the view of not the accusers (includes a few great Russian writers) but the accused.

The latest Jewish exodus may have just two similarities with Biblical Exodus from Egypt: both the Egyptian Pharaohs and the Soviet authorities did not want to let the Jews go. The second similarity is both ancient and moderns Jews had a rationale to be free from the oppression, the motivation always been relevant through history. The rest of the conditions are different. Remarkable that there is no archaeological evidence that the Exodus from Egypt took place in the way it is described in the Bible.

The book makes no pretense to describe profoundly all aspects of life and the extrinsic activities of the Jewish newcomers. The fortunes of some of them described in the book have mingled with the destinies of many people of the community. I attempt to draw the way of social adjustment of those who grew up in the autocracy and communal apartments to a completely different individualistic society. I also concentrate on the Russian Russians who shared the hardship of the Soviet socialism together with Russian Jews for so long. It is even more difficult to draw a cultural line between them as the destinies of these two peoples interlinked so closely. Yet, the Russian longtime mental tradition separates people of the non-mainstream ethnicity out. It is just given. This is Russia, the country that is very close and distant from me at the same time.

The Fifth Record has been written against the backdrop of the dramatic developments in the second half of the twentieth century. The wander is going on and only generation of our American-born grandchildren to become native to this land. I want them to know what we renounced in the old world and found in the new one.

1
The Uncommon Civilization

When you go through deep waters and great trouble, I will be with you. When you go through rivers of difficulty, you will not drown! When you walk through the fire of oppressions, you will not be burned up – the flames will not consume you

Isaiah 43:2

Who was born in Leningrad, Soviet Union may be a bit confused filling out an application while writing down the country and the city of birth: neither this country, nor the city present on today's maps. Still namely Leningrad is my homeland, and to me the name of the proletarian leader V. Lenin is not associated with the city. I am a Leningrader, and always pleased to answer where I originated from. I would say that Leningrader is my nationality if not felt there is another, more important identity, I am a Jew. It is important because albeit we are like other peoples, there is still difference in somewhat very elusive. Why this "otherness" exists and how it impacted the Jewish fortunes, in particular the Russian Jewish ones is a question not yet fully understood. I am bringing up this Jewish topic one more time.

Jews... What are they? Where did they come from? Why are they different? Why are they not loved by so many? How come they are preserved after many centuries of suffering, dissipation, extermination? Who was the first anti-Semite and why anti-Semitism on our planet is eternal? Why are there so many gifted brains among Jewish people? Thinking about these questions one can find a lot of mystical and unexplainable in what occurred in Jewish history, in Jewish consciousness, in the national character, in polyphony of their voices and actions. Questions like these still perplex philosophers, writers, politicians, historians regardless of how they treat these people. While other ancient peoples worshiped different gods, Jews had a monotheist religion of one God, which also built a foundation to Christianity and Islam. They have been sustained as an ethnos after thousand years of trials, whereas other ancient civilizations: Maya, Egypt, ancient Greeks and Romans, only remain in historical textbook. Many interpretations but no explanations – the roots go too deep into millennials.

This is a question Mark Twain asks himself in his essay *Concerning Jews*:

> "The Egyptian, the Babylonian, and the Persian rose, filled the planet with sound and splendor, then . . . passed away. The Greek and the Roman followed. The Jew saw them all, beat them all, and is now what he always was, exhibiting no decadence, no infirmities of age, no weakening of his parts. ... All things are mortal but the Jew; all other forces pass, but he remains. What is the secret of his immortality?"

French philosopher, scientist and theologian of seventeenth century Blez Pascal wrote:

> "In certain parts of the world we can see a peculiar people, separated from the other peoples of the world and this is called the

Jewish people... This people are not only of remarkable antiquity but has also lasted for a singularly long time... For whereas the people of Greece and Italy, of Sparta, Athens and Rome and others who came so much later have perished so long ago, these still exist, despite the efforts of so many powerful kings who have tried a hundred times to wipe them out, as their historians testify, and as can easily be judged by the natural order of things over such a long spell of years. They have always been preserved, however, and their preservation was foretold... My encounter with this people amazes me..."

Explaining the phenomenon of Jewish survival by a divine power is easier than understanding of why that indeed took place.

About 2000-1800 B.C. ancient Jewish tribes came from Mesopotamia and settled in Canaan between Mediterranean Sea and Jordan River. According to Bible, part of them migrated to Egypt where they had been enslaved. After four hundred years of Egyptian slavery, Jewish prophet Moses brought the people out from Egypt. That first (but not last) Exodus, though not confirmed by archaeological diggings, has nonetheless, a significant moral value in the fortune of Jews. Hard to give the benefit of the doubt that there were six hundred thousand people as the Bible stated but the number is less important than the assumption it was possible. During forty years of the wandering, Jews got Ten Commandments, formed as a people and eventually came back to Canaan soil.

In 586 B.C. Babylonians captured Jerusalem, destroyed the First Temple and took thousands of Jews as prisoners of war (Babylonian Captivity), which lasted about fifty years.

Other Jews saving themselves from slavery, went to Syria and Mesopotamia, and some to Egypt. Thereafter, Babylon was defeated and conquered by Persians. Persian king Cyrus allowed Jews to go back to Jerusalem where they founded the Second Temple in 536 B.C.

Romans began persecution of the Jews with the acceptance of Christianity as the official religion in 313 A.D. Part of the Jews still lived in the Middle Eastern countries, whereas the other part moved to European countries. The dissipation was not completed as a single action. The status of Jews was different at different times. Large Jewish communities existed in the West Roman and East Byzantium Empires in early medieval times (sixth to tenth centuries). The blossom of Jewry was viewed in Arabic Spain in the tenth to twelve centuries. Jews lived among friendly Arabs (!) in Cordoba Caliphate.

It changed during the crusades when crusaders, before going to East against the Muslims, crushed Jewish communities in many areas of Western Europe, forcing them to convert to Christianity. Roman Popes of the time played their role in the prosecutions. A series of medieval Jewish expulsions started from England and continued in France, Spain, Italy, and some other countries. Neither America, nor Israel existed then, where the expelled Jews could have found their shelter. Hostile Europe did not greet them. In European countries, the rumor spread that Jews were at fault for poisoning water in wells and infecting them with the plague or "black death", which turned out to be lie. Thousands of innocent Jews were killed in France, Austria, Switzerland, and Bohemia. Jewish migrations continued with their expulsion from many Western European countries.

In the fifteenth century, Spain and other Western European countries lost their role as a center of European Jewry, and Poland took over as primary Jewish location. Jews found better conditions in Poland because Polish kings favored them in sixteenth century. Many European Jews moved to Poland where they had better shelter and more respect from Polish kings. However, the time became tragic for Jews when Ukrainian Cossacks under Bogdan Khmelnitsky rebelled in 1648 against Poland. Khmelnitsky's rebels massacred dozens of thousands of Jews for their connections with the Poles. Another historic turn occurred at the end of the eighteen century. Jews massively found themselves in Russia after Russian Empress Ekaterina II gained large areas of the Eastern Polish territory due to dividing Poland by Russia, Austria, and Prussia.

The beginning of the nineteen century was likely the time when my paternal ancestors moved from Austria to central Russia. From that time on, the two hundred years of the common history of Russians and Jews started and lasted until the first massive Jewish emigration from Russia in 1890s–1910s when about one and a half million of Jews parted from Russia. None who fled could know that they saved themselves from the worst of the worst that laid ahead for the European Jews in the 1930s - 1940s.

The mission to survive and preserve the Jewish culture and heritage has been finally realized with reestablishing Israel, the state able to protect its citizens from the hostile environment. In 1948, after two thousand years of the destruction of Second Temple and long dissipation, Jews got an opportunity to re-build their state on their historical soil, in Palestine. Just after seventy years of existence of the Jewish democratic state it was included in eight most influential countries in the world!

What kind of enigma surrounds these people?

Mark Twain continues with his questions and answers:

"If the statistics are right, the Jews constitute but one percent of the human race. It suggests a nebulous dim puff of star dust lost in the blaze of the Milky Way. Properly the Jew ought hardly to be heard of, but he is heard of, has always been heard of. He is as prominent on the planet as any other people, and his commercial importance is extravagantly out of proportion to the smallness of his bulk. His contributions to the world's list of great names in literature, science, art, music, finance, medicine, and abstruse learning are also away out of proportion to the weakness of his numbers. He has made a marvelous fight in the world, in all the ages; and has done it with his hands tied behind him. He could be vain of himself and be excused for it. The Egyptian, the Babylonian, and the Persian rose, filled the planet with sound and splendor, then faded to dream-stuff and passed away; the Greek and the Roman followed, and made a vast noise, and they are gone; other peoples have sprung up and held their torch high for a time, but it burned out, and they sit in twilight now, or have vanished. The Jew saw them all, beat them all, and is now what he always was, exhibiting no decadence, no infirmities of age, no weakening of his parts, no slowing of his energies, no dulling of his alert and aggressive mind. All things are mortal but the Jew; all other forces pass, but he remains. What is the secret of his immortality?" (Mark Twain.

Concerning Jews. Essay, Harpers & Brothers Publishers, 1934).

Leo Tolstoy on the same issue:

> "What is the Jew?...What kind of unique creature is this whom all the rulers of all the nations of the world have disgraced and crushed and expelled and destroyed; persecuted, burned and drowned; and who, despite their anger and their fury, continues to live and to flourish. What is this Jew whom they have never succeeded in enticing with all the enticements in the world, whose oppressors and persecutors only suggested that he deny (and disown) his religion and cast aside the faithfulness of his ancestors?! The Jew – is the symbol of eternity... He is the one who for so long had guarded the prophetic message and transmitted it to all humankind. A people such as this can never disappear. The Jew is eternal. He is the embodiment of eternity."

This remarkable statement of the great Russian writer about the Jews put into words what Jewish choosiness is about. The Jewish culture has preserved after centuries of wars, separation, dissipation, persecution, and the Holocaust. Jews have kept their religious and ethnical features, as well as their otherness for over four thousand years.

This is what the outstanding Russian philosopher Nikolai Berdyaev wrote on the topic:

> "It must be said that from any materialistic and positively-historic point of view this nation should had stopped existing. Its existing is a strange, enigmatic and wonderful phenomenon indicating that the fortune of these people linked to a special predestination. This fortune cannot be explained by adjustments, which normally used to explain other people fortunes. The historic survival of Jewish people, its indestructibility, continuation of its existence as one of the most ancient in the world, its fatal role in history – all these indicates special mystical basics of its historic fate." (N.A. Berdyaev. *Meaning of History.* Obelisk, Berlin, 1923).

Jewish civilization has survived and become a symbol of eternity. Philosophers and thinkers have contemplated this subject for centuries. A non-religious person, I nevertheless often think about the incomprehensible power that has preserved this civilization. It seems like something mysterious saved Soviet Jews from deportation to Siberia right before it was going to happen in 1953. That was dictator Stalin's death. It is difficult to give a simple answer to the question of Jewish survival if at all possible. I can only bring up some points of my view on that wonder. So, the question is why relatively small ethnos have not dissolved within the centuries, not assimilated with others as it happened with many ancient tribes but preserved?

For analysis let's think of another question – who would better defend its otherness - the tribe that has more dissimilarities from people of the mainstream or less? I think the answer is obvious: the tribe with more dissimilarities. It is because the loss of unlikeness would be the loss of culture and eventually, the absorption of the unique but small ethnos by the bigger one. Someone could object to the notion pointing to Ukraine whose culture and faith are very close to Russian: why it resists to unite with Russia again? Due to historical and geographic reasons Russia has always played the role of a big brother overseeing a younger one, but what people want to be overseen?

It was easier for Jews to preserve their self-consciousness and traditions by looking, behaving and thinking differently from the locals during the dissipation. If some of them under the hard circumstances converted to a prevailing religion, they stopped being Jewish (for example, moranos in Medieval Spain). Soviet Jews represented another example. Any religion in the Soviet Union was suppressed, and at the same time the Jewry suffered anti-Semitism. However, the desire to look and sound like ordinary people or the *external* assimilation did not mean thinking likely. All gear of Jewish values: traditions, education, intellectual activities preserved. So, the *internal* assimilation among Soviet Jews did not go that far. Differences in culture, the way of life, consciousness are the main but not the only reasons of preservation of this ethnos. There are more reasons.

Strong family bonds. There are dozens of thousands abandoned childs who have the living biological parents in modern Russia. Just think about this number! How many do you think abandoned Jewish kids among them? No one! Due to historic reasons, Jews have the tightest family attachment that helped in preserving their adherence to family, tribe, and ethnicity. The closest analogy from chemistry is oxidation reactions of different metals: from the least stable Potassium that easily gives away electrons forming another chemical (by analogy, national) substance (disappeared ethnicities, weak ties) to the most stable Gold, with the strongest atomic bonds (ethnical preservation). Hence, do not say there is no connections between the natural and social science! Jews stood together during persecution, expulsion, the Holocaust, and the Soviet struggle against "cosmopolitanism". They preserved their existence as a people during the hardship of dissipation when the host nations oppressed them. The more persecution, the stronger the consolidation.

Jews of the Russian Empire transformed into Soviet Jews and became different in many aspects. However, the transformation was unnatural, even though scores of them lost their Jewishness. Many banished their Jewish identity but in the back of their minds, they had not stopped being Jewish, just changed their behavior and outlook. It was not widely known within Soviet realities that families with a living grandmother had matzo ball soup or gefilte fish on Jewish holidays. On the Simchat Torah, many Jewish boys and girls of the teens age overcrowded the synagogues in Moscow and Leningrad. That did not mean they aspired to observe traditions. It was just a consolidation against the official and unofficial Soviet anti-Semitism.

While dissipated, Jews did not freely mix with the host nation up until the twentieth century. Imagine a piece of ice (assume Jews) dropped onto hot water (assume other peoples and countries where the Jews dissipated). How fast would the ice melt? I take the liberty in saying the Jews, as an imagined piece of ice, would melt at much slower rate compared with other peoples in their place. This is because Jews, as a community, have the high rate of self-organization and self-recovery. History has proved this assumption many times.

Another important Jewish quality is an adaptable but determined state of mind capable of preserving its historical birthright even under unfavorable conditions. This specific state of people's mind has transformed this culture into the everlasting civilization. Combination of persecution and specific flexible state of mind formed a new quality of the *advanced* survival. It is not just a survival but against all the odds, making a progress in any area of activities: arts, business, science, politics, etc. They could not survive on without mutual help and aid-giving behavior and therefore, Jews developed a mindset of mitzvah – good deed to one another. We don't know how much the ancient Jews helped each other but in modern time Jewish help is very significant. According to Report of American Jewish Joint Distribution Committee for 2015, just the Joint Organization spent $192 million to help low-income Jews, $36 million for Jewish education, and so on, total of $297 million. That is only the Joint but how many other Jewish charity organizations exist!

Soviet political and social policy denied any religion and weakened historic traditions. Transformation under this policy changed Soviet Jewish life dramatically: no religion or traditions openly practiced, ignorance of Judaism, and extensive assimilation. They had to survive harsh conditions of ethnical harassment. They made it. However, many Soviet Jews gave up their culture because they wanted to build a new international community with no people separation into nations due to an enormous moral burden to surrender their cultural, religious, and ethnical identity. They hide their traditions and anything that made them look Jewish, thus tending to assimilate. How many Jews changed their names to sound Russian! The well-known Soviet writer Ilya Ehrenburg actively advocated assimilation of all peoples of Soviet Union having in mind primarily Jewish people for which that would mean full annihilation. Many Jews kept this point of view, which needs to be understood considering the social and political circumstances.

A sense of community ("state within the state") helped Jews to keep themselves as an ethnos. It also helped preserve their religion in the face of exiles and persecution. Helped but not caused!

> "To attribute "state within the state" to merely persecution and self-preservation is not enough… The most powerful civilizations in the world did not reach even half of forty centuries [of Jewish existence – L.P.] and lose their power and appearance. It is not only self-preservation, but an unspecified idea that drives and involves something global and deep, and the humanity has yet to pronounce its final statement."

Russian writer F. M. Dostoyevsky said these words about the vitality of the Jewish people (my translation). Although the general idea of his article *The Jewish Question* is anti-Semitic, this statement is objective. Times have changed but the Jewish Question exists as it did centuries ago. New generations come to receive old and new accusations.

Jews are very different, even more different than any other nation in world. There are three categories of Jewish disposition in terms of religious commitment: secular, orthodox, which are on the opposite sides of the devotion spectrum, and the rest in between. The first two are polar different, like diverse nations or even races by the appearance, life style, habits, food, etc. Honestly, their interrelationship is often unsympathetic. The first ones (secular) are almost indistinguishable with the non-Jewish people, whereas the orthodoxies read Torah all the time, they differ from others, make anti-Semites irritated by their appearance. But hey, may be their otherness and reading Torah is a secret of the Jewish survival? Remember my note on the tribe, which has more incentives to survive because of more dissimilarities from the mainstream? I think, that is about it!

The worst anti-Semitism is seen in societies with the biggest rate of intolerance or intellectual difference between the Jews and the host nation. The words attributed to Mr. Churchill "we are not so stupid to be anti-Semitic" catches the problem.

Modern Israel has absorbed cultural traditions brought in by Ashkenazi, Sephardic, and other Jewish branches from all over the world. This commonness has formed a new civilization, which combines the backgrounds Jews accumulated in different areas of the world. By the relative number of newcomers and their cultural input to society, Israel could only be compared with the US. At the same time, I regret that the Yiddish language has practically disappeared with the culture of my ancestors from the Pale of Settlement and Sholom Aleichem's touching stories.

Mordecai Kaplan defined Jewish civilization at the time when other philosophers only discussed the term civilization as opposite to barbarism. He called it the Judaic civilization even before the creation of the Israeli State, which later united almost half the world's Jewish population under the common territory.

How about the Jews not living in Israel, do they belong to the Jewish civilization? My answer is yes if they consider themselves Jewish. The example is the contemplated community of Russian Jewish Americans.

Religious and ethnical self-consciousness can exist independently in any secular or reformist Jewish soul. I may take myself as an example. Although I am not a religious person, anything associated with Jewish history, including religion, is dear to me. An ultra-religious Jew may not care about the ethnicity; to him, practicing religious law every day is a stipulation for being a Jew. This is how I see it. For thousands of years, religious and ethnical components were inseparably associated with the condition of being a Jew. Over the time, it has largely narrowed from the universal holy power (ancient and Medieval Jews, modern Orthodox Jews) to a spiritual lifestyle (European Jews of eighteenth and nineteenth centuries, residents of the Pale of Settlement and modern Conservative Jews) and then to holiday observances (modern secular and Reformist American, Israeli and European Jews).

Haskalah, the Jewish Enlightenment movement, inspired by the Jewish Prussian philosopher Moses Mendelssohn in the eighteenth century, caused reduction of the religious component in Jewish life. From the nineteenth century on, and especially in the twentieth century, the number of secular Jews increased substantially. According to Gallup, nowadays over 50% of Israeli Jews do not consider religion as important part of their everyday life. In 2005, the proportions of Jewish denomination among all American Jews are as follows: Orthodox – 13% (20% raised Orthodox in the childhood); Conservative – 26%; Reform – 34%; Reconstructionist – 3% and Just Jewish (secular) – 25% (20% were raised Just Jewish) (Jonathon Ament, *American Jewish Religious Denominations*. National Jewish Population Survey 2000–2001, February 2005, Report 10, p. 9).

The level of Jewish Orthodoxy gradually decreases in favor of secularism. Unlike the religious component, the ethnical one remains stable. If a person was born to a Jewish mother, he or she is considered a Jew by the religious laws of Halakha. According to these laws, even those who adopted other religions do not lose the status of being Jewish (does it mean if you do not identify yourself Jewish, you are still a Jew? –L.P.). Also, Halakha states that mere acceptance of the principles and practice of Judaism does not make person a Jew but only through the conversion. Even though Halakha is a religious law, it determines who is a Jew based on the ethnical belonging rather than religious.

There are some Jews who do not associate themselves with their ethnos. I think just being an ethnical Jew with no Jewish self-identification would look like an apostasy.

Another Jewish paradox: trying to apply different definitions of the nation to Russian Jewish immigrants, the definitions turn out to be inapplicable - they do belong to the Jewish ethnos but not to the Jewish nation.

"The term nation connotes a broad community of individuals, whose members consider themselves linked on the basis of shared long-standing cultural practices, ethnicity, history, memories, or traditions, who are typically associated with a specific geographical homeland, and who are predisposed to make political claims of autonomy, sovereignty, or other assertions of rights on the basis of their membership." (*International Encyclopedia of the Social Sciences, 2008*)

"Nation refers to a community of people who share a common territory and government—but who are not necessarily a sovereign state; and who often share a common language, race, descent, and/or history." (*Wikipedia*)

One more definition refers to Joseph Stalin's article "*Marxism and the National Question*" (1913) when he had yet to become a cruel dictator of a huge empire but was considered as an expert for the national problems in the Bolshevik party:

> "Nation is a historically formed stable commonness of people on the base of common language, territory, economical life, and psychological constitution that appears as a commonness of culture. Just the presence of all these attributes gives you a nation."

A. Smith defined a nation as "a named human population sharing a historic territory, common myths and historical memories, a mass, public culture, a common economy and common legal rights and duties for all members." (*National Identity. Ethnonationalism in Comparative Perspective.* University of Nevada Press, 1993)

E. Gellner's definitions:

"…A mere category of persons (say, occupants of a given territory, or speakers of a given language, for example) becomes a nation if and when the members of the category firmly recognize certain mutual rights and duties to each other in virtue of their shared membership to it…" (E. Geller. *Nations and Nationalism.* Cornell University Press, 2008)

The common in all these definitions are mutual history, territory, and culture. The shared history clause complies with the definition for all but the countries of immigrants like America, Australia, or Canada where millions of people are newcomers. In fact, in 2000, the portion of foreign-born residents was 9.5% of the US total population. Are they members of the nation if they are legal? They are. Do they have common history with other members? I doubt it, since people within just fewer than one generation cannot develop "common myths and historic memories" that discover a history.

Benedict Anderson defined a nation as "an imagined political community imagined as both inherently limited and sovereign." (*Imagined Communities: Reflections on the Origin and Spread of Nationalism.* Revised Edition Verso, 1991). The word "imagined" covers possible variances. However, under this definition, the Jews that do not live in Israel and do not share a common territory with most of the "imagined political community" cannot be members of this nation.

Russian Jews legally living in America are members of the American nation. At the same time, they belong to the Russian community. Culturally, they have much in common (I do not touch politics or religion) with ethnical Russians and not much in common with the other Jews born not in Russia. Moreover, there is little or no interest in social adhesion and upholding connections on a person-to-person level between American (at one time Eastern European Jews) and Russian Jews (recent Soviet people). Different ways of thinking and habitual life do not provide a favorable background for personal social connections between Russian and American Jews. I also know cases of friendship but those are only exceptions especially for the middle-aged or seniors. Those who started in America at the age of over twenty-five have the background aloof to average Americans. At the same time, they are drifting away from their country of origin.

There is an opinion that Jews are what the prevailing nation is with some variances. In Britain, they are British; in Iraq, they are Iraqis; in Russia, they are Russians. This is not a full truth. Even though Jews are so different culturally and yet racially, something unites them.

Same ethnos but different cultures: this is truly a Jewish feature! Look how Webster Dictionary defines ethnos: it is "people of the same race or nationality who share a distinctive culture." And Wikipedia:

> "Ethnicity is a group of people whose members identify with each other, through a common heritage, often consisting of a

common language, a common culture (often including a shared religion) and an ideology that stresses common ancestry or endogamy" (endogamy is practice of marring within a specific ethnic group –L.P.).

All these definitions of ethnos are not applicable to Jews not living in Israel. Think about two large groups of Jews who went different ways long ago. One of the groups (later called Ashkenazi) came to Europe and then most of them through the centuries found themselves in Central and Eastern European countries. They spoke the Yiddish language, a German dialect. The second group (Bukharean Jews) in the ancient times moved from Judea to the Eastern countries of Iran, Iraq, and Syria; they mainly spoke Farsi. Through the years, they migrated to Central Asia (Uzbekistan and Turkmenistan) that later became the Soviet republics. These two groups of Jewish people for decades of the twentieth century lived in one country – the USSR, had the same ethnicity, celebrated the same state holidays, but had different cultural traits. No wonder, these two groups have formed different immigrant communities in the US: Russian and Bukharean. With all that, we still have a common ancient (Judaic) and recent (Soviet) history. The number of such examples is as many as the number of Jewish communities throughout the world. However, Russian Jews by their upbringing, cultural spirits, and life habits stay apart from the others.

Dissipated all over the world, Jews do not share language or culture: say, Iranian or Ethiopian, or South American Jews look, speak and behave like different nationalities! Seemingly, they do belong to same ethnicity. But based on the definitions of ethnicity, they do not. Instead, they have something different shared, which is not covered by the common definitions. This something is recognition of a few facts: they have common ancient predecessors; they are being hated by substantial part of humanity; and they attempt to advance in both good and bad arrangements. All the above comprise a big part of the Jewishness.

Jews from the former Soviet Union are educated, secular, with a little or no knowledge of Judaism, carry Russian traits, and mostly identify self as Jewish. They used to obey the oppressive order and overcome typical Soviet obstacles. They habitually keep the similar way of thinking they had in Russia; often possess features and vices considered natural in the country of origin but seem weird to the Westerners. An ingrained habit of social equality often makes them stay away from one another in a society of the unequal individuals. However, the same features keep many of them together as carriers of the same culture. Most Russian Jews are ambitious, capable, and want to realize a dream that is no less than the highest American dream. Spirit of culture, common values, and social unity are the attributes of the community. The Russian Jew in America (Canada, Australia, Germany) is a member of the American (Canadian, Australian, German) nation, the Jewish ethnicity, and the Russian (not Jewish!) community. The case with Russian Jews in Israel is even simpler: they belong to Jewish nation and Russian community in Israel. This is who the wandering Jews of the modern-day are.

One more difficult topic is about the Jewish character of the State of Israel. It is difficult because on one hand, the nationalism, even sensible condemned by both liberals and modern conservatives, but on the other hand, can we imagine Israel a non-Jewish state? Russian writer of Jewish descend Dmitry Bykov does not like the idea of national state, he says better eat salt in soup (salt in this metaphor is Jews and soup is the rest of the world) than just eat the salt. This point of view is very common among civilized thinkers and politicians.

Political activists from a few European countries, demand fair punishment of fanatic-terrorists in their countries but when it comes to Israeli's repulse of Palestinian terrorists or Israeli's defense against HAMAS's underground passage or "marches of return", these civilized politicians loudly protest against the "disproportional response" of Israel. I can only regret that these protests often weaken Israel's decision to protect itself by all necessary means. Retaliations, yielding up lands, humanitarian help from Israel seen as its weakness by the neighbors and based on the past experience, only lead to further aggravations.

Yes, some people living far from the Israel's realities pressure against the national state idea. However, even big European powers have tremendous social and political problems as they stopped being national states due to huge refugee flows from the Middle East and Africa. What to say about a small country so much hated by surrounding peoples and nations! Those who dream about the destruction of Israel from inside - the military victory is not possible – the Jewish state is strongest in the region. Had Israel stopped being the national state, it would simply gradually disappear as dreamed by its enemies. Yasir Arafat, the late leader of Palestinian Liberation Organization, claimed that the best weapon against Israel is womb of an Arab woman. That is right.

A critical ratio exists between the number of aborigines and the aliens. Once it reached, there is a possibility of loss of the dominating culture and identity. People of the small country risk of loosing their identity due to the big inflow of the foreign culture. Imagine the unimaginable - the worst-case scenario, Israeli Jews would begin to leave their country under the "peaceful" onrush of huge mass of less civilized people. The fate of rest of the Jews is easy to envision. Jews had already come through this apocalypse about twenty centuries ago. There is no way of preserving Judaic civilization other than keeping the national character of the state.

Former Secretary of State John Kerry claimed Israel cannot be Jewish and democratic state at the same time but only one of these. Wrong! Imagine Israel implements Kerry's scenario and opens the door to everybody (surrounding Arabs). At the hypothetical new ratio of the opposite cultures, whatever the strong democratic institutes are, the very governance would be entirely different. One can only assume what kind of Premier, President and Knesset would be if they are voted by say five million Jews and ten million Arabs who were taught of hatred Jews and Israel from early childhood.

Culture and civilization have always bounded. However, not every culture could be a civilization, but every civilization should have a distinctive culture. This is what the late Harward University Professor Samuel Huntington speculated about the Jewish civilization,

> "…Most scholars hardly mention it. In terms of numbers of people, Judaism clearly is not a major civilization… It historically affiliated with both Christianity and Islam, and for several centuries Jews maintained their cultural identity within Western, Orthodox, and Islamic civilizations. With creation of Israel, Jews have all the objective accoutrements of a civilization: religion, language, customs, literature, institutions, and territorial and political home. What about the subjective identification? Jews living in other cultures have distributed themselves along a continuum stretching from total identification with Judaism and Israel to nominal Judaism and full identification with

the civilization within which they reside, the latter, however, occurring primarily among Jews living in the West." (*The Clash of Civilization and the Remaking of World Order,* Simon & Shuster, 1997)

Why the Judaic civilization seems to me the uncommon one? In normal representation, civilization is something big to a planetary scale: for example, Western, Muslim, or Chinese. Small peoples are not in that number. But what if the small people's history and culture deeply affected much bigger peoples 'cultures?

Here are some considerations. A culture becomes a civilization if it makes great and distinctive inputs in historic humans' development in various aspects. Only all these conditions and factual values make culture a civilization. These values can weigh up through the *quantitative* or *qualitative* properties. For example, the number of a population or a size of territory is the *quantitative* characteristic; an impressive achievement in science and/or arts, medicine, technology, industrial development is the *qualitative* one. Some civilizations, such as Islamic or African, are hundreds of millions in population, sizable territories but lag other nations in industries and technologies despite having the civilizations. Other civilizations like Western, Chinese, Russian Orthodox, or Japanese have both quantitative and qualitative traits.

The characteristics of the Jewish civilization are merely qualitative. Quality in development of the nation is what makes the Jewish culture a civilization. During the short historical time, Israel has reached one of the world highest levels in science and technology and provided exports of high technology products to industrially developed countries. That has made Israel a high-ranking country in any area of human activity. It does not come from nowhere, but the succession from generation to generation of people's intellectual work matters, be it in garment tailoring, banking business, musical performance, teaching, or engineering, or justice.

I must admit the fact that the number of sharp individuals among the Ashkenazi Jews is higher than the average. One of the valuable indexes of these qualities is scientific achievements. From 1906 up to 2010, the total number of Noble Prizes awarded was eight hundred and thirteen in the nominations of Literature, Chemistry, Medicine and Biology, Physics, and Peace. Of this number, Jews received one hundred and sixty-six. This represents over 20% of total number of prizes with the total Jewish population of about 0.2% of the worlds. This aspect of Jewishness has always contributed to anti-Semitism. The Jewish state achieved impressive accomplishments in technology, industries, culture, and arts for just a few decades of its existence. There may be objections that other small nations have also well-developed industry and technology like Singapore, but it is still not considered a civilization. It is because Singapore already belonged to the Southeast Asian culture at the time the British founded it in the beginning of the nineteenth century. The Jewish origin is different – they have over four thousand years of distinct history, did not lose their identity, and Judaism is a source of other world major religions. These credits make the Jewish culture a civilization.

Jewish culture has a history of four thousand years. Over the harsh centuries, the people have not loss its identity and not assimilated that much to be dissolved in other peoples. Furthermore, Jewish impact in most of human activities takes place wherever they live. World without Jews would have been different than it is.

To have the complete picture of the Jewish civilization, I must add a fly in the ointment of historical portrait of the

Jewish culture. It is about how atrocious political or religious groups of Jews treat each other when they are together. Authors of this citation, Igor Guberman and Alexander Okunev have been living in Israel for many decades and knew what they wrote about:

> "As two thousand years ago, people of Israel divided by sectors whose interests (for instance, religious and secular Jews) are very often the opposite. As two thousand years ago, each group consider that only they are right, no one else. As two thousand years ago, they hate and despise those whose opinion and position oppose. As two thousand years ago, they cannot and do not want to come to agreement, give even a little way to an opponent. And the words of sages that the hate and despise to one another were the cause of destruction of the Temple are actual today as two thousand years ago." (I. Guberman, A. Okunev. *Guidance on the Country of Zion's Sages. Limbus Press*, St. Petersburg – Moscow, 2009, p. 319 – in Russian).

Today about half of all Jews live not in Israel. Dissipated all over the world, they differ from those in Israel. But get them all together – and they would be the ones. And this is so Jewish! The uncommon people and uncommon civilization!

2
Tribal History

As the whole world reflected in just one drop of water, so these few stories if viewed at the historical background, can give a representation of Jewish living within the past 100-120 years. These tribal stories trace several generations of a Russian Jewish family. One of the brothers, by some quirk of fate, moved to America in the pre-World War I time, others remained in Russia. Their fates were so much different as different Russian and American men's destinies could be. Descendants from these two branches now live twenty-five miles from one another in the New York Metro area but have never met and hardly ever would. This is a Jewish providence: bonded by genes, descendants of the old and modern-day *Wandering Jews* are separated by the cultures.

We know what was going on with Russian Jews in the twentieth century and how strong Russian turbulent politics affected them. But we do not know and will never know what was stirring in every Jewish soul. Fortunes of people of several generations depicted in this chapter are typical for Jews lived in Russia.

STARODUB'S PALE OF SETTLEMENT AND POGROMS

Pale of Settlement was a permanent residency where the Russian government allowed Jews to live and beyond which, Jewish placement was restricted. Pale of Settlement included parts of Western Russia, Ukraine, and parts of Poland, Belorussia, Lithuania, and Moldavia and extended at the western border to Germany and Austria-Hungary. At the time Poland was he country with most numerous Jewish populations in Europe. At the end of eighteen century, due to redistribution of borders in a few Central and Eastern European countries, enormous changes occurred with Jewish locals. From 1772 to 1795, Poland was three times divided and shared between Russia, Austria and Prussia, and ceased to exist as an independent state until 1918. Hundreds of thousands of Jews unexpectedly found themselves within another state. This is how Israeli historian M. Shterenshis describes this historical event (my translation):

> "Small number of Jews in the pre-Peter's Great Rus seemingly did not even think that Russia suddenly becomes a huge Jewish center but that happened almost abruptly, after the annexation of Poland and Lithuania to the Empire" (M. Shterenshis. *Jews. History of the Nation*. Gerclia-Isradon, 2008. P. 371).

Pale of Settlement occupied 26 Southwestern Russian guberniyas with population total of over five million (1897). It was not ghetto, not only Jews lived in the Pale. Russian, Ukrainian, and mixed population townships were also there. The difference, however, was the restriction for Jews doing some type of business activities like lease land, run taverns, or receive higher education. Double taxes were also collected from Jews. Jewish residency was only allowed in provincial small townships. That shaped a deep Jewish cultural isolation from other Russian people, especially from those lived in big cities. Jews were also isolated from the major trade, industry, and social and political life. They were banned from working in public and civil services, to be a juror, or take part in the municipal council. Due to the cultural isolation, generations of Jews originated from Pale of Settlement spoke only Yiddish. They did not speak Russian or used it as a second language. Unless they converted to Russian Orthodoxy, moving out of the Pale was prohibited for them. The ordinary life in the Jewish Pale of Settlement is depicted in many details in Sholom Aleichem's stories. The famous musical *Fiddler on the Roof* is based on one of them. Within the Pale of Settlement, my parental ancestors lived in Starodub, the provincial township of Chernigov guberniya starting from the end of the eighteenth or beginning of the nineteen century.

Starodub was first mentioned in the eleventh century, after Oleg Svyatoslavovich, Rurik's descent founded the Novgorod–Seversky Knyazhestvo (Principality) in 1096. The town was ruined by the Mongols in 1240 and then built up again. In the sixteenth century, Starodub was part of the Grand Duchy of Moscow and then Poland until 1648. During the Bogdan Khmelnitsky uprising in the second part of seventeenth century, it was the center of the Starodub Cossack Regiment and remained part of the autonomous Cossack Hetmanate until 1781 when it became a district town. By the beginning of the 1860's anti-feudal reform of Alexander II, the population of Starodub accounted about twelve thousand Russians and Jews, and there were fifteen churches and four synagogues.

Cruel Jewish pogroms of 1881–1882 shook the entire Jewish community in Russia. At the end of nineteenth, beginning of the twentieth century, three hundred and fifty-eight pogroms occurred throughout the Pale of Settlement. Jews of Starodub were also the target of a pogrom. This is what Jewish historian S. M. Dubnov wrote about the Starodub's pogroms:

> "Under the effect of the officially perpetrated "legal" pogroms little attention was paid to the street pogrom which occurred on September 29, 1891, in the city of Starodub, in the government of Chernigov, recalling the horrors of the eighties. Though caused by economic factors, the pogrom of Starodub assumed a religious coloring. The Russian merchants of that city had long been gnashing their teeth at their Jewish competitors. Led by a Russian fanatic, by the name of Gladkov, they forced a regulation through the local town council barring all business on Sundays and Christian holidays. The regulation was directed against the Jews who refused to do business on Sabbath and the Jewish holidays and would have been ruined had they also refrained from trading on Sundays and the numerous Greek-Orthodox holidays, thus remaining idle on twice as many days as the Christians. The Jews appealed to the governor of Chernigov to revoke or at least to mitigate the new regulation. The governor's decision fell in favor of the Jews who allowed keep their stores open on Christian holidays from noontime until six o'clock in the evening. The reply of the local Jew-baiters took the form of a pogrom."

> "On Sunday, the day before Yom Kippur, when the Jews opened their stores for a few hours, a hired crowd of ruffians from among

the local street mob fell upon the Jewish stores and began to destroy and loot whatever goods it could lay its hands on. The stores rapidly closed, the rioters invaded the residences of the Jews, destroying the property contained there and filling the streets with fragments of broken furniture and leathers from torn bedding. Peasants who had arrived from the adjacent villages assisted the plunderers. In the evening, a drunken mob, which had assembled on the market place, laid fire to several Jewish stores and houses, inflicting on their owners a loss of many millions.

All this took place during the holy Yom Kippur eve. Jews who did not dare to worship in their synagogues or even to remain in their homes, hid themselves with their wives and children in the garrets and orchards or in the houses of strangers. Many Jews spend the night in a field outside the city, where, shivering from cold, they could watch the glare of the ghastly flames, which destroyed all their belongings. The police, small in numbers, proved "powerless" against the huge hordes of plunderers and incendiaries. On a second day, the pogrom was over, the work of destruction having been duly accomplished. The subsequent judicial inquiry brought out the fact clearly that Gladkov and his associates, a fact of which the local authorities could not have been ignorant, had engineered the pogrom. Gladkov fled from the city but returned subsequently, paying but a slight penalty for his monstrous crime."(S. M. Dubnov. *Concise Jewish History*. Fenix., 2003. Rostov-on-Don).

Although the police were warned about the forthcoming pogrom, they showed up too late. One more pogrom in Starodub occurred between October 17 and 25, 1905. The leader of the anti-Semitic group of *Chernosotentsi* (*Black Hundred*) and disguised policemen were heads of the pogrom. The noise of bells was used as a signal to start, and after that, the drunken crowd ruined Jewish stores, broke into Jewish houses, crushed furniture, dishes, and beat people. However, the young Jewish self-defense organization of one hundred fifty people emerged, and few gunshots were enough to scatter bandits. Compared with the massacres of 1881, the pogroms in Starodub did not result in killings.

Today it is hard to believe that the commerce in the holidays caused the pogrom. The deeper reason was the envy to Jewish competitors, who apparently were more successful.

Two different cultures as they seem like now, incompatible by the religion, life style, habits, holidays, and many other expressions existed side by side, had also different wealth, which made its input to the anti-Jewish sentiments of the local Russians, and eventually broke out to pogroms.

My great-great grandfather Samuel and his son Lev were winemakers. Lev's business lasted until 1914 after the prohibition (dry law) brought in during WWI. Then he switched to the cab business: he bought horses, phaetons, and hackney-cabs. I think he did not enjoy his new business for a longtime because of the socialist revolution of 1917 with a course to "expropriate of expropriators" and "rob the robbed" especially with high demand for horses in the Civil War of 1918–1921.

Lev's older son Lazar was an outerwear designer, pattern maker, and tailor rolled into one. At the beginning of twentieth century, he graduated from the Warsaw Branch of Paris Academy of Arts. I can just imagine how successful he and his wife Sarah had been in Starodub with their high-profile business, which included a tailoring shop and store. They both were master hands. After the 1917 Russian socialist revolution, the business remained intact: at first, Bolsheviks took away only the stuff needed for the battle, as well as harvest from the peasants. Later, in 1921, they announced a course change from the Military Communism to the New Economic Policy (NEP), which allowed running small businesses (up to twenty employees). Lazar and Sarah's business fell under the NEP and they kept their normal life until 1928.

In 1928, Stalin introduced the first Five Year Plan. This plan stipulated another change of the country's course from the NEP (New Economic Policy) to organizing the collective farms – *kolkhoz* - with the communal property; private property was no longer allowed. Expropriation restarted. The Bolsheviks took away anything hardworking people had gained: grain, cattle, forage, houses. The successful farmers were named *kulaks* and claimed *enemies of socialism,* and then expelled to remote regions of the country or the Gulag (Russian abbreviation that means Agency of the concentration camps, belonged to the Ministry of Internal Affairs). Left with no food and clothes, people often died on their way to Siberia. The poorest ones, who had nothing to expropriate, joined new *kolkhozes,* which were so inefficient as anything in a non-private possession. Starting from 1929 until the end of the Soviet existence, low productive communal agriculture was a big headache for leaders and especially for the commons due to the empty food stores.

In 1928, the authorities took away my granddad's tailoring shop, store, and home where they lived. The family had nowhere to life and it drifted. Starodub was no longer their place. At that point, it was not an anti-Semitic action but a common disaster for the people in Russia who owned businesses or properties and were responsible for themselves and their families. Entire families were deprived the right to vote, to study, and other political and human rights. In other words, they were blacklisted.

My grandparents endured this hard change; they were around fifty years old, which was old enough by the Russian scale of the time. The family moved to Voronezh, another city in Central Russia. Happily, they had distant relatives there, so they could stop for some time. My father and his older sister, decisively minded, moved to a bigger city to start a new life.

Bolsheviks taken away civil rights from this family as belonged to bourgeois class: they could not vote, children could not get education. The family broke up with the former Pale of Settlement and moved to Moscow and then Leningrad. My father started there as a laborer at a plant and then Soviets later allowed him access to education. On this photo: my paternal grandmother Sarah and grandfather Lazar in the front row; my father Arnold (thirteen years old) and my aunt Dvoira. Starodub, Bryansk Oblast. *(Photograph of 1926)*

My father was fifteen when he moved to Moscow and then Leningrad. I do not exactly know what made him move to Leningrad from Moscow but once he settled, he brought his parents over from Voronezh. His sister Dvoira and her husband Akiva had also moved to Leningrad.

We can distinguish two periods of Jewish life in Russia. The first one is within the Pale of Settlement and the second is mostly in big cities starting from the 1920s. They represent two different Russian Jewish cultural epochs: the culture of "shtetl" - typical small Jewish townships within the Pale of Settlement - and the culture of Soviet Jewish intelligentsia – represented by the young Jews who got educated in Soviet universities. The *first* period was characterized by Jewish retardation in the Pale of Settlement. The *second* one was distinguished by the advancement (1920s–1930s) and suppression (end of 1940s–1980s) of Soviet Jews. That was one of the Soviet paradoxes.

Generation born in the beginning of the twentieth century later became Soviet Jews and had Russian as a first language apart from the previous one speaking only Yiddish. Abolition of the Pale of Settlement and following the move of Jews to big cities made a big change in the destiny of Russian Jews and their assimilation to Russian life. Those who did not move out and stood in small towns continued keeping Jewish traditions and therefore, were not assimilated. Conversely, a certain part of the Jews – mostly new residents of cities – intermarried, and the children from such marriages grew up leaning either Russian or Jewish spiritual way of thinking. Under the Soviet political circumstances, most of the children in mixed Jewish-Russian families wanted to identify themselves as Russians, marry Russian spouses and not bare their Jewish roots. Thus, a certain number of Jews fully assimilated during the lifespan of three generations between

1917 and the 1990s. Others, less assimilated, preserved some Jewish life attributes.

I assume the older generation had a rough time after they moved out from provincial towns of Pale of Settlement to big Russian cities and started living in totally new environment thereafter. Their move was a big issue and had all aspects of emigration – language spoken (Yiddish, not Russian), no work for a certain time, emotional conditions, and the outer environment. However, the bad situation of the early Soviet period, at the same time, was the end of the damn Pale of Settlement.

Group of young Jews – last residents of the Starodub's Pale of Settlement. Very soon they would find themselves in big Soviet cities. *Bottom row, second from right is my aunt Dvoira.* (Starodub. Photograph of 1928)

Moved to Leningrad, the family started new benchmark. They all were unaware what a hardship they had yet to go through.

CATASTROPHE

The Holocaust organized and controlled by Nazis with active help of collaborationists of different nations was a great tragedy for the European Jews. Of six million Jews who perished in Holocaust, over one million were killed in the Soviet territory.

Before 1980s, the word "Holocaust" was not heard in the Soviet Union. People knew that Germans killed prisoners of war - officers, political commissars, Jews, people of another ethnicities. The words of dedication on monuments for citizens killed by Nazis did not disclose who these citizens were. There was no such a topic in the Soviet Union as extermination of Jews. The Holocaust as the inconceivably massive genocide like no one in the previous history was realized by the world after the Nurnberg Trial over the Nazi war criminals. However, it was different in the Soviet realities. Soviet government did not want people to know that millions of Jews were killed just for being Jews. The first time some people learned about the massive murders of Jews to such a huge scale was after the poem of Eugene Evtushenko *Babiy Yar* published in 1961. It was like a bombshell.

Germans and the local Ukrainian collaborationists assasinated over 50 thousand Jews in a small village Babiy Yar (yar means ravine) near Kiev (Ukraine) just within two days, on 29 and 30 September 1941. How many more of these small Ukrainian, Russian, Lithuanian, Polish, Moldovan, Belorussian and other villages where Jews lived became their massive graves! No monuments, no words, no commemoration for victims of Holocaust. On the contrary, trying to diminish this Jewish tragedy, Soviet principals ordered to top up the Babiy Yar ravine with a liquid waste pulp from a chemical plant and install a dumb to keep the liquid waste in place. In ten years the deteriorated dumb did not sustain and was destroyed by the pulp. The liquid waste rushed to nearest villages making new destructions. Something mystical was in it as if God damned those who let the waste in this massive Jewish grave: do not curse!

Massive killing of Jews took place in Vitebsk, Mogilev, Gomel, Bobruisk, Daugavpils, Riga, Liepaja, Lvov, Lutsk, Rovno, Rostov-on-Don and thousands of other big and small towns and villages. The assassinations were very much alike: initially with obscurity, then fear, horror, and finally, doom and fatality. In the Soviet territory, Jews were not kept in the concentration camps as it was in Central Europe, they were shoot in forests, glades, ravines, which were filled with the dead bodies of women, old and young people (men were mostly in the fronts fighting Nazis).

It is hard to comprehend who participated in the massive killing of Jews. Nazis were responsible for initiation and organization of Holocaust, no question about it. However, too many locals helped them and even took the foremost role in assassinations. Up to today some eastern European officials deny participation of locals in massive killing Jews. Lithuanian journalist and writer Ruta Vanagaite published unbelievably naked truth about participation of ethnic Lithuanians in Holocaust in her book *Svoi. Journey with Enemy*. During 1941-44, two hundred thousand Jews were killed in Lithuanian forests. There are 227 massive graves. Per Vanagaite, 20,000 Lithuanians participated in these killings. There were only 600 to 900 Germans in Lithuania during the occupation. Everyone knows who had organized the Holocaust but that was part of the truth. Just a few knew the whole truth of who implemented the Holocaust. I am grateful to Ruta Vanagaite's bravery to reveal this bitter truth despite of resistance and obstruction she faced in her country. To this inconvenient discovery, I would add that not only Lithuanians but also Latvians, Estonians, Russians,

Ukraineans, Polishes participated in Holocaust mass murders. That is undeniable historical truth that cannot be ignored.

I made a search on Yad Vashem website of who of my relatives died in Holocaust and found depositions of Alexandra Ulmakher, my maternal relative. The testimony stated that our relatives died in Bobruisk. Germans occupied this Belorussian provincial town on the sixth day of war. The family of relatives was killed together with other Jews some time later. In the beginning of August 1941, all Jews were moved to Ghetto where they lived 10-16 people in one room. Cooking, heating was prohibited, for any disobedience – assassination. This is how it described in the Yad Vashem website:

> "On June 28, 1941, Bobruisk was occupied by German troops. Only a small part of the Jewish population was able to evacuate itself to the Soviet hinterland. Almost immediately after the conquest, the Germans issued an order compelling Jews to wear a yellow armband. From the first weeks, they murdered large groups of Jews in unknown places. Thus, on August 5, 1941, SD members and soldiers of Police Battalion 307 assembled a large group of Jewish men under the pretext of transferring them to a labor camp. They were murdered in unknown place. In early August 1941, a ghetto was established on the open space near the airfield in the southeastern part of the city, and Jews from Starye Dorogi, Slutsk, Krichev and Glusk were brought there. The majority of Bobruisk Jewry was murdered in two big operations carried out in September and November 1941." (*The Untold Stories. Bobruisk. Yadvashem.org).*

There were 25,000 Jews murdered just in Bobruisk Ghetto. They were killed for being Jews. Here are the names of Alexandra's and my relatives killed in Bobruisk:

Sheina Khmelnik, place of death: Bobruisk, Mogilev Oblast, USSR. DOB – unknown. Circumstances of death – assassinated in 1941.

Solomon Khmelnik (husband), place of death: Bobruisk, Mogilev Oblast, USSR. DOB – unknown. Circumstances of death – assassinated in 1941.

Genia Khmelnik (wife), place of death: Bobruisk, Mogilev Oblast, USSR. DOB – unknown. Circumstances of death – assassinated in 1941.

Moisey Khmelnik (husband), place of death: Bobruisk, Mogilev Oblast, USSR. DOB – 1875. Circumstances of death – assassinated in 1941.

Bela Khmelnik (wife), place of death: Bobruisk, Mogilev Oblast, USSR. DOB – 1882. Circumstances of death – assassinated in 1941.

Elya Khmelnik (husband), place of death: Bobruisk, Mogilev Oblast, USSR. DOB – 1876. Circumstances of death – assassinated in 1941.

Bluma Khmelnik (wife), place of death: Bobruisk, Mogilev Oblast, USSR. DOB –

1878. Circumstances of death – assassinated in 1941.

Rafail Khmelnik (grandson), place of death: Bobruisk, Mogilev Oblast, USSR. DOB – 1930. Circumstances of death – assassinated in 1941.

Only one family, in one place and one day!

One-third of the entire ethnos perished in the furnace of Holocaust. I am happy that from 1948 a new country was reinstated where Jews will never be oppressed, harassed or insulted just because they are Jews. I repent the Holocaust was required to be recognized by other countries (far from unanimous) in the need of creating the State of Israel.

Unfortunately, none of that eliminated Jew-hatred.

THE AMERICAN KINFOLK

At the beginning of the twentieth century, many Russian Jewish families split into those who left Russia and later became American Jews and those who became the Soviet Jews and because of this, went through the countless hardship. Soviet ideology converted Russian Jews, previously religious inhabitants of the Pale of Settlement, into people ignorant of Judaism. Paradoxically, but at the same time, Soviet Jews became the most educated group in the population. The fortunes of the Russian and American branches of the formerly one Jewish family turned out to be different. The destiny that awaited the Soviet Jews was hard: the cruelest War of 1941–1945, the Holocaust, Stalin's purges, anti-Jewish "cosmopolitan" campaign, permanent fear, and open and then latent anti-Semitism.

Irrespective of whether a Soviet Jew did or did not hide the fact that he had a relative in America, it was bad for him in the Stalinist regime. In case he hid it and the truth was later revealed, he was persecuted for the disguise of this fact. Conversely, if he did not hide the fact that he had a relative living abroad, and moreover, he had an open correspondence with that foreigner, he was not trusted for the connection with a resident of the hostile camp or even repressed. The last correspondence between my father and his American cousin took place in 1935, before Stalin's purge of 1937, as then it became dangerous. Of course, it was not safe for my father earlier but luckily, he avoided repression.

Before I moved to the US for good, my father asked me to find if not his cousin, then his descendants. I said I would try but could not promise success. The story is the result of my longtime search. Unfortunately, I found them after my father passed away. I did what he asked me to do, even though it was too late. I changed the names of the living people to keep their privacy. The story started at the time when hundreds of thousands of European Jews moved to the US.

My grandfather was the oldest of all his siblings and his emigrated brother (my granduncle) was the youngest son in the family. Their parents – Lev and Kreina – my great-grand father and mother had five sons: Lazar (born in 1877), Moshe (1880), Mendel (1885), David (1890), and Reuven (1894). As I mentioned, they lived in the township of Starodub in central Russia. All sons were apparel patternmakers and tailors, the profession mostly occupied by Jewish people then. The family was moderately religious, prayed, and practiced Jewish holidays. By 1907, the older brother Lazar had his own tailor shop and store and married Sarah, an energetic and good-looking young woman. It was surprising for the parents and older brothers when in 1914, the youngest one

Reuven announced (he was about twenty) his aim to move to America.

Note that in 1914, World War I broke out and the Russian Army desperately needed soldiers. I initially thought that Reuven was supposed to serve and trying to avoid military draft. Later, I changed my mind. The war began after the assassination of the heir to Austro-Hungarian throne on June 28, 1914. Reuven came to New York City's Ellis Island on board the steamship "Dwinsk" from Libau (Latvia) on June 30, 1914 after crossing the ocean for a few weeks. Therefore, the beginning of the war had nothing to do with Reuven's emigration to the US.

By the way, I tracked the fortune of the steamship *Dwinsk* and it was remarkable. Built in Belfast (Northern Ireland) in 1897, it was sold to the Holland–America Line and renamed *Rotterdam*. In 1906, it was sold to the Scandinavian–American Line and renamed *C.F. Tietgen*. It was then transferred to Russian–American Line and renamed *Dwinsk* in 1913. Later, in 1917, it transferred to Cunard Line under the British flag and was eventually torpedoed by a German submarine and sunk off Bermuda in 1918.

Thus, my granduncle went to America. To get to American ports, emigrants who lived in the remote areas of the Pale of Settlement had to overcome many difficulties. To travel to the Baltic or Black Sea ports, preparing documents often was a real problem with Russian bureaucracy and spending much money for tickets. Sailing onboard a ship took many weeks to Ellis Island, and that was a real trial for many. Eventually, part of the Russian Jews found themselves in America, the first country to provide equal rights and opportunities for Jews.

This is what I found out about my American relatives. Reuven enrolled in the passengers' list under the name of Ruwin. When I looked through the listing, I thought it was he. Almost all his data that I have previously learned from my father matched the ship's document: under the item "age" was nineteen; "occupation" – tailor; and the nearest relative was Lev, his father. I said almost because one name was different – he indicated under "Last permanent residence" – Russia, Chernigov instead of Starodub and the "Address of nearest relative in country whence alien came" – again Chernigov. According to the civil division of modern Russia, Starodub belonged to Bryansk Gubernia. Why did Ruwin put Chernigov, not Starodub or even Bryansk? This was the question for which I had no answer for quite some time. But then I found out that in the beginning of the twentieth century, Starodub was part of the Chernigov Gubernia. Ruwin wrote he had come from Chernigov, not from Starodub probably to show he was from the urban area rather than the remote one he thought Starodub was. If my logic is correct, all other data about him matched. He later changed his name to become Americanized: Rubin.

 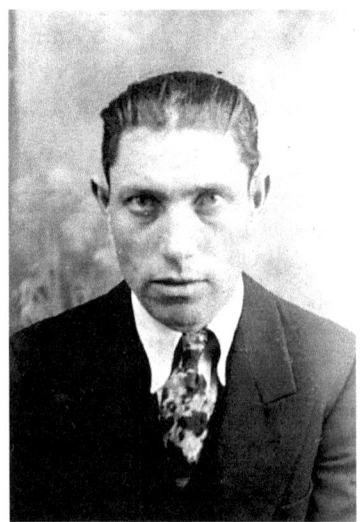

Two brothers – Lazar, photograph of 1934 (*on the left*) and Reuven (Rubin), photograph of 1926 *(on the right)* found themselves on different sides of the ocean in 1914: Lazar stayed in Russia, and Reuven moved to the US.

So, what was the fortune of the person who came to the US alone in 1914 at the age of nineteen years old? I assumed in 2005, the time when I did my search, he was supposed to be one hundred and eleven-year-old and likely, he must have been deceased. Therefore, the next step I made was to check the Social Security Death Index on Ancestry.com. Among over seventy-five million records, only five were close to his age, and one of them matched! Yes, that was he: Rubin! He lived in Brooklyn (Kings County, zip code 11232) and passed away in January 1973 at the age of seventy-eight.

Through the Kings County Clerk's office, I then found the documents for his naturalization and life events dated between June 30, 1914 (Rubin's arrival) and January 1973 (death):

> – *USA Declaration of Intention of Rubin of February 25, 1915, stated that... "It is my bona fide intention to renounce forever all allegiance and fidelity to any foreign prince, potentate, state, or sovereignty, and particularly to Nicolas II, Emperor of all the Russians, of whom I am now a subject..."*
>
> – *Certificate of Arrival – for Naturalization Purposes) for use of aliens arriving in United States after June 26, 1906. To be issued prior to petitioning for naturalization.)*
>
> *US Department of Labor. Immigration Service. Office of Commissioner of Immigration. Ellis Island, NY September 26, 1921. The document certified that Ruwin arrived in New York, NY on June 30, 1914 on vessel Dwinsk. Signed by A. F. Sherman, Chief Clerk.*

– *USA Petition for Naturalization dated October 5, 1921, stated that "I declared my intention to become a citizen of the United States on February 25, 1915. I am married, my wife's name is Celia; she was born on 15 day of August 1895 in Russia… I have 2 children…: Abraham born 10 March 1917 and Lillian born 11 January 1920. I am not a disbeliever in or opposed to organized government…, I am not a polygamist... I am attached to the principles of the Constitution of the United States, and it is my intention to become a citizen of the United States and to renounce absolutely and forever all allegiance and fidelity to any foreign prince, potentate, or sovereignty, and particularly to RUSSIA, or any Independent State within the bound of the former, of whom at this time I am a subject…"*

– *Kings County (Brooklyn, NY) Naturalization Index has identified that Rubin arrived as Ruwin.*

– *Registration Card for men born on or after April 28, 1877 and on or before February 16, 1897: Rubin, Place of residence 258 Osborn St., Brooklyn, N.Y., age 48 (means that it was issued in 1942 with a purpose of military registration), place of employment: Belmont Ave, Brooklyn, N.Y.*

I noted there were little changes in the formal language about renouncing all allegiance to the country of origin in the Declaration of Intention of 1915 and in the Petition for Naturalization of 1921. The first document renounces them to Nicolas II (Emperor), the second one renounces to Russia as a subject. The explanation comes if we consider the huge political changes that occurred during these six years in Russia: fall of the autocrat emperor (tsar), October Bolshevik's revolution of 1917, and the Civil War (1918–1921).

I also managed to trace Rubin's son Abraham after a few life events. The US Army had him registered as a pigeon trainer in 1942. The search was difficult because the names were so common among American Jews. Every time, the search results brought many dozens of names irrelevant to the people I was looking for.

All census data become open after about seventy-five years. Therefore, the last data available for the public are in the 1930 Census but unfortunately, for unknown reasons, the family of Rubin, Celia, Abraham, and Lillian in the 1930 data was not listed. I spent weeks cross-referencing these names but with no success. The nearest was the 1920 Census and I found them! The family of three (all but Lillian) lived on Thatford Av, Brooklyn, NY. Lillian was not included in the 1920 Census as it occurred on January 5 and she was born on January 11. The 1920 Census marked Rubin's occupation as a paddler, and Celia as a housewife. The Social Security Death Indexes showed that Rubin died in January 1973 and his wife Celia in March 1980.

I assumed their daughter Lillian married and changed her last name. That made it almost impossible to trace records of her life events by any available means. It appeared that Abraham was still alive in 2008: when I finished my search, he was ninety-one years old. He has two daughters: Kathy and Betty about my age.

I wrote a letter first to Abraham and received no response, and then to Betty. In a month or so, I received an email response from her:

> "Hello, my name is Betty. I received your letter and apologize for taking so long to reply. After much checking, I believe that we are related. If you wish to contact me, I can be reached at ...(email address) . Best regards, Betty."

I was so excited to receive the email that for the next few days, I was under a great impression of proving a longtime expected contact with an unknown family branch that split from my branch almost a century ago. In my imaginations, it was like a forthcoming meeting of two different civilizations.

My email to Betty started with words about how happy I was that we had such a historic event that after so much time, the descendants of two brothers, Lazar and Rubin, could communicate and even meet. Then I wrote about my findings on her granddad Rubin and her father Abraham's cases.

She never responded to my email. My next short letter in a month and another one in ten months brought no response either. I was disappointed and thought a lot about Betty's lack of reaction. Finally, I thought it is what it is. I made my way toward my American relatives; they did not even take one step. I located and tried to contact these people and it was their choice not to maintain our communication and stay away. Therefore, I stopped being frustrated. The meeting of two branches of kinfolk with different backgrounds has not happened. How deeply these branches alienated!

Although communication with my American kinfolk did not start, I have no regrets about my painstaking search. It increased my understanding how the immigration system in the US of the first quarter of twentieth century worked. I learned something about the life of the Russian Hebrew – this was the name of our ethnicity in the documents of that time. Had my entire granddad's family moved to America a century ago, I would have been one of them and probably a different person than I am now. Even though I belong to the same ethnicity and nation and have same ancestors, my culture would have been different, and my story too.

GENERATION OF "ROOTLESS COSMOPOLITANS"

They were born right before or after the Russian revolution of 1917 and passed away by the end of the century if not died in GULAG, killed in the war or in Holocaust. They lived their life in brutal conditions of totalitarian regime with fear and violence. I think they may feel happy at their young age, as young people are happy just because they are young and do not know a different life with no fear. The World War II was the hardest time they went through. It was the generation that Tom Brokaw on the other side of globe named the Greatest speaking about the Americans. That generation in the Soviet Union underwent even more tribulations.

My father fought Nazis as an officer of the Red (Soviet) Army from the first to last day of the war and had countless possibilities to die. He defended Leningrad and his division participated in the removal of the Nazi siege of this city that lasted nine hundred days, then freed Romania. He finished the war as a captain of infantry.

He enrolled in the Militia (Narodnoye Opolchenie) at the beginning of war in June 1941. After Germans invaded, the Militia was formed and consisted of divisions of volunteers in addition to regular army (later it reorganized and merged with the army). In the beginning, one rifle had been given to every third (!) member of the Militia, and the armless soldiers were told to get their weapons from the Germans in battle.

One time, my father survived the direct hit of the artillery projectile into the dugout where he and three other soldiers were. The dugout was covered with four layers of wood logs. The bombardment started, and the projectile hit through and broke them all. One of the broken logs inclined, forming a triangle with a wall and floor. My father happened to be inside this triangle that saved his life, but he was heavily contused by the explosion. The explosion instantly killed three other soldiers. The commander of regiment ordered to dig out all who died for them to be buried. When father was dug out, he opened his eyes and heard nothing but dead silence. Soldiers surrounded him were astounded when understood he was alive. Ever since he had hearing loss, which increased with time, and at the end he was almost deaf.

Another case happened when he was assigned as a commander of the company of one hundred soldiers. He had the order to take over the hill from the Germans. The hill did not play any important role in a battle, but he had to follow the order. In the heavy battle with Germans, the company lost ninety-six people, and only four – my father while severely wounded – survived. This brainless order took many people's lives as did thousands of other useless orders that cost the lives of millions more Russian people in WWII. Such was a tradition coming from the top downward: a human life did not have a value. Millions of people were exterminated in the purge of 1937–1938, as Stalin and his junta did not care for them in the battlefield.

The 268th Infantry Division where my father served defended Leningrad's suburbs close to the city approach area of Kolpino, which is about five kilometers from the border of the city. He well knew whom he defended from Nazis. His parents, older sister, and young niece lived there inside the cold and hungry city, where more than one thousand people died every day of hunger during the siege. As a deputy of command staff of regiment, he could visit them in the rare hours of hush from the front. The visit he made in early 1942 was right in time: had he comes one day later, he would have not caught them alive. To get to the city he raided a horse. When he arrived on the Third Soviet Street where they lived on the first floor, he brought the horse inside the kitchen to protect it from people who were looking for any food. There were not even dogs in the city, not to say such delicate as horse. He found his relatives bad: only 125 grams of wet fake bread a day per human was not enough to keep alive. His military food chow was much bigger, so he brought bread, butter, and condensed milk. This food saved their lives.

I keep the book *From Neva to Elba* written by the commander of 268th Infantry Division during wartime General S. N. Borshchev. This is what he wrote (p. 259): "the same 18th German Army that entered Paris as a winner in 1940 defeated at the great city of Leningrad in 1944. The 268th Infantry Division took part in its defeat" (my translation from Russian)

Interestingly, I met the son of another veteran of the 268th Division. He happens to be... my wife's relative who now live in Richmond, VA. Every time when we meet, we feel like the fellow soldiers and raise a toast for the 268th Division.

I remember one episode for which I still feel ashamed. It occurred when my parents celebrated their golden anniversary at the end of 1980s. Among the guests, there were five or six my father's friends – veterans of WWII aged about seventy-five to eighty years old. That was a time of Perestroika in Soviet Union. Television and newspapers were becoming freer, publishing challenging political articles, people went to demonstrations, and the entire country was in a bustle. We felt signs of relief. I brought this atmosphere to my parents' celebration party and blamed communists, the Soviet regime and all those who supported it. The veterans and my father just sat quietly and sadly, kept silence and that puzzled me. I had to understand that what I said was the opposite of the ideals they had in mind at the war and for some of them throughout their lives. The values they fought for in the war were now being thrown out. I should have spared the veterans' pride. It must have been a bad feeling to learn at the end that the ideals they were sacrificing their lives for the wrong reason. Stalinist regime called them to defend Soviet and communist values. The tyrant-dictator stole the family and people's values and substituted for his regime and personal name.

My mother to be (second from left) at ten years old with her brothers (from left to right) Yakov, Boris, and Mikhail. All three brothers fought in WWII; Boris was killed in September 1941 on the Karelsky Front. *(Photograph of 1927)*

No doubt, the main life event of their generation was the war of 1941–1945. I cannot miss the statistics of Jewish participation in the war. According to Soviet Ministry of

Defense, statistical reference of April 4, 1946, the number of military orders and medals awarded to Jews was exactly 123,822. I did some calculations, taking the specific number of military awards to ethnic population as the base for comparison. My assessment revealed that Jews are in third place after Russians and Ukrainians and are in advance of Belarusians, Tatars, Georgians, Armenians, Azerbaijanis, Moldavians, and other ethnical entities.

Other statistics about war captivity were disclosed recently: Germans captured millions of Soviet soldiers during the war. For Jews and communists, that meant imminent death. According to different sources, of some 5.7 million Soviet soldiers captured by the Germans, over 3 million died in captivity, while some agreed to collaborate with the Nazis, later enrolling into General Vlasov's army to fight against the Soviets.

The fate of these soldiers was unenviable. They fought against their country, and their claim that they fought the Bolshevik's misanthropic regime makes no excuse. After Germans lost the war, almost all Vlasov's soldiers were captured by the winners. Some of them captured by the Western allies and became the so-called displaced persons, and later turned over to Soviets. About 2.3 million Soviet soldiers – prisoners of war after liberation from the German concentration camps – were put into the Soviet camps. The Soviet government considered the prisoners of war equivalent to traitors. Some of the communist party members, when understood the Germans would surround them, threw their party membership ID out, and if not betrayed by other soldiers, had a chance to survive in German concentration camps. With the coming of Soviet Army, the SMERSH Secret service (Death to Spies) sent them to Gulag for being in German captivity.

The US and the Soviet Union were allies in that war; both had Jewish soldiers and officers in the armies. Following the end of the war, the fortune of the American and Soviet Jewish soldiers was poles apart. After the world learned about the Holocaust tragedy, American soldiers of Jewish descent received even more respect in their country as people whose compatriots died in a catastrophe. A different doom lay ahead for the Soviet Jewish soldiers that returned from the war. Treatment of Jews by the Soviet dictator abruptly changed for the worse. In a false mirror of the Soviet repressive machine, the political interests of the supreme leader were more important than the fortunes of his people. Stalin's logic behind the anti-Semitic campaign of 1948–1953 was supposedly the newly formed State of Israel: since it denied aligning with the communist politics as a Soviet poppy, then all Soviet Jews should pay the price.

My father once shared with me his thoughts about his surprise of not being arrested during Stalin's anti-Semitic campaign. While working as an English instructor at Marine Coast Guard School in Leningrad, he was claimed *a rootless cosmopolitan* in an article of the newspaper *Morskoy Pogranichnik* (Coast Guardian) in 1952 for his educational posters in *English* in the department he headed. The KGB officer questioned him, "Why are these posters not in Russian?" "Because I teach students English," he answered. In fact, it did not matter what he told them: the KGB officer had to report the struggle against the *rootless cosmopolitans* conducted at the Coast Guard School to his headquarters. After such blame, the arrest was usually imminent, and it was just a matter of time for collecting more "compromising materials" like my father's correspondence with his American cousin in the 1930s. He did not know what kept him free. Nobody knew at that point whose turn it was next to go to Golgotha.

In 1957, my father met his former peer of the Pedagogical Institute. Konstantin G. (this was his name) was arrested in

1937 within Stalin's purge, convicted as a British spy, and sentenced. He was freed after about twenty years. On the interrogations in NKVD (the predecessor of KGB) under torture, Konstantin was quizzed about his accomplices in spying for Britain. He initially said invented names. Agents checked, making sure there were no real people under those names, got back to Konstantin and made him suffer more. Then he gave the names of his friends who were arrested and put to Gulag. He did not give my father's name just accidently. My father and Konstantin, when they met last time, talked just a few minutes and then walked away. The last thing Konstantin told my father before they parted forever was that he was afraid to meet anyone he had betrayed. What a horrible regime the Soviet generation survived!

My father used to spend much time with me; he brought me to St. Petersburg museums: Hermitage, Navy, Ethnography, Kunst–Camera, and discussed architectural styles and politics. I received from him my first representations about the world and the cruelest war that had finished just six to seven years previously. He was straightforward and tough with the family members, especially in his best healthy years up to the mid-1970s. His hearing loss was progressing and eventually became intolerable for him after he turned sixty. His teaching job was more difficult and forced him to retire.

The last thirty years of his life (he died at eighty-five), he fought with his progressive deafness, which was the result of his three bruises. At the end of his life, he could not hear anything and did not take part in any conversation. We had a correspondence. In one of his last letters to me, he mentioned his survival at war was a miracle; he was supposed to die many times. He wrote he was not afraid of the death… he waited for it.

My mother was a person who easily got along with people. My earliest recollections refer to the time when I started going to kindergarten, I was probably four years old. Father brought me to kindergarten every day and mother took me back late afternoon. I remember how happy I was one day when all kids went to bed for daytime sleep and my parents took me from kindergarten. We went to a movie-theater on Nevsky Prospect and watched the American film *Tarzan*.

Sometimes, after my kindergarten hours, my mother took me to the large department store *Passage* at the corner of Nevsky and Sadovaya Streets. To me, it was not an interesting visit. Understanding that this shopping was for her, not for my pleasure (it still does not inspire me today), my mother used to buy a piece of cake or ice cream for me and I did not ask her to go back home. This was our agreement by default.

These photos of my father and mother were taken at about the same time (November–October 1942) respectively in Leningrad Front and Ufa, Bashkiria – four thousand kilometers away from each other. Only letters connected them: they wrote over eleven hundred letters to each other during the four years of war. They burnt all letters in 1949 in anticipation of arrests during Stalin's "rootless cosmopolitans" campaign.

My mother had the good ability to relax human emotional stress. Her nieces (my cousins) liked confessing their maiden-like secrets to her. She was a teacher of English at school. Elementary, middle, and high schools in the Soviet Union were combined in one, located in the same building, and had the same name. She graduated from the Leningrad Herzen Pedagogical Institute in 1938 (same graduation course with my father) but started as a teacher in 1950. Before that, she worked as an interpreter and during the WWII, she translated technical manuals of the US and British military equipment supplied to Russia within the Lend Lease. When the war began, and the father went to front, my mother (yet in future) went back to Ufa, Bashkiria near the Ural Mountains, which was far away from the front and where her parents lived.

The war deeply affected not only the army but also the civilians. It was not across the ocean but right here in every home for four years. Earlier I told you the story about my father's relatives in Leningrad when the Germans surrounded it. They survived the hardest winter of 1941/42 and then on spring 1942, they evacuated to Ufa. My mother's parents harbored this family of four and they lived altogether in small apartment until the end of war. The conditions were normal for any Russian family who had to move further from the warfare. My mother once told me that when my father left to war, he was a man she was used to (they were married for three years by 1941). When he came back in 1945, they had to re-build their relations from the beginning as if they had just met.

Father had written six hundred, sixty letters from the front to my mother who waited for him for these four long years, and my mother responded with four hundred fifty letters. They brought all their letters back to Leningrad after the war. Had my parents kept them, these letters could have read as a novel. They kept them only until the political campaign against the *rootless cosmopolitans* (the word Soviet authorities used for persecution of Jews) initiated by the "greatest leader of people all over the world comrade Stalin" in 1948. My parents later decided to burn them all in fear of possible arrest: anything the secret agents may find at the home search would have been used it as "blaming" evidences.

The last push for destroying the letters, as my father told me, was the central newspaper *Pravda*. The article described an extract from the letter written by a certain Rabinovitch from the front, and the KGB used the extract as crucial argument for his execution. "I think many such extracts from my letters would have found had KGB read them. So, when you were barely two years old, I and your mother decided to get rid of the letters," he said to me.

My mother used to say she did two feats in her life. The first one was when she decided to have children while most of the doctors advised her not to because of her medical problem. The second was when she started teaching in a male postwar school with no teaching experience at all at her thirty-four years. Not much for someone but much for the soft character my mother was. It was also much for Vera, my younger sister, and I. Had our mother followed those doctors' advice, we would have never existed in this world. Only one doctor said to her go for it, and she did. The doctor, Solomon Margolin, then became my parents' good friend and I remember him and his wife Anna (a doctor too) visiting our home on different occasions. I am happy my mom gave birth to my sister Vera, a person whom I have always felt I needed to protect.

Officers of the 947 Infantry Regiment soon after finishing the war under the genius military leadership of the Commander-in-Chief comrade Stalin. My father is second from the right on top row. Romania, June 1945.

My mother had one touchable quality: she was easily moved to laughter. I used to take advantage of it and when she was angry with me for something that I did wrong, I tried to make her laugh by making faces or affectation. Being a young kid, I always wondered why other kids love their mothers so much, as no other mothers could compare with my mother because she was one of a kind. I liked asking her provocative questions. At one time, I was about five years old, I asked her who do you love more – Stalin or me (at the time the dictator lived his last paranoid years). She answered in a second or two: you. I love Stalin, I said to her. She did not respond.

In her professional development, she was among the best teachers of English in her school district. As all teachers, she had both more and less favorite students. The number of the least favorite ones was getting fewer with time, whereas the number of favorite students increased. One of her girl-students once told her that she did not believe she was a regular human; she must be an angel. She was always dependable and flexible with my father. When anything bad occurred to my father, whether it was job-related troubles or his personal health problems, my mother was always sympathetic and tried to comfort him. She comforted Vera and me at any difficult time, and that was her mission. I shared my problems with her and always got genuine advice. That was my mother: understanding and loving, protective for us and defenseless for herself, easily drawn to laughter but pessimistic at the same time, a decent, beautiful Jewish woman Rebecca, a daughter of Isaac. Sounds biblical, doesn't it?

My parents belonged to first generation of Jews in Russia free from the Pale of Settlement. The price for that was life under fear of Stalin's guillotine. Their atheism was the inherent part of Soviet life.

That generation went through the terrible war, and thereafter were persecuted by the anti-Semitic Stalin's regime. Up to the last days of their life, they were very close to the family of my aunt, my father's sister. They spent together all holidays: we used to come in to the 3rd Soviet Street in Leningrad where my dad had once brought a horse in winter of 1941. That was our second home and two of my girl

Cousens lived there: Lyuda, the one who survive Leningrad's siege and Lara, the younger one. For the parents, these meetings were like a bit of fresh air - so much different from what they felt outside of this small group of the loved ones. It was like an escape from the cruel world of fear, persecution, denunciations, and hatred. They then came back again to their realities, to hostile environment of communal apartments and showcase conformism to the Soviets.

GENERATIONS X AND MILLENIALS

In immigrant families, English becomes the first language for kids if they arrive to the country before the age of ten to twelve years old. Of course, there may be some variations but generally, it is correct. There may be two languages spoken within one family, and it is funny to watch how parents and their young kids argue in different languages. It is delightful to watch how my children grew up and ripened in this country. They have some Russian background: from the complete high school to incomplete kindergarten. My older son Igor belongs to Generation X who were born in seventies-eighties of the last century. My younger son was born in the beginning of nineties representing the Millennials.

Igor grew up in an environment influenced by a big difference in approaches, views, and ways of thinking between the tandem of my first wife with her tough mother from one side and me from another. We had never agreed on any issues, and Igor's childish mind had always been bifurcated. It was like a competition of whose side the kid would take. Eventually I won because spiritual conversations that make a child think take over the everyday flat talks.

I used to spend much time with him when he was able to understand not merely the command language of parents but also absorb information. We walked a lot, spent time in museums, sometimes went to theaters, and talked about different things. His childhood was placid. He was an easygoing kid until the time came for his parents' divorce. He was fifteen when the family finally broken up.

Anybody who is going to divorce, do it either before your kid is twelve or after he/she is sixteen years old. If a kid is under twelve, he may live with one parent and not implicitly feel a moral discomfort. If he is over sixteen, he is mature enough to be independent to solve his current problems. A parents' divorce divides the immature life of those between twelve and sixteen years into two parts: before (placid and simple) and after (distressful and complicated). The child lived a normal childish life; he builds up his own world where he feels comfortable to live in. He had both father and mother next to him and he expected to solve his kiddy's problems by getting help from both parents. He knew what problems he solved with his father and the ones he solved with his mother. Everything was logical and convenient for him. Suddenly (for him!) his comfortable world ruins. From now on, his life has changed drastically.

My participation in Igor's life was gradually reducing with my longer absence at home. Obviously, my communication with him got limited to our not too often meetings and telephone calls. I understood he was going through a hard-emotional time. He once said to me, "I cannot believe this is occurring in my family. I could have thought of it as happened with some long distant guy." Then he added, "I do not want to live at times." I took his words seriously. Without getting into specifics, the relations in our family damaged and there were no chances to restore them. I made an appointment for Igor at the psychologist.

We entered a large apartment in the center of Leningrad at Petrogradskaya Storona. The doctor met us, told Igor to wait in a separate room, and invited me to his office. He asked me to tell our story, and I told him everything what was going on in our family, and then he asked his questions. He eventually said, "This is what I am going to tell Igor to distract his thoughts from the intended suicide. He must not think of his family as something that should stay intact as a condition of his well-being. Instead, he should concentrate on merely himself and his personal matters. From now on, he should not care about the relations in his family. I will have him to stay away from these bad thoughts and not to take seriously all what is between his parents. It is not his problem any longer. I understand it is selfish and you may have an issue with Igor in future, but this is the only way to save him."

Then doctor invited Igor to enter the office, spoke a little with two of us, and then asked me to wait behind the door. I went out of the room and sat down. In about thirty minutes, Igor came out. I asked him how he was. "Fine," he said. From that day on, he was a different person. He got busy with his own life and I abruptly lost my influence on him. That was the psychologist's plan to save my son that I was looking for. I was happy that I managed to prevent him from the worst. Unfortunately, the price was high: our contacts reduced to almost zero for many years ahead.

We met in New York about ten years later, just three months after our arrival from Russia. He had flown from Los Angeles where he had lived with his mother and grandmother for almost two years by the time. I found a good change in his position: he studied in college and was going to enter the University of California to become a dental doctor. He was not a teen any longer but a well-built fine young man with an ambitious plan.

However, the real change to him occurred years later when he found his vocation as… an art photographer. His making up was difficult. He graduated from university as a molecular biologist, worked for a few years, then dropped everything. He flew back and forth between St. Petersburg, Russia, and New York, took pictures, developed them, had several exhibitions in different countries, but adhered to the Russian culture more than to any other. The topics of his art clearly reflected this adherence. His photographs show his vision of reality, both ugly and beautiful but always unique. He is esoteric, talented, and irrational. "My childhood affected me much," he once said to me. Yes, we are a continuation of what we were while being kids. He has found what he looked for during his prior serpentine life and entered the art world as a mature person who has formed his own style and meaning for its expression.

Igor is a minimalist in a sense that he needs a minimum of well-being for his everyday life. All he needs is funds to cover his expenses for printing, a small Brooklyn apartment, cigarettes, and coffee, nothing extra. I like listening to him about his life philosophy, although we often keep different viewpoints on many issues. I can only add to this that for six years, Igor and Olya, his admirable wife, bring up their son Ilya who has inherited the trait of all our tribe – to be unlike others.

The story of my younger son Boris started when I met Marina, a divorced woman, at a party I was brought by a friend. She had something touchable in her appearance. On that night, we danced under the songs of Laima Vaikule (popular Latvian singer) and eyed at each other. Our relations developed slowly. I had my business trips to Riga, Tallinn, and Odessa, and then we decided to meet again. However, it took three years to take it upon myself. I was not sure about my readiness to become a father of family again. Finally, we got married and I have never regretted it.

Boris was born in April 1991 in Leningrad, Soviet Union. Neither of these two geographic names exist on the map. He lived his first five years in Russia before moving to the US with us.

Most of the immigrants' kids from Russia achieve impressive results in studies. I call it hick's syndrome: a newcomer whose starting social or economic position is lower than the average of the mainstream applies more energy and courage in studying to achieve similar or even higher results. I used to see this bigger enthusiasm yet in Russia: the university students who came from the remote provinces to big cities like Moscow or Leningrad to get higher education were more persistent, studied, and went through any obstacles easier than the local students did. They did not return to their provinces but rather stayed in the capitals and became successful.

Boris is the first in my family to have gone through the entire school system in the US. He started from kindergarten. I cannot forget his first day when I took him there. Imagine a puny little Jewish boy, like what appears in one of the episodes in the *Shindler's List* movie: piteous and unhappy. Add to this, he did not speak even a word in English, did not know anybody, and he had to leave me in a schoolyard to go to his class. They were drawn up in a column by two, and he looked at me the moment before going inside the school. His face reflected so much distress and pain that a parent, a woman who stood next to me when Boris looked at me, uttered, "He makes me cry." I was despondent, and it took time for me to come around.

Here is the same episode but seen and felt by Boris who after thirteen years wrote his essay entering the University of Michigan. I did not suspect that he would bring this topic up years later.

Here is what he wrote:

"I entered this foreign land with tears in my eyes, refusing to leave the grasp of my father's hand. Some call it elementary school, but to me it was another world. As hundreds of people walked across the gymnasium, I was shocked at just how lost I felt. I figured the other kids must have also felt this way. But for me, it was different. They knew something I did not. That something was English, a language I had hoped to one day master."

"A teacher approached me and tried to take me with her. I knew this was the end, as my father had run out the door to go to work. I tried to dry the tears from my eyes, but it only made things worse. I joined the line of kids my age and looked at each of their faces individually as the teacher took attendance. I heard the teacher butcher my name; I would have to get used to this."

"The class walked up the stairs while all the kids talked to each other. Some of them tried to talk to me, but I had nothing to say, seeing that the only words in my vocabulary were "watch" and "beach." Students took their seats and according to the teacher, we had to sit in boy girl order. I was confused as to where to sit and the teacher picked a spot for me."

"I sat there looking around the room and heard a familiar language whisper to me. I turned my head and saw a little black-haired girl speaking Russian to me. After we quickly agreed on the fact that we both spoke the same language, we had an unbreakable bond. After discovering that she knew English as well, I felt as though a bridge had just been built between me and elementary school. I wasn't alone anymore."

"A few moments later, as we were all listening to the teacher lecture us, I felt my bladder knocking. I was clueless as to how to ask if I could go to the bathroom. I looked over to my new friend and asked her if she knew how to ask; she did. I raised my hand, asked the teacher, got up from my seat, and made my way to the boy's room. Hey, maybe this place wasn't so bad after all."

"When I first came to America, it was hard not to be able to communicate with my classmates. I just wanted to be normal, but the language barrier prevented it. Life at home was completely different than life at school; in one world I felt like I belonged, and in another, I felt misplaced. But I pushed through the tough times. The people that helped me along the way, like the girl I had mentioned, were signs of hope. I learned that even in the most difficult situations, there are always tools and resources you can use to help you out."

"I feel as though this experience has made me ready for anything. I now embrace challenges rather than fear them. Although the chances of something similar happening in the future are not likely, I am still ready for anything just as challenging that comes in my way. This experience has made me a stronger person and I look forward to taking the lessons I've learned with me for the rest of my life."

This was Boris's first day at school in September. His cultural crisis lasted few months. By January, he picked up the kid's English so well that we barely could understand him – he spoke so fast. Of course, his vocabulary had just a few dozen words but he freely and easily used them to express anything he wanted to say. He was growing up along with us, his parents, in this country, and his progress was much more noticeable than ours. Indeed, we, the parents, were also like kids who had to learn how to live and survive in a new country. It was as if we got the second life on a half way and we had to learn simple: how to speak, how to behave, how to win, and how to lose. Hick's syndrome was fully applicable to us adults, and it was important to realize that it depends on the drive to achieve something. Age is an issue in the integration process, but motivation comes first. Marina and I needed to provide a decent life and security for our family, and we eventually made it.

Boris has grown up and by the time he graduated from high school, he evolved to a handsome guy with the outlook of confidence and freedom in his eyes. His culture is different from ours. He has grown up in the US, speaks his native English, has many friends, and watches American movies and television shows, so to me he culturally was one-hundred percent American. I thought that was true until we had a remarkable conversation. I would love to discuss general and philosophical issues with him more often but he usually was not inclined to engage in it. Once, as I drove my car, he sat next to me, and we talked. "All of you, [meaning his parents and older relatives] think that I belong to a different culture than you do but this is not correct. I am culturally different from the mainstream Americans; I have different habits and appreciate the cultural diversity rather than likeness. Therefore, I applied to the University of Michigan where I was looking for the diversity."

I asked him why the diversity is so important for him and what is the difference for you whom you communicate with and befriend if you and your friends grew up in the same country and had the same sports and music idols? "Pop," he answered, "you once told me about your Maritime School where you were the only Jew. How did you feel as being the only Jew over there?" I was surprised the way he caught the problem but had no further questions. Such is the generation that goes after us – smart, liberal, different.

3
In the Land of Exodus

The past is not dead. It isn't even past.

William Faulkner

Russia and other parts of the former Soviet Union is the country where almost all nowadays wandering Jews came from. Depiction of this country may help understand their profound roots, cultural character, and motivations.

In western aesthetical standards the ordinary Russia is incomprehensible. It is not true when some say that Russian and American mentalities are alike. Expediency and rationality are the basic point in the American modus vivendi, i.e. approach to problems. This kind of attitude is not an inherent part of the Russian soul. In Russia, the concepts of greatness, symbols, victory, spirituality, great power were always important, hence, so little attention devoted to human being, convenience and quality of people's life. Too many questions on Russian realities do not have answers:

Why Russian people are prone to make idols from their leaders?

Why there is no replaceability of power? Moreover, why each next leader takes over through a coup or after the death of predecessor or by the order of the previous one?

Why many people are so intolerable to those who demonstrate disagreement with the common political views but would tolerate to those who suppress the former?

Why there is a century old tradition to put interests of the authorities above interests of humans?

Why people have so little respect to others and to self?

Why value of human life is so low?

If common corruption in the society so much undermine the country and people, why ordinary people (not to mention the officials) sustain it giving bribes wherever?

I could have continued… many things seen differently when you are not there.

Russia is full of inconsistencies. It is compassionate, harsh and consenting, aggressive and spiritual, as well as indifferent, bored, tough-minded, and irrational at the same time. In 1917, Russia, took in the erroneous political way and paid an extremely high price for this terrible historical mistake. The system had periods of freezing and thaws, but the ground remained the same. In the period of severe freezing, it was a repressive order of the terror-stricken country. In the "moderate" times it was an *equal sharing of misery* associated with the growing number of despondent people who attempted to overcome this misery. Russian Jews were both participants and victims of this misanthropic system.

The epic Jewish departure from the Soviet and post-Soviet Russia needs to be examined. It has to do with specifically Jewish social and political issues in addition to a controversial coexistence of two peoples. Individuals are different but when it comes to a national unanimity, something invisible but strong brings them together or breaks apart. The relationship between two peoples – Russian and Jewish – has never been simple. The attempt to reveal and depict and compare these two common characters and traits has been made. Two hundred years together, especially the seventy years of the Soviet period, affected Russian Jewry. Certainly, the concept of national character has some limitations. Yet, the cultural habits and many common traits make up what is called the national character.

I attempt to depict the common characters of these two peoples, the generalized Russians comprised of many ethnicities populating the state, and the Jews, who lived side-by-side for such a long time. I separate the first from the latter just because this separation has existed for two hundred years and had the consequences both for the Jews and for the country. It is not a black and white picture. From the beginning I do make a provision that every human of any nation is a unique creature; what is ethically acceptable for one may not be good for another. There are always individuals whose character, habits, and mind are opposite to those I depict as national qualities. However, general commonness in national character comprises people's culture. I am going to seek this commonness as well as differences in the context of the coexistence of the two peoples. There would always be some people who may argue against these depictions and reject it. That is their choice. My prerogative is to make this analysis. Let me start this intricate work.

SAME BUT DIFFERENT

In reflection of the relationship between these two peoples Russians and Jews, I do not go so far back as hundreds of years being together, just limit it to the Soviet period. After abolishing of Pale of Settlement, during the 1930s–1950s, Soviet Jews became part of the newly formed strata of the Soviet society, which was called the intelligentsia. It later became an influential trendsetter in Soviet art, science, other activities.

A Russian (Soviet) Jew differs from the European, Middle Eastern, or South American Jews, and even from the

Russian Jewish descendants in America. The Russian Jew bears cultural likenesses to Russians more than, say British Jews have a similarity with Britons. This likeness is due to lack of cultural diversity in the authoritarian society. Soviet Jews have never fully enjoyed of being Jewish. A tiny Jewish autonomous area unnaturally formed in the 1930s in the Soviet Far East did not become center of Jewish culture. Due to political background in the totalitarian regime, Jews just wanted to assimilate into the Russian society and culture. As an outcome, Russian Jew is a carrier of the Russian culture and the Jewish mind. Two peoples are somewhat different but too many traits unite them, representing the Russian background. While discussing the question, we must consider that Russians is the *host ethnicity* in the country, and it counts for way over half of the population, whereas the Jews have never exceeded 4% (now is about 0.2%) of the total population.

Russia is a multi-ethnical country. Through the centuries, many ethnicities have assimilated, and it is now difficult to find a human who has been one hundred percent Russian in three to four generations back. Seventy years of the Soviet rule leveled ethnically different peoples to the Soviet people, "the new historic commonness" as it was officially claimed in 1972 at the fifty-year celebration of the USSR's existence. Therefore, we can only characterize this historic commonness of various ethnicities by calling them Russians. Describing a character of the entire nation is a lowly employment. Born and lived in Russia, I am culturally Russian and partially the one who does not belong to them due to my Jewish mind. Therefore, I can look at the issue both as an insider and outsider.

Generally, before the October Revolution of 1917, different categories of Russian characters viewed as a noble, a commoner, and a peasant. K. Marx called these categories social classes. The ideas and well-being of a class have predetermined the features of the character. For example, nobility, as the upper class, had their own understanding of honor and reputation, which was not likely adhered to peasants or commoners. This changed drastically after 1917. Prosecution and extermination of the former upper class, and years of fear and terror have wiped out the nobility. With it, the model of human honor that used to be the dominant notion among the nobles has gone. As a result, we have had the *Soviet type of character*, which is also not as plain as it seems. In the late Soviet period (1960–1980s), the society encompassed two unequal parts: common people (the majority by a number) and intelligentsia (the minority). The difference between these two groups within the same nation was so noticeable that we had as if two civilizations within one country (the division seems to exist up to now). The intelligentsia and the originating middle class more often have independent views on social and political problems. Paradoxically but Russian commoner sounded less anti-Semitic than some Russian intellectuals possibly because a scholar always declares louder. Jews mostly belonged to intelligentsia and often shared spiritual, social, and political views with other members of this specific part of the Soviet society.

My attention stresses the common character because the number of its carriers is prevalent. The common Russian character is tolerant to obstacles and difficulties, even to suppression from authoritative power. Moreover, he prefers it to a liberal regime. The authoritarian rulers best loved by Russian people. The representative rulers are Stalin and Putin. The unlimited power over the institutions, justice, parliament, press covered by a phraseology about the state interests, which is in fact a shield for the absolutism, made them extremely popular leaders. They used different means to establish their power, but the result is similar: unlimited power over the state institutions like justice and parliament, and common people. Other rulers like Gorbachev or Yeltsin, who did not repress the commons (to some extent, Khrushchev and Brezhnev in that number) were not loved and even despised. This puzzle spills some light to the enigmatic Russian soul.

The borderline between people's love and fear is elusive. The fear has always been a necessary feature of the strong power. The fear of supreme leader and suffering in the name of him have always been the attributes of the powerful Russian leader. Once bitten, twice shy – this is about the people under repressive dictator. The reason of this acceptance may hide in the deep Russian Orthodox notion – the sufferer is believed to go to paradise after life. This has something to do with political inactivity of most Russians. They blame others rather than selves for all wrongdoings but do not admit their personal responsibility for the wrong vote or for giving a bribe or for their indifference: that is somebody's fault, not mine.

Russian character is cheatable and distrustful at the same time. The ideas of miraculous progress of economic and political progress can easily indoctrinate into common people's consciousness. Political leaders understand this clearly and take advantage of people's credulousness using government television channels. Television seen by millions is a sphere where the leaders show up many times a day as saviors of the nation. The TV talk show hosts have been brainwashing so many common people.

In the post-Soviet period, when making money became a new religion, someone Mavrodi, a cunning crook, created Ponzi pyramid in the beginning of the 1990s. His "investment" bank bled dry thousands of witlings, giving out high "profits" to the first who applied for money return and closing his office when other people requested the same high "dividends". People's credulity was boundless. What happened next: the same group, whom he cheated and robbed, voted for him as a Member of Parliament! He then sat in Parliament until his arrest. Similar pyramid was created by Bernie Madoff in New York. The difference between Russian and American pyramids was that investors believed in Madoff only up to the financial crisis of 2008. When they checked their deposits and understood they lost the money, he was exposed and brought to justice whereas Russian depositors were still bringing their money even after Mavrodi's exposal. The credulity exists in Russian character in the political aspects as well: a unilateral propaganda penetrates people's consciousness, and they trust all what authorities want them to believe.

Distrustfulness is not the opposite but the backside of the ability to be cheated. Fear of possible harm from the people who surround is on the subconscious level. The Russian is not as open as a common American; he will not speak openly with somebody unless it is someone he knows. Here is just a typical example. A few groups of people are in an elevator. Americans within one of the groups talk naturally, without lowering their voices; Russians speak low to each other or not speak at all not to allow other people listen to their talk. The fear also caused a distinctive approach to treatment of the surrounding people in a certain way. A first time-met person is considered not a good one unless he proves he is good is a typical Russian approach – apprehensive and unfriendly.

A common Russian is generous. Once I drove my car in a remote area with no road covering and since it was a rainy day, my car slipped. I called a tractor driver who was working nearby; he hooked my car up and pulled it out. I was grateful and gave him two bottles of vodka that happened to be in my trunk. What do you think he did? He said he could not take all vodka from me and returned one bottle back to me.

The notion of fairness is deeply inside Russian character. The fairness understood as spreading the wealth equally rather than by the merits. Possibly because of that Russia was the first country where the real socialism was implemented and existed for seventy years. The rich and successful business people are not loved in Russia. The sense of fairness is predominantly higher than the law obedience on the scale of people's virtues. Hence, this cultural notion creates problems in the national and international legal field. For example, annexing of Crimea was widely supported by Russians just because people over there speak Russian, and it did not matter the peninsular belonged to Ukraine.

The more fear people feel towards the state and the leader, the louder we can hear how people must love the state. It is a big difference in Russian and Western perceptions of the relationship between people and the state. In Russian mentality, the concept of tsar and his *oprichniks* from one side and the grassroots who serve them on the other side is still popular. Freedom only starts when the common people understand that the state serves them but not the opposite.

A common Russian is kind-hearted. He is not too outgoing, but he may open his heart and unburden himself to a person he sits with. Mostly it comes about while drinking. Russians' inclination to drink is on the national level: it is like the obesity for Americans and rather their disaster than fault. One nation suffers from overeating; another one from overdrinking. The real threat for the nation's existence impends from that side, and this is not a CIA plot. Frenchman drinks no less but he realizes when to stop. Russian does not. He drinks at home, in parks, restaurants, stadiums, picnics, everywhere… for the reason, for no reason, meeting friends, relatives, alone, after workday, sometimes even before the workday. Common drinking unites people even if they barely know one another. In a company of drinking people, the one who does not drink looks suspicious for the others, as if he does not belong to their community. While drinking, people feel warm, secure, they love the world. A proverb says: Merrymaking in Russia is drinking. Meanwhile this lifelong attraction brings its bad if not tragic effects. Divorces are common on this basis but more disturbing are the crimes, stabbings in a kitchen after common drinking, deadly accidents, and suicides. That is a final phase of such merrymaking.

What really makes the difference between Russia and the West is the common practice of cutting corners in Russia. For instance, the right procedure comes first in the West, whereas the Russians often not too much worry about completing all steps of a procedure, be it business or technology or safety. Yes, the rules exist; staff of inspectors filled but… an inspector may be bought over. That is one of the possible reasons for technological backlog and inadequate quality of goods made in Russia compared with the West. It is even sadder that it leads to more corruption. If the full procedure, say for fire safety or construction inspection has not carried out for the sake of saving money on it, then an inspector who "does not see it" either does not know what he is doing or is corrupt. Either way, the results are always bad – from the lives lost to technical degradation.

Russian character combines such opposite traits as compassion and indifference at the same time. Even if someone is guilty but he suffers a lot, people sympathize with him. Politically, this peculiarity influences people's support. For example, Yeltsin suffered persecution from the communist Politburo and was elected the president of Russia. At the same time, people have astonishing indifference to the acute suffering of others. Years of socialist dominance formed people's jealousy as part of the character. There is a saying that it does not matter how well you live, it is important that your neighbor does not live better than you do. A terrible example of the indifference is the tragic incident with the passenger steamship *Bulgaria* that sunk in the Volga River during a heavy storm in July of 2011. The ship was overloaded with people and children. A big wave covered the ship from one side; it lurched to a dangerous angle, received too much water through the opened doors and portholes, then lost its stability and sunk. The captains on two passing ships saw people in the water and did not come to help. Only a third ship arrived and saved a few people but most of them died, including over thirty children. Russia, what is wrong with you?

What was the deliberations of the people on board the two ships that passed by the sinking people as if garbage floating on a river? The country is badly ill. The deep indifference comes from the late socialism. "Why do I have to help anybody if I live poorly?" Such was the sense for the conscience sake. After collapse of socialism, many people considered themselves adhered to Christian Orthodoxy and now wear the cross on their necks. I assume some members of the passing ships had the crosses on their necks.

An important feature belongs to the distinctive strata of Russian society - intelligentsia: spirituality. Arts, literature, and theater, as part of the traditional Russian culture, have always been important for the intelligentsia. Even in the dark middle of Soviet dominance, some theaters in Moscow and Leningrad made a deep impression on many of them. My obligation is not to miss this Russian feature and note that a big number of Jews were the inherent part of the Russian intellectual community.

Apart from the US, there were no neighborhoods populated by a certain dominating ethnicity or race in the Russian and former Soviet republics' cities. Russians, Tatars, Jews, Ukrainians grew up together, attended same public schools, were taught by the same teachers. Within the Soviet society, the influence of religious confessions on separation of people was minimal. All of these made Soviet Jews culturally look much alike the Russians and the other Soviets. Even though the Jews did not want to expose themselves Jewish, still almost every Soviet Jew had slightly expressed elusive distinctions. Let us see what those differences were and how they affected Jews.

A Jewish character is not easy to portray plainly. Jews are separated deeply by the civilizations they grew up with. Ashkenazim, Sephardic, Bukharian, Mountain, and Ethiopian Jews are like different nations or even races. It is not my purpose to characterize all of them but only the Russian Jews, the specific part of the Ashkenazim. Although Russian Jews are far from Judaism and deeply assimilated into the Russian culture, they suffered full-scale anti-Semitism. When it comes to a grave problem, Jews help one another and whereby hated by anti-Semites even more. I did not mean to say that all Jews are brothers between themselves. If two Jews contend each other, it is a tough struggle. Years ago, in Russia, I had a Jewish boss of retirement age. His concern was not to admit me to become a PhD to take over as a group leader. I spent years in this harsh conflict to hear from him when he retired that he was not right.

The first and main Jewish feature I would point out is a sense of belonging to the community, a consolidation. It has a historical ground. As a reason for this sense, Soviet writer, Ilya Ehrenburg (1891–1967) considered persecution. He wrote, "start chasing all the redheaded and they would consolidate." In fact, most of Jews feel obligated to help each other. I remember one episode from my childhood. I was twelve years old and we had just moved to a new room in one of the districts in Leningrad. My mother went to local school to enroll me. The deputy school director, a Jew, met her. When she gave him my name, he asked her in Yiddish, "A Jewish boy?" My mother nodded. "Bring more, bring more," he said with a smile.

Pointing to this Jewish feature Joseph Roth, an Austrian journalist noted describing the peasants' community of the first years of socialism in Russia: "The Russian peasant is a peasant first and a Russian second; the Jew is Jew first and then peasant" (*The Wandering Jews. The Classical Portrait of a Vanished People*. W.W. Norton & Company, NY-London, 2001, p.11, 110). It was noted in the 1920s but still relevant today in some countries where oppression of Jews exists. In America, such a behavioral trait is not common.

Another important Jewish trait is the tendency to take active part (excessive as some think) in the political and social life in the countries of their residence. Taking their leadership in politics in countries like Russia and Germany often brought a burst of anti-Semitism. Solzhenitsyn called Jews a "catalytic agent of any society." No doubt, this common Jewish quality to be the first in politics, arts, science, or industry is a distinctive one. Other people seemed to not like it, which is objectively reasonable: you came to our land and you take the lead. Historical development did two things to the Jews that contributed to anti-Semitism: took their land from them and gifted high intellect to a statistically significant number of them. The more fear of competition to active and sharp Jews, the more anti-Semitic the country's government and the people. The examples are medieval European countries, Germany of 1930s-1940s, Poland of the 1950s–1960s, and the Soviet Union of the 1940s–1980s influenced world history, and there are many examples, both good and bad, of this stimulus. Many books and articles describe Jews: the authors who like Jews depict mostly good deeds influenced by Jews, and the ones who do not like them describe more of the bad things promoted by Jews. Even those who do not like Jews would not deny the fact that without this nation, the world and its history would be different in every respect.

The distinctive aspect of the Jewish character is a variety of opinions on issues or problems: every Abram has his own program (for improvement of the world); and two Jews always have three opinions. It is in deep Jewish tradition to discuss anything with anybody. Even the Biblical forebear of all Jews, Abraham argued with God to save Sodom and Gomorra from the destruction. The late Israeli President Shimon Peres once said, "Leading the Jewish people is not easy– we are a divided, obstinate, highly individualistic people who have cultivated faith, sharp-wittedness and polemics to a very high level." Freedom of opinion has become a fundamental base of democracy in modern civilized world.

Another part of Jewish character is dedication to knowledge and education. No wonder the percentage of higher-educated Russian Jewish immigrants is the highest among any other immigrant communities. A typical Russian Jew is secular that proves the education has less to do with the religion but rather with the national tradition. A relatively large number of Jews took lead positions in industries, science, and arts.

Every human is unique, and the deviations from the average may be big. Further, some people often use the intelligence charged to many Jews to accusing them of cunningly taking advantage over others. They blame Jews as being sly and dishonest towards their non-Jewish partners. That may apply to any nation but for some reason, a few bad examples are enough to generalize the feature to all Jews. I will cite N. Berdyaev again about some national qualities of Jews:

> "There is Jewish self-conceit, which displeases...
> Jewish people is a people of the polar opposite

qualities combining high moral traits with the low ones, aspiration to social justice with inclination to capitalistic additions" (N.A. Berdyaev. *Christianity and Anti-Semitism. The Religious Fate of Jewry.*)

Jewish aspirations to be in advance of other peoples played both good and bad roles in Jewish fate as a people: on one hand, it promoted anti-Semitism, but on another hand, it played critical role in the development of many countries.

Russia has deeply affected the mentality and culture of her Jewish nationals. I have watched both secular Russian and American Jews here in the US. The cultural difference between them is as much as it is between Russians and Americans. American Jews are active, individualistic, dedicated to knowledge and education, talented but… unconsolidated on the platform of their Jewishness. I do not have in mind the Orthodox Jews whose primary feature is a sense of belonging to their community. The discrimination in the former country made Russian Jews consolidated. There is another game play in America: no discrimination – no consolidation. This is how the country's policy towards Jews shaped Russian Jewish national character.

A Russian Jew still has many qualities the American Jew does. However, a Russian Jew is not open. Remember the example with groups of people moving in an elevator and behaving differently? That is about us as well. We hardly openly discuss our personal issues in the presence of strangers inside an elevator or anywhere because of a subconscious fear of possible harm. This is what the culture of limits and the lack of freedom did to us. A person needs to be born in a free society not to be suspicious in the back of his mind.

Another change refers to our view of the Judaism and Jewish tradition. Communist rulers replaced religion with religious-like dogmatic political idolatry. The leaders wanted people to admire them, not to offer worship to God. It is difficult to say what a secular Russian Jew would have characterized in the cultural expression if not for the communist bondage. Communists deprived them the opportunity of their own choice and thus, they remained ignorant to Judaism as a system of values. I do not say many of them suffered for being secular but Judaism is not just religion but the Jewish culture as well.

Russians and Jews went through different political epochs: feudalism, unripe capitalism, ultra-left socialism, and then back to a crude capitalism. How it affected the Jewish character is not a one-to-one issue. Both peoples went through enormous suffering and shared the common misery. Whether they liked it or not, but the joint misfortunes and the ways they were overcome, made the Jews living in Russia in the twentieth century less Jewish than ever, at least extrinsically. That was the result of the coexisting of two peoples, big and small in the totalitarian country, and Jews did not have too many options to survive. However, there have always been reasons, both internal and external that kept Jewish national self-consciousness. The internal reason is stronger family and people-to-people bonds shaped under the persecution. The external reasons were terrible Jewish tragedies of the past century that influenced the identity of the Soviet Jews.

Some traits of the Soviet national character developed under social circumstances. For example, cutting corners are a typical result of the history of violence grown under the condition of fear and indifference. A wish for security for self at the cost of others made people prone to violate fundamental commandments: do not thieve, do not bribe, do not lie, and help your neighbor. The dominating concept of the communal property (was factually considered as nobody's property) penetrated people's minds and developed a system of the dishonest values. According to this wrong thinking, stealing anything belonging to the state or taking bribes was considered customary business.

I would like to add just one cultural feature. It is lack of tolerance to one another. It takes place anywhere – in municipal transportation, department stores, or official buildings. It is especially noticeable when it comes to political discussion. People often overreact and cross the limits of a civilized discussion. The reason being is no tradition of holding the correct political debates. Emotions go too far, which is fraught with a sour of lose friends. This breach in attitude is because of intolerance to the opposite political viewpoint. We pay the price as being deficient in respect to others.

Two peoples lived together side-by-side for two centuries. Something clearly Russian is inside every Russian Jewish character. That did not diminish their bitter humiliation from anti-Semitism: the compassionate Russian soul could coexist with ill feelings toward the Jews.

RUSSIAN ARGUMENTS OF THE PAST CENTURY

Russia belongs to both Europe and Asia, and Russian soul torn between two civilizations. What it takes from each is easy to watch: rationality, liberties and technology come from West; autocracy, hypertrophic role of religion, suppress of freedom invade from East and South. These winds blowing in opposite directions have always challenged Russia on which way to go. Within the reign of emperors Peter the Great and Alexander II and at the later times with leadership of Gorbachev or Yeltsin, political vector turned closer to west. On the contrary, at the time of Alexander III, Nicolas II, Stalin and Putin that vector switched to east.

After the Russian revolution of 1917, humanity watched the transition from capitalism to socialism when all properties, industries, land taken from the owners and nationalized. That way turned out to be dead ended. The opposite way, from socialism as a bankrupt system to capitalism, after collapsing of the Soviet Union was new and extremely painful. This was the price for madness of 1917, for Russian Civil War, for collectivization of agriculture and extermination of millions who opposed to Bolsheviks, for politics of primitive idolatry of autocrat leaders.

I hesitated if I need to write about the Russian past. So much was said about the communism and its hatred nature! Is it worth talking about it again? Eventually, I decided to say on this topic in my own words. Let me underscore that this is not a historical manuscript but afterthoughts on the recent past in context of Russian and Jewish fortunes. I wanted to be unbiased, but it does not turn out, still painful!

Soviet Union, the country where the Russian Jews originated, is no longer exists. The Soviet society is now perceived as a mixture of triumphant boorishness, almost religious faith for fairness of sharing equally, and a cruelty in the name of this fairness. From the very beginning, this regime ground the ideas of a common fairness down into a slavish tyranny and genocide. At the end, it had transformed into a society of apathetic and skeptical people longing to get anything basic to provide their primitive life.

In 1917, common Russians, Ukrainians, Jews, Kazakhs, Tatars – the peoples populated Russia – bought the Bolsheviks' rhetoric that they had only take wealth away from a few rich and share it with all… and then a good and fair life will come in forever. Russia has always believed in miracles. That miracle held out for over seventy years and took millions of lives.

The reason Russia has not transformed to a real democracy is traditional people's inclination to autocracy and adoration of leaders cultivated with generations of absolute and cruel power. In addition to autocracy, the Soviet regime became misanthropic. Now, after decades of one of the most inhuman repressive rules in history, surprisingly, but many Russians feel nostalgia for the dictator Stalin and the fearful superpower – the Soviet Union. Some Western intellectuals adhere to the far-left ideas, notwithstanding the Soviet experiment has shown how these ideas may turn out if realized. One of the proponents of such ideas happened to be a friend of mine.

I met Russell Steam, a talented medical doctor and patriot of his native Bronx, in New York on spring 1999. Since the 1980s, he has permanently lived in Japan, practiced medicine there, but he often travels to New York and calls himself the Bronx expatriate. My colleague and good friend Gaylord, a longtime friend of Russell's, introduced him to me.

We met in the Bronx Botanical Garden. We talked for several hours, then met on different occasions at his apartment at Gun Hill Road and at my home, and then continually exchanged emails for years. Russell likes writing on medical topics, art, politics, literature, and social themes. Often, I do not have enough time to respond. However, sometimes, I could keep silence because what he wrote was often opposite to what I think is right. He considers himself a communist, which is rare now but was popular forty or fifty years ago when many Europeans romanticized communism (I had a chance to see it in Europe in the 1960s). Russell and I keep opposite political views. Notwithstanding this fact, I patiently read his opinions on different issues just to realize what logic stays behind such opinionated views. Once, after reading his letter – it was something very negative about America and Israel and friendly to their enemies – I felt a wave of indignation overweighs the decorum and responded with advice to include the Al-Qaeda leaders into his mailing list but exclude me. In a few weeks, he wrote back saying he thought our political differences should not break our longtime communication. I responded that I agreed and was glad he did not take it personally.

Anyway, it is even more disturbing that Russell's leftist viewpoint becomes popular within a certain group of intellectuals who expose themselves as liberals struggling for fairness and equality. Exactly the words claimed by the Bolsheviks in 1917, and consequently we got the country with the uncontrolled and irremovable leaders, and common people suffered the despotism.

One needs to understand that a corner habitude of Soviet society was inclined to have small but equal pieces of possessions. The October Revolution of 1917 and the events that followed had to do with people's equality. Still in the distant 1960s, the word *equality* has magical importance to most Russians. In 1961, General Secretary of Communist Party Nikita Khrushchev announced that the current generation of Soviet people would live in a communist society where everyone is equal. What it meant was the transition from the formula of socialism "from everyone according to his abilities, to everyone according to his labor" to formula of communism "from everyone according to his abilities, to everyone according to his needs." It sounded pleasant and nobody discussed these formulas or the question seriously. But what if someone has too little capabilities and too big needs, would he still deserve to have more than others?

People just liked to hear they would live in such a good society where you could do little but get much. Communist theorists counted on forming a new human being who would have high consciousness dedicated to communist ideology. However, human nature is different; a man is not an angel but a mixture of angel and evil. It is not likely this nature changed during thousands of years. Humanity has just become more experienced after going through it all. The communist agenda of forming a new human with the false thesis on the sharpening of the class struggle upon developing socialism was a big excuse that caused Stalin's purges of killing and jailing innocent people in the 1920s–1950s.

It is so Russian to believe in fairy tales that a good magician comes down and gives the people all they need. Taken seriously in the 1960s about the modern generation that would live in communism, it became a topic of anecdotes in the 1970s and nobody even recalled this promise in the 1980s. Who of the Soviet people had even imagined that the Empire would collapse so soon? With all those missiles and nuclear shields, the army of more than four million soldiers and three hundred million populations, the Soviet Empire seemed as unshakable as a cliff and everlasting as universe. However, the finish stole up humbly. Could it be different if people spoke one way but thought and behaved another way? The communist country has never had a human-oriented ideology. Collapse of this political system just proved that any repressive regime is doomed to disappear. Still some people believe in the "ideal communism". They are convinced that Russian communists just spoiled a good and fair idea.

The communist ideals are common to many Russians missing the Great Soviet Empire or some older ones missing the Communist party. I found a sincere apologist of this conception in Dr. Russell Steam. I am going to quote our written discussion with his permission almost in full reflecting the main argument of the twentieth century.

> "…Yes, it is obvious from my writings, that communism has an attraction for me. But no, I have never said or implied that I

contrast my attraction to communism with a lack of (or less of an attraction to) democracy. This is a common mistake from persons who are brainwashed contra communism: that it is a system whose opposite is democracy. So, to these types of brainwashed persons if you seem in favor of communism you must either dislike democracy or like it less than the average educated person. Especially in the USA where 99+% of persons on the left or the right politically are brainwashed contra communism, an answer to the question needs to first educate them what is communism."

"Also, important to keep aware is that "-ism", a suffix which means a doctrine or a teaching - of a way of life, a philosophy or political system – has in English acquired a subconscious negative feeling. Examples, "Nazism", "Hitlerism", "Satanism", Atheism (and belief in all non-Christian faiths, all originally words made by Christians), "Hooliganism", "Capitalism" – all these negative implications contrast with good ones for the modifiers like "democratic", "Christian", "pro-life", for things Americans either admire or at least feel neutral about."

"Well, we have to live with using "communism" but just keep aware when you ask me about it that your feelings are being manipulated by the language."

"Communism can be reduced to a teaching of an idea of "share and share alike." It can be contrasted with Me-ism, Individualism or even Libertarianism, each of which have their own separate twists but essentially mean that in your own life behavior or the government you prefer the individual; that is, you as an individual are either all important or majorly dominant over others."

"Communism considers the good of the community as of equal or greater importance than the good of the one individual. It advocates arranging the power in society so that, for example, gifted or financially rich or stronger persons do not have a share of the wealth or control that is in proportion to their wealth or strength or giftedness. So, in a communist society – a millionaire would not be allowed – no Michael Jacksons, no Madonnas, no Obamas, no Rockefellers (These persons would not be deleted, they would be reduced to normal status (in power, possessions, etc.)"

"Being a communist can simply mean sharing as much as possible in your life and behavior. On a political level it means working to advance a system of government where the electorate controls the means of power – like the banks, the major industry factories, the major services – like telephone and electricity and water, and offshore drilling etc.) and gives socialized services free, like medical and dental, postal, banking, etc. We do not have that today under our system that promotes individualism and libertarianism."

"I was attracted to communism as a long-term result of my independent childhood education starting with reading HG Wells's

The Outline of History at age 9. HG Wells was not a communist and his book does not promote it, but it gave me an un-brainwashed view of the Earth and of the progress of human history and of the possible human future. And that view was reinforced as I became more educated. Especially as I saw that humanity was entering a crisis period because of overpopulation and its effects such as Global Warming."

"Communism as a political idea arose among the European peasants in the middle ages in their struggle against the tyranny of power. In the 1800s various writers who represented movements for freedom, like the Anarchists and Socialists developed the ideas of political communism. In the mid-1800s, Engels and Marx wrote the first great works that put down the ideas of communism as an economic and political system. Until the 1900s, it was never in control as a government. The world systems have evolved as humanity developed from primitivism that you might have seen in central African tribes as late as 1700 to Slave Systems like Ancient Greece and Rome to semi-slave Feudalism like European middle ages and Russia up to mid-1800s to the present control by capitalism sometimes in a democratic form, sometimes in a totalitarian form up to the present. In the 1900s after the World War I the first communist states developed. For historical reasons the communist countries – Russia, China – developed in the most undemocratic populations that had just before been ruled by Kings or other dictators. So, they tended to be more totalitarian regimes than many capitalist regimes in the West. But within each communist nation's own area each one was an advance in terms of freedom over what had come before (Russian communism over czarism, Chinese communism over the Chin Empire). So, these communist states were and are very imperfect."

"Communism is not against democracy. In fact, the two should go hand in hand. In the communist state of the future, elections will be free, and communism will be chosen by the electorate. But before that can happen the apparatus of capitalism and the power of the few rich individuals must be destroyed and that is going to mean a lot of killing and destruction of property whether you or I like it or not."

"Like Christianity, communism (which has philosophical connections with the Jesus ideas of human behavior) is fighting an uphill battle, but it will, in my opinion, – like Christianity – probably be successful. Keep in mind that the historic Jesus (probably not a real person but an agit/prop character) started in about 0 AD and it took 300+ years of persecutions until Constantine the Great converted his late Roman Empire to it, and even then, another thousand years were needed for its complete triumph. So, politically, communism is not doing badly if we consider 1848 its birth date. Meanwhile each of us living in the capitalist society can be communist in our behavior as best we can manage. Share and share alike. Back communist systems. Educate the people by your own life and by writing and showing."

Russell's letter draws the ideal communism as conceived by Karl Marx. Once forcefully implemented, it soon evolved into its terrible but logical consequence: dictatorship and repressions instead of freedom, slavery instead of free labor, and common poverty instead of well-being. This was my response to Russell:

"I have always envied the defenders of communism because all their slogans sound fair and convincing. In fact, it is easy to persuade the ignorant people with the statements like there would not be rich and poor individuals or the rich should share their wealth with the poor. Of course, it is excellent if there is no poverty. However, these catchy calls are against the human nature. Implementation of these slogans into the real life cuts out the incentive to achieve something good – work harder, think smarter, and do job better. Why would someone do better if anything extra received for his/her outstanding entrepreneurial ability or invention or performance would anyway be shared with other people who have less capability or desire or talent to achieve anything good? Thus, this first condition of the communism would cut the incentive of the most successful and talented.

That in turn would make the progress slower, limit the initiative and as a result, would not provide any prosperity for a nation."

"Let us set the mental economic experiment: may income taxes increase up to 90% from the rich. In this case, we would have most of the tax money shared with other less successive population, have a huge government to control the distribution and... stoppage of the economy. Drifting to more taxes will bring more socialism that eventually would come to a system failure." You say: "Communism…advocates arranging the power in society so that … gifted or rich persons do not have a share of the wealth or control that is in proportion of their wealth or giftedness. So, in communist society – a millionaire would not be allowed…" How familiar it sounds! We have already gone through it in long-suffered Russia. With just one predicament: wealthy and rich people did not want to voluntarily give up their power and control. Consequently, it was taken away from them forcefully."

"To achieve the goal of humans' equality in a literal sense the bloodshed was necessary or that goal would never achieve. Your words "apparatus of capitalism … must be destroyed and that is going to mean a lot of killing and destruction of property whether you or I like it or not" means the civil war is imminent. In Russian Civil War of 1918–1921 four million people died from both sides. After millions of killing, the "Jesus ideas of human behavior" would not be possible like it was not possible in the real Soviet socialism."

"Communism is not against the democracy, you say. Yes, communists never say they are against it. Why do you think, "Elections will be free, and communism will be chosen by the electorate"? What if the electorate does not choose them? Then "…a lot of killings", and "destroy the apparatus of capitalism" follow. They would never give up the power in case they lose the democratic elections. They seize power not to give it up but to keep it. Such is the forceful nature of the communism. As a result, the renaissance of Gulag for dissidents and psychiatric clinics for those who think, and act differently would return."

"I never understood your sympathy to the misanthropic communistic regime in the Soviet Union. Probably you got freedom of expression and other freedoms as granted because you were born in the US. I did not. I know what it is to live in that stuffy atmosphere of KGB dominance and understand the value of the real freedom."

I do not seriously think that Marxist ideas would ever again be imposed on Russia but any radical left models are possible in the Third World countries. The examples are North Korea, Cuba, Nicaragua, Venezuela and others where leftist governments are in power. Except the oil-extracting Venezuela, what we see there now is a dictatorship and poverty. It looks familiar to what we have already seen in our past.

The Soviet regime and its specific way of life is a unique historical experience and needs to be understood and analyzed from today's positions. Most of those who lived in that country and watched how the Soviet empire crashed have become immune to communism and the Marxist type of socialism. They do not want it to return except for the invariable 10–15% of Russians that continually vote for communists.

There was an entire generation born about the time Russian communism burst in. The generation that fully absorbed it, lived in it, and went away with its downfall. They had never known the life free of violence. A great riddle of that Soviet generation was that they simultaneously believed in and feared the same entity. In this dual affection, the fear was a prevailed feeling over the belief. This was a typical eminence of the slavish people – belief through fear and idolatry.

Next time, Russell's other letter described his view on the Soviet Union, Cold War, and Stalin's leadership. Believe it or not, many older people and you may be surprised, the young ones too think similarly in Russia. I quote Russell's letter again with his permission.

> "...Communism in Russia in 1917 had been a surprise – it was the worst place according to Marx for a new communist regime because it was undeveloped – but the beginning with Lenin was as good as could be expected under the circumstance. Stalin was a necessary brutal leader for the very stupid and backward Russians and contra the brutal rightist opposition. He was uncorrupted and had a good vision of the future and he literally beat the Russians

into industrialization. He made mistakes but also, he did good stuff and especially during WW2 was a brilliant military leader contra Hitler. The problem that developed related to USA President F.D. Roosevelt's death. Stalin, understandably paranoid against the West, trusted Roosevelt; but FDR's sudden death in April 1945 upset the applecart. The vicious anti-Communism movement in the USA, also in the Democratic Party had maneuvered at the Demo Convention in Summer 1944 to replace the USSR-friendly Vice President Henry Wallace with an ignorant manageable country bumpkin Senator from Missouri, Harry Truman, and Truman took over in 1945 and, starting with his big mouth and then his ignorant use of the A-bomb in Japan, stimulated Stalin's paranoia and the Cold War was on. Especially, the unnecessary start of the Korean War, which occurred because of Truman's bad signals – again his big mouth – that the US might tolerate a North Korean invasion and Stalin's mistrust from the Berlin blockade, solidified the Cold War as an almost nuclear arms hot war."

"Stalin died in early 1953 and our good president Eisenhower, who had Soviet good will from WW2, tried hard to end the Cold War with the help of former Governor and Presidential candidate Harold Stassen of Minnesota, but they were frustrated by the bad anti-communist Republican Party during a period when America went crazy in favor of anti-communism. Eisenhower had prevented a U.S. Attack on Castro Cuba, but the inexperienced and sex-crazy President Kennedy incompetently allowed it and the Cold War further deteriorated. On the Russian side, under the ignoramus country bumpkin Khrushchev and succeeded by the corrupt apparatchik Brezhnev, the Communist Regime deteriorated and became corrupt, justifying Stalin's worst fears in his paranoid years."

"Came 1991 and the USSR was reeling from the shock of the Gorbachev Glasnost reforms. The Russian people justifiably had become angry and discontented with their corrupt communist regime but under the incessant US CIA propaganda were misled into backing the drunkard, equally corrupt Boris Yeltsin – a tool of the CIA and the US President Bush Sr. (former head of the CIA) American Policy of dismembering the USSR as part of a power play that would put USA on top of the world with no super power rival."

So, the Yeltsin coup happened, and was responded by a counter-coup of the communist regime leaders trying to dump Gorbachev. Only the French leader Mitterrand had the good judgment and foresight to recognize the communist countercoup leaders. But they were overwhelmed because the CIA-bribed Russian military sided with Yeltsin."

"The result of the Yeltsin-US victory was the immediate dismemberment of the USSR and its "satellite empire" and not only that but even the non-satellite Communist regime in former Tito Yugoslavia. In addition to the terrible suffering of the Russian people because of the fall of communism, and in addition to the rise of militant Islam and Osama because of the liberation of millions of potential radical Islamists in former USSR, we had the dismemberment of Yugoslavia and Albania. The formerly contented inhabitants of Yugoslavia and Albania were split up with the help of the USA into the old nationalist and ethnic minority subculture countries and we had a return to the Serbia, Croatia, Macedonia and a new Muslim enclave bordering Albania with ethnic Albanians called Kosovo, all with their constant internecine wars."

"And that is the tragic story. And the blame goes directly to the crazy, vicious anti-communism of the Americans that supported the dirty policy of divide and conquer against the USSR and other communist nations. And, the triumphalism of the present Neo-Conservatives who have gone crazy with dreams of world conquest starting in Iraq."

"Be honest. Look at the world of 1990 on the verge of the end of the USSR and look at the world since 1991 and today after the Cold War. In terms of human suffering on earth which was a better, happier time? In terms of democracy? In any terms. Was the end of the Cold War good for you as an individual? Or would you like those old, good days back again (If Humpty-Dumpty could be?) Who made mistakes? And who was correct and right as rain?..."

I must note there are some people in Russia missing the standoff between the superpowers who call for multi-polar world order. I am not against the multi-polar world order but with one pre-condition: each polar should represent the responsible democracy. This is not the case for the old as well as the modern Russia.

Communism and the Cold War is now a history of continuous standoffs between two giants. Whatever political movement in any Third World country one of these governments supports – another government supports the opposite. I do not know how the Soviets had been painted in the US but remember the caricatures of President Truman with a bloody axe in the Soviet satirical magazine *Crocodile* in the early 1950s. That was the time of Korean War. Some people loved the external attributes of the Soviet superpower and wanted it back. It does not matter if there would be new Stalin or new czar. They just need Russia "to get up from knees" and be the frightful empire as opponent to the US. "Philosophy of failure" is still alive.

Most people learn from their mistakes. The Russian experience with its real socialism demonstrated it as a dead-ended way. We could distinguish another belief in the communism: some people think the basics of the communism were just badly performed in the Soviet Union, but the theory developed by Marx and Engels, if applied correctly and in the right country, had the ability to provide a happy and wealthy life for everyone. Wrong!

The key to understanding this disparity is in unnaturally making people equal, whereas they are not and should not be equal in many aspects. We do not have to switch the equality with the equal opportunity as it changes the idea to its opposite. Theoretical communism described by the classics drew the society where people had to hold the equality, goodwill, and fairness. Indeed, the real socialism (communism) had been endowed with the chronic shortfall of food and clothes, had inefficient industry, and transformed poor and angry people into rude and thievish ones. Besides, everyone expected to glorify the Soviet regime. What a mockery!

The Soviet Union of 1950–1960s had much similarity with modern North Korea: atomic weaponry, rockets, ideology, and isolation from the world. The majority of Soviet people had no idea that somewhere beyond the Iron Curtain another life exists without communal apartments and no shortage of goods and food. Most of them believed their living standard would soon go above the West's. What was outside of the drape two hundred and fifty thousand million people lived in, I got a chance to see in 1965.

BEYOND THE IRON CURTAIN

A very few people could look behind the Iron Curtain. I still do not understand why I was so lucky to see Western Europe at the time Soviet political and cultural isolation was at its strongest. Only diplomats and mariners had the privilege to peek around the guarded state borderline. Travels abroad (to the countries other than those belonging to Soviet political allies) were basically impossible for regular people. If a fruit is forbidden, it seems much more attractive. That curtain was drawn a little over and then put down to me. Yet, at my eighteen, I had no doubt all doors were opened for me.

Teenagers dream about romantic professions. I did about sea travels. It was very unusual that a Jewish teen was admitted to maritime school because it had to do with the exit visa to sail overseas, and Soviet system usually did not allow Jews to go abroad. But I was given leave to enter, and I must grant credit to my father for that because he worked at that school. Thus, in 1963, I entered the Maritime School in Leningrad.

The Fifth Record

I studied marine engineering and liked the subject. I went to my first sea apprenticeship in July 1965. I was happy with the opportunity to go abroad and kept travel notes of my sailing. I thought I lost it longtime ago.

What a surprise was to find my diary after decades, eight moves, and emigration! It was originally written in Russian. I quote a few pieces of it here to bring up the spirit of mid 1960s. Some of my descriptions of European towns and people sound naive today but what I paid attention to in Western Europe was quite different in the Soviet Union's drab existence, uniformity and grayness. It was my discovery of 1965 Europe.

I turn the time machine on.

2 June, 1965, Leningrad, USSR

In the morning, Deputy Dean announced where the students of our class are going to go for apprenticeship. Four places scheduled: Baltic Steamship Co, Murmansk Icebreaker Fleet, polar Port of Tiksi, and the motor ship *Zenith* that belonged to the Maritime School. *Zenith* scheduled to go to Algeria to take part in the World Youth & Students Festival of 1965. I am so excited that I am among those listed in motor ship *Zenith!* I wish time would run faster and my final exams would finish sooner.

7 July 1965, Leningrad, USSR

Second grade of the Maritime School left behind, and I am onboarded the apprentice motor ship *Zenith*. It is a relatively big ship – 6,000 tons of deadweight designed specifically for the apprenticeship of future navigation officers and marine engineers. We are about 40 students of the School, first time sea goers, dreamed so much about sailing. It starts, finally.

We are not going to Algeria as it was announced to us earlier due to military coup and power shift occurred in June; we will go to Denmark.

9 July 1965, Baltic Sea

At 23:38, we put off from port of Leningrad. From 4:00 in the morning, I worked my first marine watch in the engine room. The main engine and two auxiliary engines are running. Noise of the main one is not too loud but auxiliary engines are noisy. Weather is rainy; the sea calm, just slightly sways.

10 July 1965, Baltic Sea

Bitterly sways in the morning. Every one of us, maritime students, reacted differently: someone joked; others kept silence. Someone said I looked pale. Indeed, I felt unwell. Nonetheless, as a mariner, I must get used to it. We passed the time zone, 1 hour late compared to home time.

11 July 1965, Baltic Sea

A shore is visible for all day long. That is Sweden. We are close to it and I can see the cars and houses with red roofs and churches. After lunch, we worked in training engine room with compressor and diesel-generator. We are passing by Copenhagen in the evening. Europe is small.

12 July 1965, Norresundbu, Denmark

The country of Prince Hamlet! At 2 in the morning, all of us who slept at the snout cabin woke up by the dropping anchor. We came to port with a strange name of Norresundbu.

I am free from watch in the morning. Every one of us, who was going to go down to town, was given 12 crones and within the group of three dismissed for a few hours. I had never been a foreigner and now I was in this country.

I surprised by the brightness and motley of colors in everything: commercials, people's clothes, shop windows, etc. Cigarettes, books, movie and public transport are expensive, not affordable for the money everyone got. Movies are mostly American westerns advertised by the placards with beautiful women, rubbers or murderers. Topless women are on ball pens, screwdrivers, can openers and other stuff. People look friendly and smiley. Is it a capitalistic monarchy and the enemy of Soviet Union? It does not look like that.

My comment of 2018: Soviet morals of the time did not encourage showing even a low neck on the pictures of women. Images showing anything lower than that were considered shameless or even dirty. But how about naked Delilah, or Bathsheba, or Eva on paintings of the Renaissance great masters exposed in a few Soviet museums, a reader may ask. It was believed to be an art of the past but the Soviet "socialist realism" art after 1917 was supposed to call for struggle for the communist ideals. The exclusion was the sportswomen. Typical was sculpture of a 'Girl with Oar' exposed in city parks. Even though she wore a bathing suit, her puritanical appearance was impassive. A modest and even sexless attitude was an officially desirable outward style of the Soviet women.

14 July 1965, Kattegat Strait

Morning, calm sea, we are moving in fog, water edge is not visible, and the impression is that we are in center of a homogeneous sphere. The fog got strong by the evening and there was no ski or water seen. The ship issues sound blasts every 3 minutes.

16 July 1965, Kaliningrad, USSR

    Last night we came back to this Soviet city. After my engine room watch finished, I dressed up and went out to city with two of my friends. Kaliningrad (former Konigsberg and capital of East Prussia) did not impress me: rambles still not restored after WWII, and modern 3–4 story monotonous buildings. We had nothing to do in the city and came by a park. I saw a girl of my age, asked what her name is. She said her name is Anna. She worked in a department store. I suggested her to join us, so four of us walk together for some time. Soon after, my friends left us alone understanding her choice. We at first had not too much to talk about, just walked. It was evening, and we needed to spend our time somehow. We stopped by a café, drunk a cup of coffee. I took her hand, she did not object. Unexpectedly, she suggested going home with her. Her parents and younger brother were at home. Then she told me, let us go to backyard, I will give you a hug. We hugged and kissed until midnight, then we came back home. Everybody slept, and we went to her room. I did not sleep that night.

    In the morning, I run late to my watch. The apprentice whom I had to relieve stayed late and I was grateful to him and let him go. After the watch, chief engineer called me and said that he will dismiss me from the ship for coming late if happens again. I ensured him this will not happen. He let me go back to the crew's quarters.

17 July 1965, Baltic Sea

    It is rolling in a heavy sea. We are all seasick. On the watch from 4:00 in the engine room, I felt crummy all morning. It is even worse there – less fresh air. Sometimes I climbed up on the deck to breathe in some fresh air and get water. I did not smoke for full daylong.

18 July 1965, Kiel Canal, West Germany

Kiel Canal separates Jutland Peninsular from the European mainland. Weather is nice and West Germany is just beautiful. We waited for the sluice about an hour. I stood on the deck and saw the town of Kiel. I saw father and daughter who stayed and watched our ship. The father was one-legged. He watched us, people on board the Soviet ship through his binoculars. What did he think about? Maybe he recalled something that happened to him more than 20 years ago on the Eastern front? Many ships from different countries: Norway, Sweden, Denmark, East Germany are passing by us. Here is British tanker from Gull, all crew is on deck, and they wave to us and shout something. We wave in response.

Our ship is in lockage in the Canal's sluice. Next to us a big ship with many white and black people staying. Its name is *Kulpaun River* from Ghana. Our group of students stood at the railing right in front of a few black mariners from the *Kulpaun River* crew. We exchanged greetings, they saw a red flag at the stern of our ship; they shouted like communism good and capitalism no-good. We shouted something in response that they liked.

Then we went across the deck on another side, looked at Germans on the embankment. In May 1965, it was 20 years of the victory over Germany and I do not see any traces of war here apart from the now Soviet city of Kaliningrad where many old buildings still rambled. We stood on the deck and freaked thinking up Nazi military ranks to Germans that stood on the embankment but stopped doing so after we saw a crowd of Germans waved to us and two girls even blew a kiss to us. How can it be: our fathers killed yours and you blow kisses?

At 20:40, we came out from the canal and got to North Sea. The seagulls here differ from those that fly over the Baltic Sea: they are light gray on the top and over there are black.

3 August 1965, Rotterdam, Holland

At 19:30, we moored in Rotterdam. Local children play at the ship's ramp. They are telling us something, but we do not understand. A girl of 16–17 stays farer and shies to come closer. We, several maritime students, give badges and post cards to kids and communicate with a girl. She said her name is Dora and then she came closer to ramp. We spoke, laughed and joked. Then somebody asked her for fun which one of us she picks. When she pointed on me, all guys laughed loudly. I felt I must respond to her playful show of affection and gave her the last badge I had. She gave me the aluminum ring. The Third Mate suddenly emerged and chased all of us back to the ship saying the deck work starts.

4 August 1965, Rotterdam, Holland

In the evening when *Zenith* moored out from the pier, I came up on deck and saw Dora again but alone. She saw me and waved her hand. I see her for second and the last time and we will never be able to meet. What is not even started, now left behind. Somebody turned on radio. The group performed very nice song. These were Beatles; I never heard them before and liked.

23 August 1965, Saint-Louis-Duron, France (Mediterranean Coast)

On the 10th day of our sailing, the *Zenith* entered French port of Saint–Louis–Duron. As soon as the gangplank set up, a few people got up to the ship. A woman of extraordinary beauty of about 30 was among them. They went to mess hall and talked to officers. Later I learned they were French communists. Boatswain opens the holds and about 20 French Dockers start unloading the pulp.

My comment of 2018. In 1960s, the communist ideas were still popular in France, Italy, and other European countries. The attractiveness of the Soviet socialism for the European leftists lasted until 1968 invasion of Soviet tanks to Czechoslovakia.

24 August 1965, Saint-Louis-Duron, France

Today is a very busy day. In the morning, many French guests came to see the *Zenith* but allowed coming onboard only from 18:00. In a minute or two all, the decks filled with guests. All of them excited, spoke and laughed. I assigned to be one of the guides. My sightseers were six girls from 14 to 18 years old. All of them were pretty and one was just incredibly handsome. Mary-Françoise, that was her name, spoke English better than others and I communicated mostly with her. I showed them pilothouse, training house gyrocompass room and library, and then we walked on different decks. I spent with them about 2 hours, and then brought them to a small cinema hall where they stayed to see a movie "*Melodies of Dunaevsky*".

My next guests were a couple: she was French about 40 and he was from Spain of about 50 years old. She spoke English well and told me that her husband fought in Spain in 1936 civil war against Franco, then fled to France. During the collaborationists' dominance, he was in the Dachau concentration camp and barely survived. They both are communists. She teaches French in school. The Soviet Union and our ship enchanted her. We exchanged the addresses.

After she read my last name, she asked me why it does not sound Russian. "I am a Jew," I responded. At the end, she said thanks much in Russian. The movie finished, and the girls again came to me. I showed them photos of Soviet astronauts and was surprised they knew all of them by names! At late night I saw them off.

My comment of 2018. French communist activists in 1965 (not the chiefs of course) were communists by the sideline: they did another job for their living and party membership was their leisure pursuit.

31 August 1965, Atlantic Ocean at Biscay Gulf

Heavy storm started yesterday. Rocking is so strong that all the stuff tossed from one to another side of the cabin. Mariners were mostly pale and gloomy. I also felt bad especially at 5 o'clock in the morning when worked in the stern part of the engine room where rocking is highest. Ok, I will tolerate, just want to go back home. It is not long to wait, just a day and I am home!

6 September 1965, Baltic Sea

There was a big rush job from the morning to lunchtime: everything on the ship was washing and holystoning up to shine. That means we are coming back to homeport. Thus, my first sailing practice is about to finish. I saw and learned a lot during these two months. On my next sailing, I will work not as a trainee but a member of a ship's crew.

8 September 1965, Leningrad, USSR

At 8:30 morning time, we moored to pier #3 in the port of Leningrad. After all formalities, I finally step down to my native land. I do not say goodbye to sea, we will meet again.

In 1965, I discovered a different world existed in parallel with the one we lived in. It did not look as it was described in our Soviet realm. At my nineteen, when subjects were understood straightforwardly, this was a riddle for me: from our scientific communism subject, we learned the capitalist society should have a class struggle between poor workers and rich capitalists. Where were poor workers suffering the acute poverty? The first little doubt in my socialist well-being came to me after my discovery of 1965 Europe. This rationale was a reasoning why the Soviet authorities treated people applying for the exit visa selectively: trustworthy or untrustworthy. Although I saw a huge difference in the quality of life in the Western world and the Soviet Union, I still believed that socialism was a fare political system, and that we would catch the West up with the living standards and then prevail. The 1960s were the years of the last economic stability before the long years of stagnation that started shaking the country in the 1970s and eventually felling down by the end of the 1980s.

Leo Pevsner

Remembrance of the Cold War: American Air Scout over the motor ship *Krasnogvardeysk* heading to Cuba. Atlantic Ocean, November 1967 (my last sailing before my exit visa was closed).

Yet, in 1965, my future looked promising to me. I had yet to know that sailing on ships abroad would end for me in just two years. A long twenty-three-years' ban would last until 1990, followed by Perestroika.

PORTRAITS OF THE REAL SOCIALISM

Socialism is a philosophy of failure …
the equal sharing of misery.

Winston Churchill

Communal Life

After finishing the Great Patriotic War (the name for World War II in the Soviet territory), veterans started coming back to Leningrad from the front back to their apartments. Other people evacuated at the beginning of war to eastern regions were also returning to the city. Only two years passed since Leningrad's siege finished, about one million people died of hunger, deceases, and German bombardments in the city. Many rooms remained empty. My parents bought a small room on Nevsky Prospect for the money my father received for four years' service in the war front line. Soon after my birth, they traded the room for the bigger one on Fontanka.

For the first eleven years of my life, our family lived at 26, Fontanka, right in front of the Leningrad Circus. The building designed by the well-known architect Zakharov, was erected in 1804–1806 and known as Merchant Mizhuev's House. It represented Russian classicism, the architectural style of eighteen-beginning of nineteen century imposed by Peter the Great and then by Ekaterina II.

The room our family occupied was part of a huge apartment, which in the first half of nineteenth century, belonged to Elizaveta Khitrovo (1783–1839). She was a daughter of famous Russian General Mikhail Kutuzov, a hero and Commander-in-Chief of the Russian Army in the Patriotic War of 1812–1813 against Napoleon. She kept a high society saloon where the great poet Alexander Pushkin and well-known Russian writers Zhukovsky and Gogol were often her guests.

The large apartment was transformed into the communal one after the revolution of 1917 so that instead of one, five different families lived in rooms, which was typical for the time. Communal apartment became a symbol of the Soviet socialism.

Communalization of apartments by populating them with families not related to each other is a Soviet invention. Eviction of noble families and moving in several other families into one apartment was called the "tightening". Now after a hundred years, communal apartments still exist in cities. Different families (from three to ten or more) of various backgrounds, ages, cultural levels, and habits found themselves in an apartment with shared kitchen, toilet, and access to telephone and bathtub (if existed). Hence, private life of a family or an individual was often a subject of watching by neighbors. Such a coexistence was often a cause of standoffs, fights and even court litigations. Reasons for hatred between neighbors could be different but they were always grave. Hard to imagine what brutal incidents ignited on those wars – from the exchange of hits to adding vinegar to the neighbor's soup. Whether the relations between neighbors were good or bad, the number of electric meters demonstrated it. If there was only one meter for all neighbors, the relationship was good. Many meters meant neighbors had bad relations and did not trust each other. This could indicate that members of one family thought the other family might take advantage by consuming more energy but paying equally.

It is worth it to put in the picture of all inhabitants of this communal apartment.

Next to our room was a smaller room, where the old man Fyodor Matveevich and his son Konstantin lived. Then, in the early 1950s, Konstantin was about thirty-five, divorced and shy. I never heard a word from him. He was busy at his work and sometimes I, then four or five years old, visited Fyodor Matveevich whom I called grandfather. The grandfather was kind to me, gave me candies, told me stories, and I liked talking to him and asking questions. He was deeply religious, as were most of the Russians who were over forty by 1917 when the Bolsheviks started suppressing any religion. One time, in response to my question, "Who is that woman with baby on the icon," he patiently told me a biblical story of Jesus Christ. He also said every human must believe in God and if he does not, then it is bad. My childish mind needed to know what is good – what is bad. Trying to clarify it, I asked him who is better, Stalin or God, not even having any idea about the relevance of my question. He did not answer but got upset.

Leningrad–St. Petersburg. 26 Fontanka River – former Merchant Mizhuev's House (built in 1806). Our communal apartment (1946–1957) was on the third floor at balcony level. *Photo of 2010.*

On that day, the grandfather talked to me about the importance of the Christian Orthodox faith. "And what if I would not believe?", I asked him. He said that if I did not believe in what he believed in, I would go to hell and be burnt on a pan. (I guess he knew I was from a Jewish family). I just imagined how I would burn on a pan, started crying, ran out of his room, and rushed to my mother. She had to calm me down and told me I do not have to believe and will never burn on a pan. That was my last visit to the neighbor-grandfather, and I declined all his further invitations. I just did not want to hear his chills.

In the room farther from us lived a childless couple of younger age than my parents, Vladimir, a lieutenant, correction officer, and Valentina Parshins. My parents had good relations with them. When my father bought one of the first television sets, they used to come to us by 7:30 PM at the beginning of a single television program and leave at 10:00 PM by the end of it. My father allowed me to watch television only up to 9 PM, and after that, I had an argument every day about going to bed. He and Vladimir often discussed foreign and domestic politics, which meant they trusted each other; otherwise, it was not safe. Many people who openly discussed politics and even told anecdotes paid a high price by being arrested and sent to Gulag.

In the room in front of Parshins, a family of three lived: mother, father, and daughter; they always were quiet and harmless. As if keeping a natural balance, next to them another family of three lived: mother, father, and son of about eighteen years old. The mother, Galina Sergeevna was a 'damned wretch' as my father named her. One need only look at her appearance. It was clear from distance that she was a nasty piece of work: her eyes were witless, her voice was screaming and stubbing, and her moves were quick and sharp. Nobody wanted to deal with her, they were afraid of her, as was her husband Nikon Nikonovich Lobyzenko, a legless lawyer who moved around in a cart. Their son Victor was a hoodlum, he did not study or work. Sure thing, Galina was a damn Jew-hater, insulted all of us, especially my defenseless mother. Once I was a witness when she told her acquaintance, pointing to our room, "These Zhidy (offensive name of Jews in Russia) have a daughter of three years old, and she still cannot speak."

Galina did not feel comfortable without a fight, and she picked on my mother for the abuse by ill luck. One day when I was five and my mother and I entered the apartment, she hit my mother's head on an electric meter, my mother and I cried. I thought she was going to do it to me too and ran away. Another time – I was already attending first grade – I came back from school and realized I had forgotten the key of the apartment, so I rang the bell. Galina was home, but she did not let me get in – just opened the door, saw me and closed it right back. I stood alone and waited until another neighbor came back and opened the door for me.

Remembering all this, I wonder why my parents could tolerate it so long until they found a room to trade in another communal apartment. Before that, there were eleven long years of suffering and abuse. Several times my parents applied to court but unsuccessfully because either there were no witnesses to her outrage or our neighbors –witnesses – were afraid of Galina, fearing her post-revenge. The third reason was her husband Nikon, who as a lawyer, had befriended the judges and knew all Leningrad's judicial community. In Soviet realities, this left my parents with no chance to win the case.

Finally, our family left the unhappy apartment in that beautiful historic building. The next communal apartment on 138 Griboedov Canal was the last one where I lived with my parents and my younger sister. Our neighbors in the new apartment were a family of three: parents and the adult daughter, a lawyer in her thirties. My parents' early relations to them were understandably cautious: they had just come out of hell with the horrible neighbors.

My parents' lifelong friendship with new neighbors started from the moment my mother baked *piroshkies,* a

Russian meal looking like a small loaf of white bread with mincemeat or fish or mushrooms inside. My mother gave it to them to try. In response, they left a short note in the kitchen table: "For *piroshkies,* you got 5+". This was the beginning, and they celebrated the New Year of 1958 together.

1st grade class, School #190 - Typical Leningrad elementary school, 1954, the last year of separate boys' and girls' classes. Combined classes and school uniforms were established in Soviet schools. Three years later, in 1957, students were instructed to rip off the pages in their textbooks that contained portraits of Stalin. The author is third from the left on the upper row.

All these family members had hearty qualities. The chief was, of course, a mother, Taisiya Konstantinovna. She combined the best qualities of a real Russian woman: cleverness, decisiveness, benignity, and self-devotion. In addition, she was a character, so her husband, Ivan Andreevich, a straightforward man, was under her full control.

Before and during WWII, the family lived in Siberia, where Ivan Andreevich worked as a chief on the Baikalo–Amur railroad construction. Thousands of Stalin's prisoners worked there in the harsh environment of an extremely cold winters and mosquito summers. Whatever the chief he was, his boss was always his wife. Their daughter, Valentina was a smart and experienced lawyer. My parents had a few friends of youth, and this family became the last new friends they made in their forties. They kept relations for many years even after they had both moved out of that apartment. That was luck for both families to find one another within one apartment but it was the exception rather than common event.

Families may have been lucky or unlucky with their neighbors, it was always a lottery. The communal coexistence had a big impact on people's private lives. Since the contacts between neighbors were unavoidable, many families felt deeply unhappy about their life with no privacy. Communal apartment life is a creation of socialism. If normal social life helps people to accentuate their privacy and independence, the communal life kills it.

Blat

Seventy-four years of the domination of Soviet social style created its heroes and anti-heroes. It generated a culture based on the shortage of anything from consciousness to food. In terms of communist ideology, it had more degraded with every next generation. Believers of the ideas of common fairness in the 1920s changed to become the most fearful people in 1930–1950s, and then transformed to the cynic pickers and the communal merchandise stealers in 1970–1980s. The latest twenty-five to thirty years were especially revealing in the way the country declined.

Economy of the totalitarian regime with the central planning and distribution was so inefficient that starting from the early 1970s, it stopped doing any progress. Manufacturing of the low-grade steel, cast-iron, as well as men and women's shoes and dresses that looked alike were still increasing. Warehouses and storages were full of unused outdated equipment and at the same time, the industry did not produce or sell quality goods.

In normal economy, the market regulates the nomenclature and quantities of all goods; in the centralized economy, only clerks decide. The question was who needed all that? By the 1980s, troubles with food provision became serious, especially in smaller towns: food other than bread and macaroni was sold only in big cities. I still remember *sausage trains* when people from the provincial towns and villages filled trains going to Moscow, Leningrad, and other big cities to buy some food and bring it home. This could not last forever even with the Russian tolerance to complications. In Russia, seniors and veterans used to say: anything but not a war. Common people lived their life separate from the Communist Party bosses. To survive the shortage of food and goods, Soviet people extensively used the system of *blat*.

Blat in the Soviet society was the most powerful advantage for any personal or business dealings. If not for *blat,* the quality of life for some influential people would have been as poor as for the rest of the population. *Blat* is an idiom meaning preference that someone could get through his connection with the person(s) occupied certain positions. Those who had useful connections called *blatnik*. Connections could be different: through cognate relations work, friend, friend of a friend, relative, relative of a relative, etc. *Blat* is a kind of corruption: getting unearned privileges, unlawful ordinances, and undeserved promotions. *Blat* created a cluster of all these big and small services for covering each other's backs.

Conditions that originated the *blat cluster* were lack of everything. The person in charge of the distribution had full power. Great Soviet comedy actor Arkady Raikin, master of acting miniatures, made fun of the *blatniks* in one of them. The general paraphrase is this: I am a warehouse manager in charge of distribution of goods and you are a store director in charge of selling goods. I want all people to have enough of everything but I would like that some stuff, which I distribute out and you sell, be in shortage. This will make you and me more powerful and respectable men.

The official ideology claimed there were only two social classes in the Soviet Union: workers (proletariat) and collective farmers (peasants) with a sub layer of intelligentsia (white collars). However, the real social classes were subdivided by their ability to obtain something important, useful, or delicious for the household. It was not enough if someone had a good salary like miners, mariners, senior military officers, etc.; you could not buy anything you want just by having money and stopping by a store. Useful connections meant more than money, and only for someone with connections the special back entrance to a store was available. *Blat* meant the power.

In fact, there were four different social classes in Soviet society graded by the power. The highest level included chief leaders – the "sacred" ones who made decisions (members of Politburo, members of the Party Central Committee, ministers, secretaries of region committees, and their servants). They had all conceivable and unconceivable privileges, special stores separate from others, hunting areas, personal free dachas, and luxury automobiles, and so on. The free "communism" had maintained for them. They needed to be good wrigglers and intriguers and have good connections to get up to the highest level, which was named the "nomenclature". Once they were on the top, they obtained these privileges automatically. They did not even need any money. Their only concern was to keep this dreamland position.

Next level belonged to local party bosses, regional and city bosses, and KGB officers of high and middle levels, chiefs of manufacturing, police bosses – prominent people who put their signatures under the executive orders. Their power extended to any circumstances from awarding free apartments to shielding from criminal prosecution.

The third level included smaller people participating in different kind of services like directors of food and department stores, storage warehouses managers, butchers, doctors of certain specialties like dentists, chiefs of logistic departments, military commissariat officers, chiefs of police departments, and some other categories of specialties – people of lower category of services who could provide better treatment without a line or prevent something unwanted in exchange for other favors. The examples were dentists that may fill your tooth with a material of higher quality or military commissar who could shield your son from the military drafting, butchers giving you a better piece of meat for the same price as for the bones.

And finally, the fourth level included those who were unable to do any favor to other people through their professional occupation, such as workers, engineers, scientists, librarians, drafters, collective farmers, and many others. They could not get any value that had merit in the hierarchy of Soviet denomination, whether it be a fur coat or salami or new car or lady's stylish shoes. Since these people could not offer any goods or services in shortage, they were not in the loop of the *blat* system. It meant simple: they eat potato, macaroni, and preserves only; they worn primitive domestic manufactured clothes; they always stand in line for months or even years to buy something big like a refrigerator or washing machine.

This is an example to describe shortage of goods and its reflection on the common people. Recently I watched old Soviet movie of 1981 (once again) *Mechanic Gavrilov's Beloved Woman*. There is an episode with the main character (performed by the famous Russian actress Lyudmila Gurchenko) where she was standing in line (not the proper verb, the more correct, she was pushed and jammed) for... Japanese enameled pelvis. Finally, she gets it and does not know what to do with it. She might not need it at all – the old one was probably still fine. The comprehensive deficit of anything developed specific Soviet mind: whether you need something or not, you had to buy if it is available. It was not about the Japanese pelvis that might have specific extraordinary properties; it was about lack of anything.

The unbelievably good feeling when you obtained something through the *blat* is difficult to describe. Your self-esteem rose, and your family loved you more; your co-workers respected and envied you. If you got something that was in shortage for your boss, you received more respect from him. It did not matter whether you were a big communist apparatchik making passionate speeches or a butcher from a dirty meat shop, both felt happy if they got anything through the system of *blat*.

Eventually, people, fed up with the shortfall of everything, voluntarily organized flea markets where anybody could buy anything: from automotive parts to electronics and from books to women's dress. All these goods of course were absent in regular stores: some of them were stolen from the manufacturers, others made up by handymen, and all sold for the market prices, which were higher than the ones assigned by the state. In the beginning, authorities persecuted the independent markets but then just did not pay attention as they were not able to manage deficits of everything.

Connections with influential people played a role in getting a better job or promoting in any country but the concept of *Blat* made a difference. In the Soviet Union, *blat* was the mean for surviving, furthermore, providing an easier life for some in account of the others.

The standard package to express gratitude for the exceptional service performed through *blat* connections was a box of chocolate candies and/or a bottle of cognac. How many chocolate candies can the person who receives these gifts every day eat? Not too much even with a big family. The cognac does not spoil and could stay but the chocolate spoils after some time. Having director of a food store as a friend, where these boxes of chocolate candies could sell following recirculation was another important necessity of *blatnik*. The *blat* machine was moving on adding the new services and goods, which were getting less available for the common people.

From the economical prospective, *blat* is a kind of natural trade, however, with peculiarity. In addition to getting a stuff in exchange for another stuff, you are obtaining a power or influence over the regular people who do not have useful connections. This was an ugly mode of existence for "successful" people. It was especially observable with automobile ownership.

Luxury of a Vehicle

Until the 1990s, the owner of a used but still drivable automobile was thought a well-off man, not to say the one who owned a new car. If you think of about half of cars being repaired by their owners rather than driven, the number of lucky owners lessens twice. Car failures occurred often, and since nobody knew when it might happen next time, every owner was supposed to have basic mechanical skills for the car repair. Nothing like roadside assistance existed. The likelihood of car failure and the fear of helplessness made it difficult for women to be drivers. That is why women rarely drove cars independently in the Soviet Union.

The reliability of domestic automobiles was always an issue, and a driver could expect any mechanical problem emerged at any time and in any place. It was good if a failure caught you in a city where you could hire a truck to bring the car to a safe place (bringing it to shop was no reason – you needed a scheduled appointment before; leaving it at the shop was unsafe). It was bad if a failure found you outside a city. My car once stopped near the city of Kaunas (Lithuania) because of the water pump brake. I had to drop the car, take a bus to the flea market to buy a pump, then return and spend half a day staying on the road shoulder to install the new one.

Another time my car stopped at a busy intersection of Obvodny Canal and Lermontov Prospect in Leningrad because of a coupling engagement failure. Since the car was unmovable, it blocked the way for a line of rail trams behind me. The tram drivers cursed and honked but I could not move until some truck driver agreed to tag my car to a garage for modest pay.

When someone decided to buy a car, he should have understood what enormous problem he was picking up with a car. There was saying the automobile owner is happy only two times: when he buys a car and sells it.

Soviet cars were ranked by comfort and reliability. Automobile *Volga* took first place in comfort, then *Zhiguli (Lada)* went, and then *Moskvich*; *Zaporozhets* took the last place. The latter was the least reliable, and nearly all owners spent all their free time repairing it. None of these brands was competitive to foreign car manufacturers: the most reliable Soviet automobile was far worse than the least reliable American car, not to say anything about the Japanese ones.

All Soviet automobile owners were divided into three groups. One group consisted of well-off car riders whose income was above their official salary and who had good connections with useful people that helped with car spare parts and repair. This group of people had better and newer cars than the other two groups. The group, however, could not compete with even higher level of "party nomenclature" (apparatchiks) or the big bosses who had personal drivers and used the cars belonging to state.

The second group of automobile owners included commoners with fixed and limited income with no *blat* or useful connections. They did small repairs by themselves and only brought their car to a shop or hired somebody else if the car needed a large repair. The car was a family asset and used mainly on weekends for driving to a summerhouse or vacation. Some people in this category used their car for commuting to work but spending money on gas may risk the family budget. To compensate what they spent for gas they had to gain something by private cabbing. Having a shortage of taxicabs people often stopped personal cars to get a ride. Some car owners used this business so much that it became their second if not the first job by the earnings.

The third group of car owners was the ones who had the old and the least reliable cars like *Zaporozhets*. These owners spent their time repairing rather than driving. They served their cars; their cars did not serve them.

These three groups of automobile owners reflected an insignificant class of owners who had courage, drive, and patience to save the money to buy a car. Below the social layer of auto owners, there was much bigger class of workers, clerks, peasants, as well as engineers, medical doctors, and teachers that could only dream about a car.

The Soviet Union was likely to be the only country where the used car may cost more than a new one. This was because of the nature of its economy, where the real market prices were different from the unnatural ones assigned by the officials. For example, a new car of *Zhiguli* brand cost five thousand rubles in the 1970s, and same brand but the used car of three years old sold on the market for 10-20% more.

To buy a new car, a buyer should have stayed in line for years: only one out of seven families had a car in Russia in the 1980s. The comprehensive shortage in goods and services was a subject of an anecdote that President Reagan (who collected sayings and anecdotes) told after returning from the Soviet Union at the end of the 1980s:

> A man wanted to buy a car, he came to a store, and the sales clerk tells him to pay all money in advance and come back in ten years to take the car. A man pays and then asks a sales clerk, what time to come – in the morning or afternoon? Well, the sales clerk says to him, what is the difference if it is going to be in ten years from now! Yes, but on that morning, a plumber should come in, the man responds.

Possession of a car was always a big deal, a sign of prestige, and a cause for jealousy. Indeed, a car changed your life style: it was not a problem to get anywhere; a man who owned a car was more attractive for women because he could provide more adventure and luxury compared with a man with no car. A car and everything connected to automobile issues was always a good topic for communication between men.

I bought my first car with my parents' partial help. Otherwise, I had to work for three years not spending for food, clothes, and all other stuff to be able to buy a car with my engineering salary as no financing existed. Anyway, that was a great occasion. I had never dreamed of having my own car before, and in the first few months while I drove it, my thoughts were like *what did I do so well that made me deserve a car?* For a long time, I could not get rid of the feeling that it was too good to be true.

None of the colleagues in my department had a car. I just could read behind their delighted words, *where did this guy get so much money?*

In Soviet reality, a car served nearly forever and became a family member for the life. Nobody wasted any old car, whatever its age or condition was. Cars sold and resold from the higher income group to lower and then again to the lowest one. Eventually, when the car became non-repairable, it was still not wasted but held on bricks (instead of tires) and decayed. The country of the won socialism was exactly like those old cars: decaying and immovable but still durable.

Redundant People

Even a hugely industrialized economy does not need millions of engineers. Nevertheless, all Soviet engineers were employed, and therefore, engineering institutes and design bureaus overstaffed.

Ministries released money to finance research and development (after all, this was *nobody's* money distributed by the Gosplan – State Agency for Planning). If the purpose was formulating requirements for a new product, most of the time, the product had never been created. If the purpose was designing an experimental unit, chances are it had never been pulled in series. And if the purpose was implementation of a new product, it was not unusual for the product never to be operationally developed. The reasons were different but always excusable: non-specified quality of parts or materials supplied, or a necessity to continue finishing the work or the product was out of date when manufacturing began, and so on and so forth.

Only three industries produced successfully: military, mineral extraction, and ideological propaganda. For the country rich with nature given resources, this was enough to keep the image of a superpower.

Most of the engineering staff had never been promoted. The few who were promoted had to fit minimum requirements, which included membership in the Communist Party, not being a Jew, and subordinating with higher-ups. Some career-oriented people wanted to enter the Party but… nothing of the sort: there was a line for the white collars: engineers, scientists, etc. (This, however, did not refer to the blue collars; they were always welcome to become party members). Some midlevel engineers waited for years and if lucky enough, eventually obtained a Party card and became candidates for promotion.

Some people were not busy at all. There were three distinct categories of employees: first one – those who worked hard and made something out. The second one included those who worked a little, helping the first ones but spending more time smoking and talking to others. Third category included those who had never done anything, just pretended to be busy with a social work but mostly talked or visited nearby stores.

The observable fact of that time: even though food stores carried only potato, bread, macaroni, and preserves, regular people found their moral shelter getting together behind a table for a friendly meeting with elementary snack and drinks. The usual snack included boiled potato, herring with onion, salad with potato and peas and mayonnaise, bread, sometimes sausages (if lucky enough); drinks: vodka for men and dry or sweet wine for women.

The reasons for getting together were different but frequent. One day monthly, all engineers, scientists, and administrative staff had to take part in helping a vegetable warehouse, where these products stored and decayed.

The vegetable warehouses were huge storages filled with potato and cabbage mostly. In a moist environment, these vegetables were doomed to spoil: in wintertime, they froze; in summer, they rotted. The role of all employees, whether you were a Doctor of Science or a junior laboratory assistant, was manually check and sort each potato and separate the good from bad ones. It was like labor conscription that nobody could miss, even head of departments.

Coldness, high humidity, and mosquitoes inside the storage during the entire workday made people feel so miserable that it was natural to buy some food and drink jointly and get together after this nasty workday in someone's room or apartment. Someone most social invited all and if it was not too far from the warehouse, the invitation was accepted with enthusiasm. Cooking did not take long, just the time to boil potatoes, everything else like cutting herring or salad was a matter of minutes. In about thirty to forty minutes, everybody is at the table.

Placement of people at the table was meaningful rather than random. The ratio between men and women was most of the time in favor of women in any department. No one had ever heard about such aggravation as sexual harassment. So, the relations between different sexes within a department were sometimes romantic. No one discussed those relations openly, but people knew who was with whom and what was going on between them. The formed couples may have had families in their homes but… Relations like these could last for years. For other employees, it may become so familiar to see the couple together but if they sat separately at the table, it meant they had a variance.

Finally, all people took their places, and the improvised feast started. Toasts, drinks, talks, laugh; the primitive food tasted delicious... When the first hunger was gone, the mood became romantic, and a soul needed songs. The chorus singing was uniting even for the people who could otherwise barely stand one another. Deeply touched and lyrical over the informal meeting, people start leaving. The head of department leaves first, then his deputy leaves, and then the other people express their gratitude to the host and leave. The day overall was good.

The next morning everybody comes back to work. Some pretended that nothing occurred yesterday and just kept their business attitude. Others discussed the previous evening in every detail until next occasion outdoes the last one.

This picture was typical. However, I do not want the reader think that the entire engineering and applied science community was useless. I must say there were (I am sure still are) many gifted people working in scientific research. With a little compensation, they worked for their ideas to get the new result, discovery, or invention. Some laboratories, departments, and even institutes were successful. I know scientists who did breakthrough inventions and research in Russian applied scientific institutes and eventually became the world leaders in their industries. However, during the Soviet years, the bureaucrats and schemers of science often took the lead, having neither talents nor skills to achieve anything important. With the collapse of the Soviet Union, some of the scientists emigrated; other ones became suitcase traders or gatekeepers. Turning the country from the upside down was painful.

PERESTROIKAS

There were two short periods, each lasted 5-6 years during seventy years of Soviet Union when some political relaxation took place. First, known as Khrushchev's Thaw started in 1956 and finished in early 1960s and the second, Gorbachev's Perestroika, started in 1985 and finished with collapsing of the Soviet Union in 1991. They both are alike by the causes and consequences. Both started because of discontent of the ruling elites for political and economical situation in the country. Both were possible after the death of a previous leader. Both were initiated from the top. Both Khrushchev and Gorbachev thought socialism is the best political system for humanity. Both frightened when understood that they went too far in political changes. Both Khrushchev's Thaw and Gorbachev's Perestroika finished by replacing the leaders initiated it. In the beginning, it seemed that the consequences of Thaw and Perestroika are different – first finished with failure, and the latter finished with victory of the democratic Russia. No, from the farer prospective, they both failed. However, both had started promising.

Khrushchev's Thaw

The adolescence and youth of the Soviet boomers' generation fall onto *Khrushchev's thaw*, which was a specific Soviet epoch of the 1960s. Soviet writer Ilya Ehrenburg named it *thaw* in his book *People, Years, Life* (*Lyudi, Gody, Zhizn*), recounting period between the mid-50s and mid-60s, and then the name was picked up widely. It characterizes the time when the post-Stalin leader Khrushchev gave some relief from a prison-like regime after so many years of fear, repressions, Gulag, and uniformity.

To take in the attitude of the Soviet boomers who spent their life in the Soviet Union, someone needs to try their shoes. They lived not as harsh life as their parents did. Stalin's tyranny and the war did not affect them directly. Soviet life isolated by the Iron Curtain from the rest of the world was the only reality the people knew. Everything beyond the Curtain was thought to be hostile and bad. However, communist ideology, which grasped generation of the 1930s–1940s, was no longer able to take hold most of the young people in the 1960s.

First who massively broke up with Stalin's ideological dogmas were the young *stilyagi* (the hipsters) at the end of the 1950s. In two words, they had idolized Western, especially the American culture, dress style, and behavior. I was too young but clearly remember the propaganda machine gave damns and curses on poor Soviet hipsters. By the mid-1960s, this movement faded out. Beatles, American, and European pop-music, and a few foreign movies penetrated the Soviet Union after the filter of the Ministry of Culture became our next favorite style. It influenced a generation of young folks, making them stay away from the everlasting ideology. Many of them opposed the dominating political system non-actively. Only a very few brave people had the temerity to resist the *system* openly, and their names are now known.

Most of the boys and girls of the time were far from the politics; they met at parties, made friends, felt in love. The official ideology was on the different pole from them. By their thirties, they believed neither communism nor religion. Therefore, that generation is the agnostic one.

The political thaw started from Khrushchev's historic speech on the Twentieth Congress of Communist party in 1956 with the disclosure of Stalin's cult of personality. For the first but not the last time in Soviet history, the communist leader admitted mistakes the party has made. People were dismayed and believed it was not the political system at fault but the wrong leader. They wanted to believe it. Next time (during Gorbachev's Perestroika), it would not happen. The understanding that this political organization will continually produce irreplaceable leaders came up later. Some other Russians still believe that if not for Stalin, the USSR would have not been a superpower, as if being a superpower made their miserable lives better.

The year of 1956 was special; everyone breathed a sigh of relief and thought that from now on, their life would turn to be better. However, Khrushchev did not end the agenda of socialism. His approach was the same but without the bloodthirsty Stalin. Soviet people, with a few exceptions, were so happy having the fear of night arrests and assassinations or jailing gone that they felt their life got much better.

To follow up with revocation of the personality cult, my fourth grade teacher, Sofia Markovna, one day ordered that the class take our textbook *Rodnaya Rech* (literature readings), open pages with portraits of Stalin, and rip them all out. All pupils – about forty of us – did what she said. She then collected all ripped portraits and left the classroom for a minute. She returned to the class without the textbook pages. Surely, it was not her idea but the order from the Department of Education and higher. That was the post-Stalin action in Soviet schools.

In about fifteen years, next Soviet political leaders who removed Khrushchev from power would make believe that the Stalinist regime was not so bad, and the country was enforced during his leadership but the grains of distrust to the leaders penetrated to people's thoughts. So-called de-Stalinization (or removal of Stalinism) continually moved back and forth, and the direction depended on the country's rulers.

Still the end of the 1950s and beginning of the 1960s were different from the decades before and after. The spirit of the time was specific. By the end of the 1950s, part of the Gulag was demobilized, survived prisoners came back to free but ruined lives; other people felt some good changes. Arts and literature started to get up from the long-standing vapid and glorifying trash, spiritual life was awakening; new novels and poems previously unconceivable were published in "thick" magazines. The country learned the new writers' names of Vladimir Dudintsev, Aleksandr Solzhenitsyn, Vassily Grossman, Lev Razgon, Fazil Iskander, Vasily Aksenov, and Yury Trifonov; poets Andrey Voznesensky, Robert Rozhdestvensky, Evgeny Evtushenko, and Bella Akhmadullina (the list is far from closed) later became symbols of the *thaw* era. Alexander Galitch, Bulat Okudzhava, Vladimir Vysotsky, and other new Russian bards began with their songs.

Never had the poets gathered such a huge audience: thousands of young people in stadiums listened to poets reading their poems. Many new theaters opened. Oleg Efremov's Moscow theater *Sovremennik*, later Yury Lyubimov's *Theater on Taganka*, and in Leningrad, Tovstonogov's *Great Drama Theater* on Fontanka, *Theater Lensoveta* directed by Igor Vladimirov, and many others. These theaters set up new dramas that reflected people's problems with the light implications to the consequences of the Soviet political regime. The language of monologs was ambiguous, so the officials could not find fault with the text. The audience caught every word and then discussed how fearless the play was.

This was not a freedom in art creation or writing; it was a stopping of a bleeding but in the people's mind it was thought of as a great relaxation after a cruel winter.

The apotheosis of political actions that followed Khrushchev's *thaw* was the removal of Stalin's body from the mausoleum in 1961. Russian historian Roy Medvedev in his book *Nikita Khrushchev: A Father or a Step-Father of Soviet*

"Thaw"? published in Russian, refers to the remembrance of journalist V. Strelkov:

> "At the time I worked as a correspondent of the News Agency APN. I learned there was a demand at the 22nd Congress of Communist party to remove Stalin's body from the Mausoleum. Immediately after that I went to Red Square (where mausoleum located – L.P.) However, I did not see anything on that day. Only on the third day with my friends, I was a witness of this occasion… There were about 200 people near the mausoleum. It was cold. We thought the authorities would bring sarcophagus with Stalin's body through the main entrance. Nobody paid attention that from the left side of Mausoleum there were wooden shields, and the electrical light was on at that side. Late evening a military truck came to the right side of the mausoleum. All people who stood in front of the entrance run to the right side. Somebody shouted, "They bring it out!" My two friends and I did not run but distantly watched. Somewhere the militiamen showed up, lined up as a chain, and cut the crowd from the mausoleum. We kept staying behind the chain. From the side door of the mausoleum, soldiers brought out the glass sarcophagus and put it to the truck. We took advantage of our position and stepped out to the left by the shields. Right there we saw soldiers digging the grave behind the shields. Here was a man in dark gray coat and hat. About 10 – beginning 11th o'clock night, a woman showed

up (I think it was S. Allilueva (Stalin's daughter – L.P.)). She was nervous, and her movements were sharp. Nobody stopped her when she entered behind the Mausoleum. Then a black car came over and a high military officer (either Marshal or General, we could not distinct his face and title) passed behind the Mausoleum. I asked the young soldier, a black car driver, who the General is. He smiled instead the answer, I repeated my question, and again he smiled. About 11 o'clock, a military chief came back to car and left… Now, a man in dark gray coat and hat approached to us and politely asked to leave the Red Square... No TV-reporters were near the Mausoleum. After 1961–1962, it was noticeable that Khrushchev encouraged people praising him. It was too obvious that once again, the cult of the personality was coming. Then all words with Stalin's disclosure stopped. Again, newspapers and party functionaries began putting on a pedestal and mouth honoring the leader – not too many years passed after Stalin's cult finished with his death and it was still not forgotten."

Even during the *thaw*, a huge totalitarian machine continued to run uninterrupted with all its features: communist hardline ideology, KGB, institute of informers, suppression of dissidents, and so on. Leaders tried to persuade people that the cult of personality (this is how they named Stalin's idolatry) had merely stuck on to this person but indeed Marxism–Leninism rejects and condemns it.

Even though I knew more than others about the West after visiting European countries and Canada, I still believed in the 1960s we would have a better future. After Praga's Spring Standoff of 1968 in Czechoslovakia, with Soviet soldiers on tanks entered the streets, all nuts were screwed back in. By the 1970s, nobody even thought about the brighter future, just maintained the unpretentious present. By the middle of the 1980s, with Gorbachev's coming, something turned in people's mind.

Gorbachev's Perestroika

I bring up the tragic story of the passenger ship *Admiral Nakhimov*, as the ship symbolized the Soviet orderliness and the passengers were the longsuffering Soviet people. The fate of the ship signified the last years of the agony of the late socialism of 1980s: sinking ship - dying country.

Not many people recall now *Admiral Nakhimov's* catastrophe though the scale of the tragedy was the same as in the *Titanic* case of 1912, with the difference that the *Titanic* sunk in one hundred and eighty minutes and the *Admiral Nakhimov* did just in seven minutes.

The *Admiral Nakhimov* was one of the ships that the USSR received as part of the reparation from Germany after WWII in 1945. It was built in 1925 with the initial name *Berlin*, able to carry about one thousand passengers onboard. Many years later, I watched the movie *Titanic,* and everything reminded me of the *Admiral Nakhimov*: same luxury style, crowds of passengers, and… the same fortune. One thing though was different: the *Titanic* was newly built and was making its very first trip; the *Admiral Nakhimov* was built more than sixty years prior to its last voyage and its life cycle was long overdue.

Passengers and crew had little time to escape, and 423 of the 1,234 on board perished. Sixty-four of those died were the crewmembers, and 359 were the passengers. The event was not reported in the news for five days.

What happened to the *Admiral Nakhimov* was not only a human factor. A secondary cause was the mindset of cutting corners because of people's security so frequently seen in Russia. The Black Sea Shipping Company's bosses ordered not to scrap the old ship but to continue making money to report good results to the Ministry. They just did not send it to foreign ports not to be detained due its unbelievably poor technical condition. Some repairs were made earlier that year in Varna, Bulgaria. The Marine Register of the USSR, which depended upon and reported to the Ministry of Marine, performed the technical oversight for the repair. Obviously, the Ministry was interested in looking better in front of the party leaders by bringing in more money but ignoring safety. A classical conflict of interests!

The victims of collision with another ship and of this conflict were the ship's passengers. The former Chief Mate of the ship deposited that safe boat davit pedestals had been destroyed by the corrosion and could break and fall off. That happened on the ship during the training alarm. Then the Black Sea Shipping Company ordered the launch of no more boats. The order was for a passenger ship carrying over fifteen hundred people! Of course, seven minutes before the ship went down was not enough time to launch any boat but the case clearly shows in what mode big and small officials and the whole country functioned. The collision took place only fifteen kilometers from the shore near Novorossiysk. Marine dispatchers were able to observe the two ships approaching each other and could interfere to prevent the catastrophe. They did nothing at all.

Negligence to human life in aspiration for getting benefits, indifference, and permanent cutting corners are just a few attributes that eventually lead to a catastrophe. The quantity of wrongdoings gradually transferred to a new quality – the line of devastations that took thousands of lives. The biggest ones were the nuclear catastrophe in Chernobyl, the gas explosion at the railroad trains near the Ural Mountains, and the steamship *Admiral Nakhimov*. The Soviet superpower was getting into agony.

To characterize conditions that preceded the initiation of Perestroika in one word, I would say *a lie*. Lies were everywhere and with everyone. Big leaders lied to people about the country that was going fast to communism. Party apparatchiks lied to big leaders about good harvests, about factories and plants that ostensibly worked efficiently. Mid-level bosses lied to higher bosses about the work quality and completion. Common people falsely showed their support of the communist party at the state holidays on November 7 and May 1. Nepotism, bribes and *blat* in occupational promotion bloomed everywhere. This could not last too long.

An inefficient economy, nine years of the Afghan war with fifteen thousand sons killed, dropped oil prices, industrial disasters, and lack of food undermined the country. Even the most bullet-headed communists understood the country badly needed change. As opposed to the epoch of the 1960s, nobody recalled the communist ideals anymore. When Brezhnev died in 1982, people took it calmly and then in response to every next death of Kremlin's old leader, people just joked.

People understood Mikhail Gorbachev's first speeches after he became Secretary General of Communist Party in spring of 1985 just as slightly more human-oriented words of a party apparatchik. Nobody took him seriously as a reformer and nothing changed during his first months. The long lines in food and liquor stores, food quotes, "sausage trains" from small Russian hungry towns to Moscow to get some meat, sausage, cheese did not lessen. However, compared with all previous leaders, there were fewer words glorifying the communist party and the government.

Newspapers began publishing articles criticizing anything and even indirectly, the political system. I once spoke with an editor of a technical magazine where my scientific article was going to be published. She told me that in expectation, the strict party-liners would soon come back and stop this revelry, her husband cut out and collected all sharp and politically challenging articles as a proof this was real.

Glasnost and Perestroika were coming into the country, and this was something very new. No doubt, it was an outstanding affair of the twentieth century. Although Gorbachev neither expected, nor wanted the collapse of communist system, what he did made him a historical person. He loosened the arrangement and then did not know what to do with the awakened superpower that had been kept merely on the constraint. He had many supporters and much more enemies inside the Party members. He had to maneuver between two contrasts – democrats and hard-liners communists – and as a result, he was left alone by both. His destiny turned back on him: he was unfairly hated by most people in post-Soviet Russia. History has yet to evaluate what he did for Russia. Had he chosen to reign as Brezhnev did, he would have found the way to make it. But he did what he did. All this made him a tragic person.

Gorbachev's Perestroika tentatively has been divided into two periods by the people's inspirations: the first one of 1985–1988, a romantic period characterized by giving more freedom, the weakening of the KGB, liberation of the main dissident of the country Andrei Sakharov, and removal of obstacles for promotion of Jews. The second period of 1989–1991, came when the people felt no good words were coming true. The low but accustomed and stable living standard of the old Soviet time dropped unbelievably low and people just tired of the empty shelves.

Soviet Jewry, as always, was divided: one part still wanted to emigrate and made all efforts to do that within 1981–1988 period when the exit doors were still closed; another part believed that good changes were going to come. Eventually most people from both parts emigrated but that was later. At that point, we knew the most important events on our planet occurred in Russia. Every day brought breaking political news.

Gorbachev claimed that economic reforms should go along with political changes. However, while the latter moved fast, the economy stalled. Any verbal calls to improve, increase, intensify, or speed up did not work at all. The huge lines for everything, including vodka and the empty shelves in food and department stores made people angry, rude, and intolerant. This was how the crowds of people felt like at the second period of Perestroika, at its final stage.

What made crowds of people like this? It was a huge gap between the quality of life for the party functionaries and the *blatniks* from one side, and the common people from another side. Impoverishment of commons by the end of the 1980s had become countrywide. With food given out only by quotations, no goods in department stores, and money devaluated, people did not believe the communist ideals, nor Gorbachev or other party leaders. As a result, tens of thousands came out on to the streets. A resolve to the political mess was coming.

At the end of 1990, after a long period of the taboo, I finally got an exit visa due to Perestroika. I went to sea on board a containership. The purpose was a sea trial of an improved main engine control device. The containership *Professor Tovstykh* served the shipping line Hamburg–Singapore–Hong Kong. I had to make two roundtrip voyages from Western Europe to Southeastern Asia. At the beginning of the second one, the Gulf War of 1991 broke out. The ship was in the Atlantic Ocean going around Europe. As we got the news about the war and having no idea about the limits of the warfare, our captain said that we possibly would not go through the Suez

Canal but around Africa, which may extend the trip for several weeks. From the beginning, I did not believe the war might affect the whole Middle East. When the ship's crew learned that within several days, the Americans had defeated Saddam Hussein in Kuwait, we relaxed.

After three weeks of sailing, we reached South East Asia. Singapore and Hong Kong amazed me with their grandeur, ski-scrapers, and wealth. What a contrast with Russia of 1990, where the pre-revolutionary chaos was taking place, people were in rage, and the anti-Semitic movement "Pamyat" (Remembrance) was revived. Looking at this liveliness, I thought about Russia's poor fate that took over seventy years, millions of lives, and immeasurable sufferings to understand the falsehood of communism.

In early spring of 1991, we came to Hamburg, Germany and I had an opportunity to walk in the city. I paid attention that here and there on the city squares were containers, and people brought goods, preserves, dress, etc. I came close to one of them and saw placard in German: HELP LENINGRAD. I left Leningrad about five months ago. Was it so bad there? At that moment, I thought something big and dangerous had impended Russia. After 46 years of victory over Germany, the country-looser collects charity for the country-winner. What a historic twist!

Meanwhile, the sea trial finished. In March 1991, I finally came back home. The country changed to worse during my 5 months absence: the food as if disappeared from the grocery stores – bread and thick macaroni; people in the streets were outraged and angry with the situation in the country. That special time, as any revolution, produced passionate orators: Yeltsin, Sobchak, Travkin, Afanasiev, Starovoitova, and many more. They appealed to set up new democratic institutions, provide all human rights, and remove the domination of the Communist party. These calls were understood by most of the people who supported the democratic leaders. The Russian political specter of that time had only two colors: if someone supported liberals, he was a friend; if he stood with communists, he was an enemy. How clear and naïve! What was not clear is how people could meet the ends. Without reforms, the placards did not work. The naive representations that political freedom automatically brings economic prosperity were ruined. Since the situation in the country became worse, the quotes were limited to almost all food. There were huge lines even for the plain food like bread or macaroni that had never formed lines before.

Gorbachev's personal and political destiny resulted from his lack of economic reforms based on the conception that he could renovate and repaint Soviet socialism. He believed that he needed to fulfill a few non-comprehensive changes and bring a human face to socialism, and then the Soviet political and economic system would renew to come closer to the Western type. Relieving more and more freedom was like releasing the genie from the bottle. Fast changes in politics, much faster than those in the economy, made a misbalance between the political liberation of the people and their living standard that dropped very low. This brought hundreds of thousand people to the streets in 1990–1991.

Pro-Soviet Putsch and Thereafter

It was agonizing: the republics of the Union fought to separate from the Soviet central dictate. Terrible events occurred in Tbilisi, Georgia, where soldiers smashed and killed people with entrenching shovels. In Baku, Azerbaijan, military tanks entered the city. In Vilnius, Lithuania, local people liberated the television center and then the Soviet troops killed or arrested some. Russia, the binding member of the Union, also was in a bustle. The explosion of the Empire was imminent.

It broke out on August 19, 1991. I turned on the television and instead of the passionate speeches we used to hear during the last years, I saw the Tchaikovsky ballet *Swan Lake*. The first moment I did not pay attention but then the radio broadcast press conference of the newly formed Emergency Committee (GKChP) consisted of Politburo members, military commanders, and the KGB chairperson. They announced that this committee has formed to restore the order in the USSR and to prevent the country from chaos and catastrophe. A State of Emergency was proclaimed. Troops were ordered to enter Moscow and other big cities. The hardline communist bosses took on bringing the country to old rails. That was putsch!

Leningrad free radio station had not been shut down yet. The station called for a total strike, for everyone to go to Dvortsovaya Square! I deeply rooted for changes and could not stay home. I headed to Dvortsovaya. While the subway train was bringing me to Nevsky Prospect, I did not know if troops were ordered to enter the city. If so, then... would soldiers be shooting people? I got off the train and had to walk about fifteen minutes to Dvortsovaya. I came up on the escalator, went out to sidewalk. So far there were no tanks and no soldiers.

The square barely housed all the people gathered. I guess there were twenty thousand or more. The Mayor of Leningrad Anatoly Sobchak appeared first. He said that we were there to prove people are not cattle, the communist backward would not go through, and we would defend freedom conquered so hard. Then academician Dmitry Likhachev and other people made speeches. I looked at the faces of people next to me and farther. These were beautiful and spiritual faces. I thought so many people shared the same values. The most inspirational moment came when a huge placard WE ARE WITH YOU appeared at the facade of the Military Chief Staff building. Everybody applauded. I understood we are winning this battle.

In Moscow, the putsch turned out to be more dramatic. Tanks occupied positions along the central streets. Dozens of thousands of people came out. Everyone saw pictures on television: Yeltsin stays on a tank and speaks against the putschists. That was the moment of his highest popularity. People, not Yeltsin won this battle. Yeltsin as President of Russia (not the USSR) ordered military commanders who went over to his side to bring tanks out from Moscow. Three young guys died in an accident with tanks. Symbolically, these young men who standoff the last quake of the Soviet Empire, the disappearing superpower, became the last heroes of the Soviet Union.

Gorbachev's Perestroika failed. The country leader tried to improve socialism. The political system within the socialism is unviable. The scheme has fully decayed and could not be enhanced in general. No economic reforms had even started. At the backdrop of falling oil prices and depletion of the gold reserve, Soviet economy had collapsed. August 21, 1991 was final day of the communist dominancy.

After putsch was suppressed, Yeltsin formed a new government of the Russian Federation to conduct a new policy in economy, and one of the government's first decrees was setting up a free market with free prices for all foods and goods. By this time, the food stores were literally empty, just a few goods lay on the store's shelves. Hunger was real that winter.

On December 1991, after signing the agreement on formation of the Commonwealth of Independent States, Gorbachev resigned as its first and the last president of the USSR. This was his personal tragedy. One could only imagine what he thought when spoke his resignation speech on television. Years later, Alexander Yakovlev, a person responsible for the ideology in Gorbachev's Politburo and the "architect of the Soviet Perestroika" recollected in one of the shows that after the resignation speech Gorbachev met with him. His eyes were red; he could not keep in his feelings, Yakovlev, recalls. At the end, Gorbachev said to him, "that is what we got, Sasha" (the nickname of Alexander). That was his finish as an active politician.

The collapse of the world superpower was not like an earthquake. However, it was difficult to comprehend the new realities of 1991–1992 with a formally different country but the same people. Many of them thought the changes that occurred were better for all of us; others regret. Common people were busy with their everyday problems, and the actual collapse of the country occured just by signing papers with no demonstrations or strikes. It was like the next executive order.

During these disorderly and restless years of changes, people's well-being dropped incredibly. Majority of people did not know how they are going to feed their families. Paradoxically, life was interesting. Every day brought breaking political news. The tectonic changes occurred in the newly born democratic country. I felt as if I was a participant of a huge political and social experiment.

In January 1992, the new Russian government consisted of the young economists-liberals with Egor Gaidar as a Prime Minister, and the economic reform plans started to implement… as shock therapy. It started with the release of all prices from fixed by the state to free market prices. Just one example: one kilogram of potato cost sixty kopeks (0.6 ruble) on December 30, 1991; on January 3 of 1992, it costs five rubles; in February – twenty rubles; in March – fifty and so on. That was in parallel with hyperinflation: one dollar by the end of 1992 rose from sixty up to five thousand rubles during just a few months.

The number one problem was simply how to survive the sky-rocketing food prices. Almost all (millions) suddenly became poor, no matter whether you worked or not, and families could not meet the ends. It was so bad that many felt abashed and lost. At the time, it was not about the absence of food or goods in stores but rather about the lack of money to buy them. Further, both food and goods started to fill store shelves and within two to three months, what we saw was incredible: full shelves of food in stores! In addition, flea markets were full of goods, mostly Turkish and Chinese but still unaffordable. The misfortune, however, was that people had no money to fulfill their basic needs for life.

Crowds of white collars quit their intellectual jobs and became suitcase traders or *chelnoks* (shuttles*)* – that was how they were named for their back and forth travels for the goods. That was a major issue: a former huge superpower transfers to a different economical track. Factories, industrial facilities, and research and design institutes, military manufacturers – all superstructures – slowed down drastically and many of them stopped production. Millions of people lost their jobs or did not get paid for months and had to survive this economic hardship. Those who were younger or more active did "buy & sell" type of work; physically strong guys joined mob gangs doing racketeering; less active and older unemployed engineers applied for guards or did not work at all. The birthrate in the country abruptly dropped and the mortality rate rose dramatically. Once the world superpower, Russia had evolved to a third-grade regional country.

Some anti-Semitic groups, politicians, and media raised their voices. Most of the commons who were busy with their own survival did not support these calls, directing their anger against President Boris Yeltsin and Prime Minister Egor Gaidar. These two politicians became the most hated, and they had to have much courage to continue with their shocking reforms. An epoch of the initial capitalization has never been smooth.

The credibility ratings of Yeltsin and Gaidar dropped to their lowest points by the middle of 1992. Right in front of the building where I lived in St. Petersburg, I saw large paint writing, "Yeltsin is murderer". Nevertheless, freedom of meetings, press, television, and other mass media really existed, and Yeltsin never suppressed it.

The country had to go through this hardship for our people's slavish outlook and the stupidity of 1917 and later. There was a strong opposition to Yeltsin in the Supreme Council (parliament). Members of the Council refused to support him and the government in conducting reforms and always voted against his decrees. They just torpedoed government resolutions. The opposition rose between Yeltsin and the Supreme Council and reached its peak in October 1993. It eventually transformed into an open standoff.

Council members called to form a militia, seizing the central television center in Ostankino to announce that Yeltsin had been overthrown. At that point, hundreds of the council supporters stormed the television center, and many of them died. In response, the President ordered the tank division to come to Moscow (the second time in two years!) The crunch came when Yeltsin ordered shooting from tanks to the Supreme Council building where most of the members of the council were barricaded. Shooting the Supreme Council building from the tank main gun sobered up the rebels and their resistance broke. Yeltsin won this battle, which was the second putsch.

My support of Yeltsin finished with his order of shooting the Parliament. That was typical Soviet way of fixing political situation: gun down the opponents and a problem is eliminated. I was on my business trip to Moscow one week after the standoff. I saw the results of the tank's volley. The sight was impressive: a few feet in size hole in the wall with a large black surrounding halo because of fire, somewhere about the level of tenth floor. Politics is a big game and the stakes are life and freedom from jail. This was a special Russian way to resolve political disagreements at the end of the twentieth century: it did not matter whether they fought for the right or wrong values... the methods are the same.

On that evening of fall 1993, I walked in Moscow streets and incidentally came up to the Maly Theater, between Neglinnaya and Petrovka Streets. I checked if there were tickets for any play. I was lucky; a premier of the new Solzhenitsyn's play *Pir Pobeditelei (Feast of the Winners)* was on. I bought a ticket and entered. When the theater was full and before the play started, the administrator announced that the great Russian writer Alexander Solzhenitsyn is here to watch the premier. People applauded, and then the play started. The plot was about the end of the World War II, several Soviet officers got together to celebrate finish of fighting Germans. They naively dreamed how good their life would be after coming home with a victory but the realities ruined their dreams.

After the performance, Solzhenitsyn went up on the stage and said a few words about the play. His speech was about the political situation in Russia. He criticized reforms conducted in Russia. I just thought it is good that anyone can openly criticize the authorities for dropping the living standard. But how can we shift to the free market economy and democracy other than through these painful liberal reforms? The time to gather stones had come.

Meanwhile, the next step after the release of prices was a privatization. Privatization of big and small subjects had never been done on such a big scale. Factories, warehouses, department stores, different businesses, apartments, houses and many more estates and equipment were given to private hands with help of the vouchers. Every citizen, including children, received vouchers as an equivalent of a certain value. The price of one voucher was a quotient of all national estate divided by the number of populations in the country. It was not much. Anyone could sell it, give it in the exchange of piece of property, buy it, or do nothing. Formally, the voucher scheme as it was created was right: there were no legally rich enough people in Russia to buy properties previously belonging to the state. The way this scheme was realized was gruff.

I put all my family vouchers to a new widely advertised oil company Hermes. Next year, this company turned out to be nonexistent. Cases like mine happened so often that millions of people felt cheated. At the same time, another group of super active people emerged; they bought in as many vouchers as they could. Having thousands or even millions of vouchers bought the nimble people to invest them to buy out real factories and companies. This was the beginning of the origin of a new class of owners. Like in America, at the initial capital formation, much criminality was involved. That was time of the disorderly and lawless get-rich-quick.

Part of the new Russian economy controlled by the vast and branched criminal structure who penetrated each pore of big and small business. Locally, they did trader catches, racketeering, collected money for the "roofing" (protection from other gangs), sold drugs, etc. Killings of businessmen, bankers, and criminal chiefs occurred nearly every day. Fights for businesses, properties, land, and areas of influence were going on. Mobsters could be recognized by their appearance: they dressed in sport suits or silk shirts or maroon jackets and had the short haircut or shaved heads in the beginning of the 1990s. A decade later, many of them moved to the luxury offices of regional and federal bosses.

Humanity has already learned and experienced the transition from capitalism to socialism when all factories and agriculture had been taken away from the owners and nationalized. However, the opposite way, from socialism back to capitalism was new in the world history. Shock therapy in the economy brought much suffering. However, such was the price for decades of "taking away and sharing", leveling all people, extermination of those who spiritually stood above the level predetermined by leaders, for the policy of the primitive idolatry. Unfortunately, none of the reforms was finished after removal of the first government of Egor Gaidar, which conducted the real monetary policy. This put Russia after 2000 into a position of "semi": semi-democratic, semi-capitalistic, and semi-advanced country.

Russian Jews were getting along differently during the hardship. Some of them continued working in semi-dying scientific organizations, design, or other little paid intellectual jobs getting more impoverished. Some found themselves in the yet embryonic and unripe business, dealing with corrupted clerks and police, mobsters, and gang shooting. Within the unrestricted and unseen before economic freedom, some people began to make money. A relatively big disproportional number of Jews was among those. Several Jewish names were constantly heard as the richest new tycoons understandably created anxiety in other Jews in fear of being harassed. Others either left Russia or were going to leave – the beginning of the 1990s was the time of massive emigration. That was time when most of Jews populated former Soviet Union became Wandering Jews of the modern-day. In 1990s, Jews fled not from the persecution but from a complete economic turmoil, criminality and poverty. Who can blame people for their aspiration for a better life?

Some people say it was Yeltsin and his helpers that collapsed the Soviet Union on December 1991 in Belovezhskaya Pushcha signing the protocol on the formation of the Commonwealth of Independent States instead of the Union of Republics. No, that was the time for the Soviet

Empire to collapse since it had crumbled from the inside. Soviet Perestroika came to its logical finish because any tries to bring a human face to the decayed but hawkish organism doomed to fail. People lost initiative, they had to depend on a state not themselves, and thus, the state produced dependents.

Russian history has given a lesson to world politicians and philosophers who like talking about the equality and calling for socialism. The state that keeps all business and gives out money to people just to survive or takes almost all money as taxes can never survive. This was a history warning based on the real social experiment lasted for 70 years that finished in the dead end.

POST-SOVIET RUSSIA IN SEARCH OF THE NATIONAL IDEA

After years of turmoil, by 2000, most Russians wanted strong central authority. The country got it in the person of young President Putin, KGB native, who was literally assigned by the declining Yeltsin to be president. I assume Yeltsin had realized his mistake during his last years.

When the new leader restricted freedom of mass media, people did not protest. Most admired him. He well knew inclination of common Russians to have a strongman as a supreme leader and used it for his purpose. The message delivered by him through now controlled television and the press was the following: *liberties must be limited to avoid the turmoil. Do you need the damn Yeltsin's 1990s and his "freedoms" back again?* This warning worked effectively. The policy changed to autocracy and luckily for him, oil prices sky-rocketed, making the former KGB officer a national leader, the savior of a homeland.

When I think of what occurred in Russia during the last twenty years, I speculate about the missing opportunities to become a Western style democracy through integration with the free world. Huge oil and gas natural resources spoiled the country; they erase the incentive to develop technologies for the twenty-first century. The notorious "vertical of power" along with enormous corruption increased Russia's technological lag.

The fundamental difference between the Russian and Western supreme power starts with election of a leader. The pendulum of public opinion in the US and Western countries varies mostly from the moderate left to the moderate right with some marginal exclusions. In the West, if people and the elite are not satisfied with the economic and political outcome of the president and/or parliament, they simply change their mind and next time vote for those who have a different political approach in the hope they would solve problems more effectively.

In Russia, a leader is more like a prophet of the supreme being, he is not just performing his duty but holding the supreme power. People are expected to idolize him, and many of them do not want to replace him until it is too late to make it in the civilian way. Whoever the Russian leader is, he has always been a monarch. Gorbachev was the exclusion not loved by both the elite and people. Removal from the power occurred either because of death of a leader or through a coup. In the Soviet times, people did not elect political leaders. Any change in the leadership was always tectonic for the entire country.

Throughout centuries, the state has always been suppressive to its own people. At first, it was for the religion deviations, then for political dissidence, and the newest trend is for nonconformity of protesters by using crafty selective justice. The citizens must not protest, if not then welcome to jail, the guilt will be found anyway.

Russian domestic politics from the 2000s and on widely uses anti-Western rhetoric, which is not as innocent as some may think. Although progress and civilization have come from the West during the last few centuries, anti-Western sentiments go along with Western-phobia in anything of not Russian style: culture, politics, and behavior. The traditional division of the society is the conservative Russo-phils and pro-Western liberals (Russo-fobs as they are now called in Russia). Russian leaders traditionally support the first ones. The second ones are considered as open or secret enemies. The Western world has annoyed Russia with its technological advance and cultural front running, their friendly smiles (believed to be false), prudence, and frugality.

The concept in its modern terms suggests that Russian political development should have an *exceptional way*, different from the Western countries. It should be based on the role of Russian Orthodoxy and strengthening the state's governing and political power. Western-phobia is being imposed by the Russian rulers, but the same rulers send their children to study in the western universities. Isn't it a hypocrisy? What could this *exceptional way* suggest to people? Nothing but disrespect, dislike and distrust to the western values. The alternative to western values can be autocracy, oppressions, and hypertrophic role of religion which are the consequences of this *exceptional way* so desirable by the influential Russian elite and leaders.

In the eyes of Russians, the US has changed its image many times. It has transformed from the implacable enemy in the 1950s to the never seen fabulous country in the 1960s–1980s to the teacher of capitalism in the 1990s. Eventually it altered to a disliked country after Russia *rose from her knees* and a huge flow of petrodollars fell with the boosted oil prices from the sky in the 2000s. The modern Russia's approach to the West, especially to the US, is dual. The pinched consciousness of the former superpower causes envy and inferiority complex. Therefore, the unfriendly rhetoric towards Americans is popular in modern Russia, and the chauvinists and officials heat it up. On another hand, Russians like to expose themselves in the eyes of the West. Any modernization or big construction work is always limited by the project location, where its exposure to the foreigners is most likely. The rest of the Russian provinces will stay as they are – dirty, leaky, stalled. The Russian pinched attitude of the frustrated state with a dominant position in the international system has often been a cause of the love-hate relationship and anti-American rhetoric used by Russian leaders. Imaging the US as a foe is gainful for the current Russian leaders. Traditionally, anything that proclaimed by leaders is not necessarily the same what common people had in mind. That is not the case in the attitude towards United States. Today even the common Russians dislike America. Why? There are a few reasons for that.

First, quite recently, in the nineties, the former superpower felt humiliation while poor and cut off, it studied the lessons from big and small countries on how to conduct business. It was intolerable and so suffering for ultra-patriots who got used to trumpet how great the Soviet Union is! Hatred to America initially was only proclaimed by them. Then they were joint by the Russian leader and his elite who understood that western values, human rights and other freedoms are just a headache for them. It is much easier and safer to manually control all aspects of "democracy", which was named a "sovereign democracy". Their missed view of Russia as superpower comes back and certainly, it helps to distract people's attention from their despair with the economic stagnation, channeling it to the external political grounds. A considerable part of the population buys it. This new Russia's grandeure approach coincided with oil and gas skyrocketed prices. Huge oil money woke up the imperial consciousness. At the time, Putin claimed that fall of the Soviet Union was the greatest geopolitical catastrophe of the twentieth century. Grievance and nostalgia about the past greatness is the base of any revanchism. The wounded mindfulness of the former superpower could not tolerate that, and the spirit of greatness eventually returned along with the strong incline to militarization.

Second reason could be formulated as a response to so called "russo-phobia". Many in Russia are certain that the US and West captured by russo-phobia because they don't want competition and need weak Russia. However, the weak means unstable and unpredictable, which is not in the best interest of West. The West is too pragmatic to have a luxury of imposing sanctions just because it dislikes a country. The term "russo-phobia" has been invented by Russian elite as an attempt to respond to western accusations for the violations of international law. Some in Russia even equalize "russo-phobia" to anti-Semitism! Wrong! Not the "russo-phobia" but violations of Helsinki-1975 basic rules for security and borders by Russians in Ukraine is the reason for accusations and sanctions.

Third, the standoff with America flatters Russia. Rivalry on the edge of feud with America, the first and most powerful country makes Russia as if one more political pole in the world.

Russian government and people are united in dislike of the United States due to *fourth reason* as well. It is because the country dropped Soviet internationalism and starting from 2000s accepted Russian nationalism. It took about ten years for the new ideology to ripe. Nationalism called patriotism in Russia turned up to be the only one unmistakable alternative to died socialism. For very short time, it has united people on the base of a national identity. It worked out effectively by claiming patriotism as a new national idea. The new Russian nationalism and national identity have made what Soviet internationalism was never able to make – now the United States is being considered a foe not only by Russian leaders but also by the commons. Sad to say but some intellectuals also support these anti-Western sentiments.

Fifth reason is the unprecedented before political propaganda coming from Federal TV channels in the form of talk shows, news, monologs and dialogs with carefully selected people. Soviet political culture could not even dream of such an effectiveness! To be honest, part of the motive of antipathy is American fault for invasion to Iraq, bombardment of Serbia, Libya, other stupid moves like leaving Afghanistan, then returning there…

Humanity has collected their experience, learning from mistakes made in the past. It is just a common sense not to make them again. Historical spiral comes back on a higher level and seemingly, on that next level, people should consider all that went wrong in the past to avoid same mistakes. It is true in different countries but Russia. Experience is nothing but the past: just forget if it is bad. Most Russians vote for the autocratic president. Russia at this point deserves Putin as much as any country deserves its government. The ruler of a nation typically matches its prevailing culture. Neither Gorbachev, nor Yeltsin who attempted to conduct liberal reforms matched Russian cultural traditions and thus, turned out to be non-apropos leaders. If the majority still chooses an irremovable authoritarian leader, a puppet-style parliament, and supports a ruling close-minded party, that means most of Russians still need the autocracy. The ruler would solve Russian people's problems rather than the people doing it themselves – this hope still exists within the Russian culture.

The Russian state has never protected the security and civil rights of their people. On the contrary, those who fell out from any of the state's political or economic ideas had to defend themselves from the state: there has never been real protection from the outrage of bureaucrats. It all comes from the tradition that citizens must serve national leaders, not the converse.

With years, more educated people feel annoyed with the irreplaceable leader. Unfortunately, it may take too long until the lid of people's patience comes off and they realize what the leader says is opposite of what he does. Whatever good politician or personality he is, the nation needs the replacement of leaders, a renewal of administration and a refreshment of the course to avoid stagnation and put fresh ideas into practice. The question is why Russians still want to vote for the same person again? It may take them long and be too late to finally realize that this misfortune is due to their misperception.

I watched the birth of new Russia. The newly born country was distressing but there was a hope for stretching out and improvement. The same country after twenty years remains upsetting, and the hope flies away. The Russian exceptional way is not invented by the ruling Russian politicians and would not be removed with the current leader as it has to do with the culture. I do not believe the next sovereign after Putin or someone thereafter would succeed as being pro-western. Even if he accomplishes something good, his time would be limited because the core Russia's value is an "exceptional" way, be it good or bad for the people.

This is one more strive to develop the national idea by the ruling United Russia party. The old communistic slogan p*eople and the party united* has gone and no national idea in the modern Russia other than the oldest czarist o*rthodoxy, autocracy and nationalism* that is now called *patriotism,* can be suggested. Russians are not supposed to die for the idea of liberty for the individual and society – that is the Western way. They do not need this malicious idea – liberty is not the most important point; they are supposed to die for the state and faith. Ironically, in the country where common people's dislike and fear of their state takes place, we can hear much more talks about how people should love their state. The tradition comes from the history of massive executions in the name of state and ideology imposed by Ivan the Terrible, Peter the Great, and Stalin. The "exceptional Russian way" ideology is maintained under the President Vladimir Putin. In a very short time, it has rallied the people on the ground of national identity.

National idea is not something that can be invented deliberately but it comes from the longtime development of a nation. At this period of the modern history Russia has made its choice: stay autocratic, have unchangeable leaders and limited "sovereign" democracy. I do not rule out that in the future, not too distant, Russia will admit the real democracy, elections, and freedom of mass media. When the final choice is made, then a new national idea appears self-induced. The choice will be made, no doubt.

How about the Jews? How were they treated during those seventy years of the existence of the Soviet Union? We know from the Russian history: bad treatment of Jews at one time changed to worst with altering political, social or economic situations. The scapegoats are always in demand and Jews have always been very easy target. Let's talk about that.

4
The Fifth Record and the Common Anti-Semitism

The real ideology of anti-Semitism is the racial one, which is the most widely spread form of hostility towards the Jews.

Nikolai Berdyaev,
Russian Philosopher

The notorious *fifth record,* an epitome of the Russian anti-Semitism, was used in the Soviet Union as a determination of ethnical belonging. The *fifth* came from the number 5 record in the Soviet passport: #1 was the last name; #2 first name; #3 middle name (otchestvo); #4 date of birth and #5 nationality (not the citizenship but ethnicity). This substitution mainly impacted the Jewry. Writing about the Russian anti-Semitism is a bitter topic. I am positive that a great number of Russian people do not draw a dividing line between them and their Jewish compatriots. Unfortunately, those who are hostile toward the Jews are also Russians. Soviet and Russian ant-Semitism shown up as both the government supported and the grassroot one. It raised and then slowed down to raise again depending upon the policy of current ruling higher-ups. When the government used to resume its anti-Semitic policy, it always followed by outbreak of the grassroot (or street) anti-Semitism. We will discuss both types.

THE STATE'S ANTI-SEMITISM

The Jewish identity of a Soviet Jew was formed under anti-Semitic policy of the Soviet government. Soviet anti-Semitism had different forms in different times. The earlier one of 1940s–1950s was repressive and bloody. The late one of 1960s–1980s was concealed, quiet, but nonetheless, base. It was normal practice that a Jew was rejected for certain positions because of his "fifth record". Nobody even asked the question why they were oppressed: without saying, Jews could not exercise the same rights. Persecution of Jews started long before the Soviet and even Medieval Europian anti-Semitism shown up.

First records of anti-Semitism dated third century B.C. in ancient Egypt. As historian R. Wistrich noted, anti-Semitism in the ancient time,

> "…always draw on the fact that no other nation in antiquity, apart from the Jews, so consistently refused to acknowledge the gods of its neighbors, partake in their sacrifices, and send gifts to their temples… As if to compound the insult, Jews claimed superiority over the "heathens" in the religious sphere (something that Judaism involuntary bequeathed to Christianity and Islam) – committed as it was to a transcendent monotheistic faith and a rational code of ethics." (Robert Wistrich. *A Lethal Obsession. Anti-Semitism from Antiquity to the Global Jihad.* Random House, New York. 2010, p.81).

The new type of anti-Semitism began after Jews lost their state because of the Roman conquest, and most of them dissipated throughout Europe, Middle East, and other areas. For the residents the new aliens were obviously unwanted and therefore, hated. They were seen competitors, had different appearance and unusual habits, different faith, they built synagogues, and were too active in commerce and trade. All that eventually caused local nations to expel Jews from different European countries through the centuries. As a condition to stay, the persecutors wanted them to abandon their culture and religion.

Dennis Prager and Joseph Telushkin emphasized that

> "Since Judaism is the root of anti-Semitism, Jews, *unlike victims of racial or ethnic prejudice* (their Italic) could in almost every instance of anti-Semitism, except Nazism (and the Marranos and Conversos in Spain in 14th and 15th centuries) escape prosecution. For thousands of years and until today, Jews who abandoned their Jewish identity and assumed the majority's religious and national identity were no longer prosecuted." (Dennis Prager and Joseph Telushkin *Why the Jews? The Reason of Antisemitism.* Simon & Shuster, 2003)

Per Pragin and Telushkin, the exclusion was Nazi Germany where Jews were persecuted with no connection to their religion. I would add the Soviet regime to these exceptions. Even though Soviet Jews were the most assimilated ever, they nonetheless, were oppressed especially from the 1940s to the end of the 1980s. Even if a Jew changed his identity, KGB knew who you were and your Jewish roots would be a problem for your advancement at work.

In Soviet Union, the state supported anti-Semitism was unique in terms of its reason and results. It existed during all Soviet leaders from Joseph Stalin to Mikhail Gorbachev. From the moment the Bolsheviks came to power in 1917, they suppressed any existing religion. Judaism was one of those.

Three generations of Jews brought up in a forceful atheistic environment and most of them distanced from the Jewish culture and Judaism. The YIVO Encyclopedia of Jews in Eastern Europe, in the article *Soviet Yiddish Language Schools* states that by 1951, the last Yiddish schools in the Soviet Union – in Birobidzhan – closed. The exceptions were a few passionate Jews who secretly learned Hebrew, attended private seminars on Jewish culture, and practiced traditions. Nearly all of them repatriated to Israel at the end of 1960s and during the 1970s. Anti-Semitism widely expanded in the Soviet Union, especially after the end of Second World War from 1945 later transforming from the repressive to latent form in the 1960s–1980s. Officials had promoted anti-Jewish sentiments among common people. Satirical stories (*felietons*) published in central and local newspapers accused people with Jewish names of economic crimes or blaming them for Zionism or "rootless cosmopolitanism".

In the beginning, Soviet anti-Semitism overlapped with Germany's invasion to Russia in 1941. My father told me that in 1942 at the front, he saw Nazi airplanes scattering fliers with picture shown an ugly Jew and the following text: "Beat a *Jew–Politruk*, his snoot asks a brick". Still fighting Nazis on the front, he felt anti-Jewish sentiments among some of the Red Army officers and commanders. One of them, a real anti-Semite, crossed his name out seven times from the listings of soldiers suggested for the military orders.

Later, in 1945 my father was coming back from war. He made a stop in Moscow where he learned from a newspaper job advertisement that Ministry of Foreign Affairs was looking for an English–Russian interpreter (he was a teacher of English before the war). He called up and asked if they needed someone who spoke English and got the answer "Yes". When they heard his Jewish last name, a short silence ensued and then they said the advertisement was obsolete and they already hired someone. That was just the beginning.

By 1948, Stalin openly started anti-Jewish campaign. It had to do with the excitement a few Soviet Jewish art activists exposed due to the formation of the State of Israel in 1948. I am talking about the Jewish Anti-Fascistic Committee – organization of prominent Soviet writers, actors, journalists who did so much fundraising abroad (in the US specifically) to help the Red (Soviet) Army buy arms during the war.

At first, the USSR supported formation of Israel, hoping it would be the Soviet political puppet. About six months after the new state formed, it became clear that Israel would not be a Soviet ally but rather would attach itself to the West. Stalin got mad at this news. He could not directly punish Israel and his anger pointed against the prominent Soviet Jews.

Stalin's anti-Semitism reached its real cannibalistic form with his order to murder the Jewish Anti-Fascistic Committee members. It's chief, the great Jewish actor Solomon Mikhoels was strangled and then dropped under truck in 1948. That was officially announced as an automobile accident. Thereafter, the open persecution of Jews restarted along with a wide anti-Semitic and anti-Zionist campaign. Its repressive phase lasted until Stalin's death in 1953. Many Jews were fired from their jobs, sent to Gulag, or assassinated by Stalin's brutal machine. To avoid blaming them of anti-Semitism, persecutors used the term *rootless cosmopolitans* instead of Jews. Aggrieved were Jewish professionals: doctors, scientists, engineers, and teachers.

The culmination of the state anti-Semitism was marked by the so-called *Doctors Plot*. About a dozen of well-known doctors of mostly Jewish names who worked in the Kremlin hospital and cured the Soviet highest-ups were accused in the attempt to murder Stalin and other Soviet leaders by giving them the wrong cures. The groundless accusations were too obvious. Lavrenti Beria, the notorious KGB's butcher ordered to release and justify all these doctors immediately after Stalin's death in March 1953.

Accusations like these are not new in Jewish history. Prager and Telushkin cite multiple occasions of medieval baseless accusations of Jews in Europe of poisoning Christians: in Bohemia (1161), in Switzerland (1348), in Vienna (1610), etc. No evidences, other than those gotten under torture ever existed. Certainly, the accused were tortured and murdered.

There was a discussion among Russian historians whether Stalin was going to deport Soviet Jews to Siberia after the planned execution of Jewish doctors within the *Doctors Plot*. Some authors reject the opinion that Stalin's plan was real. They state that no written documents of the topic were found in KGB archives; other scholars are certain that the preparation was in progress at the beginning of 1953. I believe the latter because it was in Stalin's manner to solve ethnical problems the way he did– by the verbal order. Even if documents existed, they may have been destroyed later by the order of those who did not want disclosure of them. In 1944, Stalin ordered deportation of Chechens, Ingushs, Crimean Tatars, and other peoples, altogether fourteen ethnicities to Kazakhstan and Siberia (J. Brent and V. Naumov. *Stalin's Last Crime. The Plot Against Jewish Doctors, 1948–1953,* Perennial – an Imprint of Harper Collins Publishers, 2003).

This is how historian Yakov Etinger (2001), son of one of the Kremlin's doctors accused within the Doctors Plot, describes his meeting with Bulganin in 1970 (was the Soviet Prime Minister in 1953):

"Bulganin confirmed the longtime rumors about the scheduled massive deportation of Jews to Siberia and the Far East. In the middle of February 1953, Stalin called him and ordered sending several hundred military freight trains to Moscow for deportation. At that, there was planning to organize train crushes with Jews on their way to Siberia, as well as the "voluntary" attacks on Jews to finish with part of them yet on their way… I asked Bulganin a question: were there any written directions from Stalin regarding the Jewish deportation? He smiled and said, Stalin was not a fool to leave written orders on these issues. Stalin often gave verbal orders especially while communicated with members of Politburo…

N.S. Khrushchev deposited after his removal from his General Secretary position about his conversation with Stalin on the plan for the "people's actions" against Jews: the plan contemplated that bands of criminals organized by KGB had to break into trains to kill Jews on their way to deportation. Per Khrushchev, based on Stalin's instructions, only half of all deporting Jews was supposed to get to the place.

There is evidence from Nikolai Nikolaevich Polyakov, a former member of Communist Party's apparat and former KGB officer… Stalin's decision of full deportation of Jews was in principal made at the end of 1940s – beginning of 1950s. N.N. Polyakov was a participant in actions of preparation for the eviction of Jewish population. To organize the action, a special commission was formed, which reported directly to Stalin. The Secretary of the Communist Party M.A. Suslov was appointed as the chairman and N.N. Polyakov as the secretary of that commission. To accommodate the deported people, a concentrate camp-type barracks were being built in the far regions of the country, and the territories were separated within the secret zones. At the same time, special listing of the Jewish population formed by the places of residence. Two lists existed: for the full-blooded and the half-blooded Jews. The eviction was supposed to be done in two phases: the full-blooded in the first phase and the half-blooded in the second phase. All these was very much alike the Hitlerian practice of Jewish "final solution".

A.N. Yakovlev, the architect of Gorbachov's Perestroika, wrote in his memoires:

"It (planning for deportation of Jews) was represented in Stalin Jesuit's manner as if a group of Jews prepared the letter addressed to the Soviet Government asking to perform mass deportation of Jews to save them of a justified anger of Soviet people".

A.N. Yakovlev wrote that General Director of TASS Y. Havinson and the Academician M. Mitin (both are Jewish) were the organizers of the letter. Y. Etinger published draft of that letter, which was brought by the daughter of a secretary of one of the central newspapers editorial office where it was preparing to publish. This is the text of the draft-letter:

"To all Jews of the Soviet Union

Dear brothers and sisters, Jews! We, the scientists and engineers, actors, doers of science and arts – Jews by the nationality – at this sore period of our life apply to you. You all well know that the state security service recently exposed group of the doctors-exasperators, spies and traitors served the American and British intelligence, international Zionism in the face of the disruptive organization Joint. They killed the prominent doers of the Party and State – A.A. Zhdanov and A.S. Shcherbakov, cut the lives of many other responsible doers of our country including military commanders. The sinister shadow of murderers in white suits covered all Jewish population of the USSR. Every Soviet human must feel anger and outrage. These monstrous atrocities of the doctors-murderers understandably caused hostility among the substantial part of the Soviet population. Shame fell on the Jewish population of Soviet Union. Actions of the band of killers triggered special anger among the great Russian people. Exactly Russian people had saved Jews from full extermination by German-fascist invaders in the years of the Great Patriotic War. In these circumstances, only a selfless work wherever we would be directed by the Party and Government, great leader of the Soviet people comrade J.V. Stalin may erase this shameful stain on the Jewish population of the USSR. This is why we fully accept justified measures of the Party and Government for the developing of the areas of the Eastern Siberia, the Far East and the Far North. The Jews may only prove their devotion to Motherland, the great and beloved comrade Stalin and to restore their good name in the eyes of the Soviet people just by their honest and selfless work." (Y.Y. Etinger. *This Cannot Be Forgotten (Eto Nevozmozhno Zabyt* – in Russian) Memoires, Moscow, Ves Mir, 2001, p.272).

Stalin's death in March 1953 saved Jews from the deportation. The government also stopped the so-called Doctors Plot. While being a child, I remember a few Russian friends of my father praising him with the rehabilitating of Jewish doctors.

During the post-Stalin era, the Soviets did not implement the open barbaric actions against the Jews, but until the collapse of the Soviet Union, the Jews were exposed to state-promoted unspoken anti-Semitism. Soviet officials never admitted it, stating there was no Jewish problem in the country. From the openly repressive (end of 1940s to 1950s) it transformed to the latent in 1960s-1980s. The authorities encouraged ant-Semitic fel'etons (satiric stories) published in central and local newspapers making fun of the people with Jewish names based on absurd "economical" accusations or claimed them members of Zionist plot or as "rootless cosmopolitans". The officials had never said anything about the grassroot anti-Jewish sentiments. "The Jewish question does not exist in our country" (N. Khrushchev). "This is one more attempt of the psychological attack on the Soviet Union", M. Gorbachev said answering the question somewhere between 1985 and 1987 of why the Jews are not allowed to emigrate.

The bloody time of *rootless cosmopolitans* and *Doctors' Plot* passed away, but the state's anti-Semitism heated up by Khrushchev's personal anti-Semitism remained. In the beginning of 1960s some Jews were prosecuted for the "economic crimes". A new draconian law was issued for reprisal over the group of Jews already sentenced and served their terms. They were sued again and sentenced for capital punishment:

> "...In 1961 a new campaign against theft of socialistic properties started. The campaign was openly anti-Semitic. To make sentences crueler for the defendants, the authorities violated the laws. It became obvious in the first in a row trial in Summer of 1961 in the case of Rokotov. A few people of Jewish names: Y. Rokotov, Faibishenko, N. Edlis and others were convicted in violation of the currency operations. By the time they were arrested the maximum punishment for this type of crime was three years in prison. On June 15, 1961 they all were sentenced for 15 years in prison based on the Executive Order of the Presidium of the Supreme Council of May 5, 1961, although they allegedly committed the crimes before issuance of the Order. So, the Order was applied retroactively. Furthermore, on July 6, 1961 another Executive Order was issued provided the "use of capital punishment for profiteering of currency and bonds". In accordance with protestation of the USSR Attorney General, the court applied the new Order to sentence Y. Rokotov and V. Faibishenko to death. In

the cases of the economic crimes in 1961-1964 the suspects were sentenced based on the laws introduced after the crimes were committed. Most of the convicted were Jews... In 1961-1964 for economic crimes there were executed 39 Jews in Russia, 79 in Ukraine, 8 in Kirgyzia, 6 in Belorussia, 6 in Moldavia, 2 in Kazakhstan, 6 in Uzbekistan, 2 in Latvia, 2 in Estonia, 2 in Azerbaijan, 2 in Georgia. (*Jews in in Soviet Union in 1953-1967*. Electronic Jewish Library).

Of four hundred court trials on so called economic crimes the main accused were Jews. From 1961 to 1967, 1676 Jews were convicted and 163 of them (almost every tenth) sentenced to death penalty (*History of Israeli Jews. Anti-Semitism in Soviet Union in post-Stalin period.* www.istoki.ru).

Zionism and Judaism underwent the most vicious attacks, being blamed in aiding to American imperialism. The propagandist books like *Reactionary Gist of Judaism, or Judaism Unvarnished, or Be Careful, it is Zionism* published in hundreds of thousand copies. State supported anti-Semitism continued in the post-Stalin epoch, it just transformed to another form: from the flesh-eater of the Doctors Plot's time it evolved to latent persecution of Jews and to fight with inexistent enemy – Zionism. Hatred towards Jews encouraged by the government and KGB stood behind the Soviet anti-Semitism.

In the early 1970s, I met a professor of mechanical engineering department at the Maritime School (the one I graduated from). He told me that there was an opportunity in one of the laboratories and he thought of me to occupy the position. The head of the laboratory also wanted me to fill this opening – he knew me from the time I prepared my final pre-graduation project in this laboratory. After my conversation with the head of laboratory, I inspired and waited for the offer. No offer followed. In couple of weeks, I stopped by the Human Resources to inquire and got the answer that the opening does not exist anymore. Then I called head of the laboratory asking if that was true. He told me they were still looking for a person to fill the position.

In 1972, I applied for an extension of the exit visa for sailing on ships. I waited for several months, and then after many requests, a man from the Communist Party Committee (affiliated with local KGB) said that no visa would be given to me.

"I used to have exit visa before, what is the reason for the refusal this time around," I asked him. He did not respond. Every time I was bounced, I asked myself, *why does my country do this to me? What did I do wrong? Is this really my country?*

Soviet Jews were attached to Russian culture, tied in to Russian life, spoke Russian native language, and had Russian friends. Nonetheless, they were identified as something adverse and treated discriminantly. Jews were not admitted to prestigious universities. There was a tiny quote for them allowed to enter educational institutes. By the order of higher authorities, firms or scientific institutes did not promote them in their professional career, nor did they hire Jews after their graduation. The discriminatory acts were conducted covertly, without any comments, words, or explanations. The bitter truth is that Soviet officials and public opinion got Jews used to anti-Semitism. Jews perceived it as evil necessity. Many of them felt like the second-rate quality people because of restrictions in professional activities.

The government's harsh policy towards the Jews had always been absorbed by the common people.

THE GRASSROOTS' ANTI-SEMITISM

The grassroots' anti-Semitism flourished. People with the pronounced Jewish last names especially suffered. Everyone knows that kids at school do not watch their language when they communicate with their peers. Having a last name sounded too Jewish like Rosenwasser or Shmulenson was a misfortune. Peers not only teased them but sometimes teachers distorted their names intentionally so that they sounded bizarre for Slavic ear to sound even weirder. I say nothing about the first names: many parents did not give their child a Jewish name not wishing them to be an object for harassment.

In every grade from elementary to high school, a class journal held all pupils' data, grades, and other information. On the last page of class journal, there were records of nationality (ethnicity) of every student. Any student occasionally or intentionally could get access to that page and learn who was who in the class. This was a source of harassment of Jewish kids by other kids. My older son Igor studied in the Soviet school, and he once confessed me that during his school years, his biggest fear was that somebody opened the last page of the journal and learnt what his nationality was. That was torture for the young teen.

The first time I realized that my identity could be different from most of other people was in kindergarten when I was five years old. A boy from my group (I still remember his name: Kostya Danilov) said to me that I am a Jew. "Why?" I asked him not even knowing what it means. "Because you have a black hair," he answered. He said this as if it was something shameful. The boy's judgment reflected what he listened at home and the way boy's parents treated Jews. Coming home, I asked my father what a Jew is. He explained it to me as much as the boy of five was able to comprehend it. I then had thousands of questions and I suspect my father had a hard time answering them. Such was my first introduction to ethnical identity.

Soviet realities influenced and caused the identity confusion among Jews in Russia. Still being a boy, I felt I had a *wrong nationality* but had no idea what was wrong with it. The wrongness was in the atmosphere of children's street games in school, when some pupils found a record of the Jewish nationality of someone in the class register book and started making fun of him. The explanations of my parents that it was not fair to suppress Jews did not satisfy me.

A Soviet teenager of the 1960s, I always asked myself: *do I want to be a Jew*. On one side, I was a son of decent parents-teachers and I always saw respect, care, and prudence at home. On the other side, I heard and felt negativism if not hatred aimed at my nationality from some people and officials. My mother always told me that to have an equal opportunity with the Russian guys, I had to be above them in my studies. I did not want to be above all, I just wanted to be the same as anyone. Why did people make up different nations, I thought, could we live, study, work, and behave as one ethnos? These questions came to my mind until I understood by the end of my teen age years, that different nations were formed under historical and natural circumstances. It is normal that ethnicities are different, in the same way as any family may look and behave differently within the nation. I do not have to be shy of being Jewish even in the Soviet Union, where many Jews obscured their Jewish identity. This was my breakthrough in self-identification and my role confusion crisis.

I have already mentioned the uniqueness of the Soviet anti-Semitism. It was not connected to Jewish religion or traditions – these almost did not exist in the Soviet times, nor was it because of the specific Jewish occupations or line of work – Jews did the same jobs as others. In my mind, I asked Soviet anti-Semites: suppose you hate specifically Jewish attributes but if our clothes and appearance were like yours, if we spoke neither Hebrew, nor Yiddish, if we were not the money lenders, and not religious, then why in the world would you still hate us?

There are three possible answers to this observable fact. The *first reason* is the Jewish tendency to play an active role in politics, industry, science, and the arts. That made anti-Semites mad. By the 1970s, Soviet policy toward Jews had shaped to "three not": not to hire (for the middle and senior level positions in institutions, industries, science, and education), not to promote, and not to fire (to demonstrate that Jews have not been discriminated). Research institutes, design bureaus, and other organizations that employed intellectual workers had special directives not to employ Jewish professionals. Anti-Semite hates Jewish tendency to be too active. This is exactly what he is afraid of – compete and lose.

The *second possible reason* is a historically biased treatment of Jews as dishonest individuals who always cheat on other people to take commercial advantage of them. I do not say it has no basis at all: some Jews involved in the trade and commerce indeed made money in the crony business. I must admit it was a bitter truth for some Jewish merchants.

Not going too far back, in just a few months of my coming to New York, I met my former coworker by the Institute in Leningrad. He came to the US a few months earlier than I did and tried to establish his own small construction business. Since he just started, he had no credit history yet and received cash for his work. He completed a few projects renovating apartments and got some money to hire workers for a bigger project. His last client was a religious Jew from Brooklyn's Borough Park. After completion of all work, the client refused to pay and brassily claimed that he did not owe anything, using little defects as an excuse. Unfortunately, no contract agreement had been made and as a result, my friend lost all the money he had saved for business development. His business has ruined. I was upset when I heard this story and especially with the fact that a Jew had committed this dirty trick. The truth is whereas any ethnos has dishonest people, the Jews are the only ones charged with this low trait because of their ethnicity. In other words, only Jews have been blamed. Other honest, helpful, and hardworking Jews innocently suffer from this bias opinion.

In a wasteful society like the Soviet Union, there was always a need to blame for anything that went wrong, and Jews were easy target. In the permanent economic and social failure like lack of harvest, poor quality of any domestic products, it was important to distract people's attention from the real economic and social problems. Raising the Jewish issue was a perfect cure. It was easy to condemn Jews because too many people thought badly of them from an academician, writer, or party apparatchik to a laborer or a merchandiser. For anti-Semite, Jews are cunning but not clever; full of intrigue but not energetic and active; a huckster but not economical.

In the early 1970s, a *third reason* added to the first two: retaliation for emigration from the Soviet Union to Israel, US, Canada, and Australia. They all became potential traitors! Protecting state secrets was used as an excuse for providing a "three not" policy, as well as refusing some of the Jews an exit visa. It was like the mix of envy and hatred. The envy was because only Jews had been given the opportunity to leave the country that was repulsive to many of their citizens, including Jews haters.

Up to today's day, there are different forms of anti-Semitism depending on what aspect of Jewish being is most hateful by obscurantists: religious, grassroots', and racial. Whereas religious anti-Semitism formed still in ancient times and grassroots' in early medieval time, the racial anti-Semitism is a product of pseudo-scientific fantasies created in the nineteen century and developed in the twentieth. Here is what Russian philosopher N. Berdyaev wrote about this racial component:

> "The real ideology of anti-Semitism is the racial one, which is the most widely spread form of hostility towards the Jews. Germany is a classic country of such ideology. Great Germans like Luther, Fichte, Wagner were apologists of this ideology. Jews are claimed the inferior, miserable race hostile to the rest of humanity. However, it turns out that this low race is the strongest and winning other races in free competition." (N.A. Berdyaev. *Christianity and Anti-Semitism. The Religious Fate of Jewry*).

Let us be honest and acknowledge the fact that the number of gifted people among Ashkenazi-Jews higher than average. Truly, there is no statistics on how many fools among the Jews. I take the liberty to assume that many. Chosen people must be chosen in any aspect!

The worst anti-Jewish sentiments are observed in the least tolerant societies with deep traditions of envy. Regrettably, the last decades show this trend in the civilized countries with high tolerance to other races and nationals the anti-Semitism can also flourish. Some European countries surpassed a few Arabic states with traditional anti-Jewish inclination. Whatever the reason for anti-Semitism, the words Mr. Churchill said that we are not so stupid to be anti-Semitic accurately caught the issue.

It is distressing to recognize that several classical Russian writers made their input to specifically Russian anti-Semitism in the nineteenth century. They consistently described Jews in their novels and stories as greedy, dishonest, and cunning dealers. I have no intention to make any objections about F. M. Dostoyevsky's talent as a great writer as his psychological portraits are incredibly impressive, but unfortunately, his essay *The Jewish Question* is as hateful toward the Jews as anti-Semitism itself.

The book of Alexander Solzhenitsyn, *Two Hundred Years Together* (published in Russian) depicts coexistence between the Russian and Jewish peoples on Russian territory. It covers the time from the end of the eighteenth century, when hundreds of thousands of Jews from Poland and other parts of Central Europe found themselves in areas of Russia and Ukraine, until the end of the twentieth century, the second massive Jewish migration from Russia. It also discusses the Jewish role in the newest Russian history. However, if someone asks me whether this book is anti-Semitic, I would say literary no… but spiritually it is. I nonetheless, must underline that to me, Solzhenitsyn is a Great Russian thinker, historian, and writer who portrayed Stalin's inhuman repressive system. So, I try to be unbiased. I did not count how many times he tells bad and good stories about the Jewish activity in Russia; obviously bad stories are recounted overwhelmingly more times than the good ones. All his bad stories on the Jewish role are backed up by the references. Trying to be objective, he took nearly all his anti-Jewish references from the Jewish authors as if saying: look, they wrote this about themselves, it is real! Communist party newspaper *Pravda* ("Truth") used to exploit the similar ploy: blame the West, referring to free Western mass media. Same false line of attack: if they said it about themselves, they are bad!

This longtime negative attitude toward Soviet Jews was a reason for some to self-dissociate from the Jewry. They hide their Jewish ancestry or changed their last name to sound more Slavic. This action, however, did not improve their fate: the *fifth record* in passport was still the same.

The mixed (half-Jewish) individuals with one non-Jewish parent had specific status. Almost all of them picked a non-Jewish nationality for the record – so damage for life and future career was to list officially as a Jew. The situation also depended on who was a non-Jewish parent – mother or father. If a father was Jewish and a mother was Russian then a child kept father's Jewish last name and even if they recorded Russian in his/her *fifth record* in passport, he/she still suffered anti-Semitism. Sometimes the child when they reached sixteen years of age (the time of receiving passport) chose the mother's last name and became Russian by the name and passport. Do not think this child had no more problems. It depended on his appearance: if he looked like his father, there may be further problems but if he had a Slavic appearance, he did not have any problems.

When a child had a non-Jewish father and a Jewish mother, the result was different: this child carried a Russian (Ukrainian, Tatar, etc.) last name and the "right" record in his passport even though he might account as a Jew by the Halakha. The Soviet cosmonaut (astronaut) of the 1970s, Boris Volynov had Russian father but a Jewish mother, the "right" record in his passport, and a Slavic appearance. He obviously had no problem with the KGB as he was admitted to the squadron of Soviet cosmonauts. At the same time, he was formally eligible to get Israeli citizenship by the Halakha (Jewish religious law) if applied.

The more Jewish qualities someone held, the less chances for any promotion he or she had. Those like me who had Jewish name, both Jewish parents, Jewish appearance, was recorded as a Jew, was not a member of Communist Party, had zero chances in that fun-house realm.

Something really changed in the Soviet Jewish self-consciousness after the 1967 six-day Arab-Israeli War, when a tiny Jewish State conducted an instant victorious military action against three much bigger Arab armies just within few days. The Soviet mass media presented this military action as less serious as was possible and at the same time, compared Israelis to Nazis. Nonetheless, all in the Soviet Union were shocked. This victory ruined all conceivable anti-Semitic representations about the Jews as poor soldiers and people who avoid fighting trying to save themselves.

My distant relative Boris had just retired from the Soviet Army as a lieutenant colonel in 1967. When we discussed the Israeli victory, he told me that he did not care who was right and wrong politically in that war but that he was happy the Jews finally proved their great military skills, bravery, and boldness. Of course, what happened in the Middle East in 1967 did not make Soviet anti-Semites change their mindset but we felt much better knowing the Jewish state and nation was capable of kicking back strongly.

Anecdotes on the Jewish topics were popular. With that, the anecdotes of the 1950s–1960s differed much from those of the 1970s–1980s. The first described Jews as cunning and sneaky, whereas the latter (after the Arab-Israeli Six-Day War of 1967) showed them rather sharp and clever, with a covert jealousy toward Jews about an opportunity to emigrate that Russians did not have.

The favorite theme for the Jew-haters was the large, disproportional Jewish participation in the socialist revolution and repressions. Yes, Jews played a substantial role in the Bolshevik Revolution and in establishing the repressive state. Anti-Semites blamed Jews for the Russian Revolution in 1917 and further, making up what evil Jews did to the

Russian people. Jewish writers also discuss this painful topic, and some even call Jews to ask for forgiveness. As Jewish participation in Russian revolution is widely known, so little is known on their role in creation of Soviet military superpower. I will not spell out the names of chief engineers designed aircrafts, helicopters, atomic submarines, tanks, and anti-missile systems – the number of Jewish names is overwhelming. Why is it still almost unknown in Russia?

I must admit the truth that too many Jewish revolutionary fighters performed their misdeeds in 1920s–1930s in Russia in the name of communism.

A few considerations on this painful issue.

First, not only the Jews performed the revolution and participated in the carnage and the repressions. A great disproportional number of Latvians and Poles also took part. Do not forget that it was Russian revolution: if it was not supported by most of the Russian grassroots, it had not taken place at all.

Second, Jews suffered cruel pogroms and humiliation for decades. They wished to get rid of the authoritarian brutal and anti-Semitic czarist regime and gain equality with other peoples of the Russian Empire. For over a century, they lived in the restricted areas of Pale of Settlement. They hoped the social revolution would release them and help gain them the freedom to live anywhere and do everything permitted to others but not to them. What would someone expect from the people locked-in the Pale for over a century, suffering cruel pogroms, doomed to degrade with no development, no access to higher education and freedom to move? Downtrodden people, fed up of harassment from the tsarist regime, believed that the new communist rule would set the community and the nation free. Jews naturally fought for their social rights, and at that point, there were no opportunities to succeed other than through proving and reinforcing the new Soviet regime, which at first was thought not to be as terrible as it turned out.

Besides, during the first years of the Soviet regime, Bolsheviks declared equal rights to all ethnicities. Jews finally saw the light of hope in the new political order. Many of them wanted to give up their culture and tradition, break up with the ethnical identities in favor of the new international community. This reason brought many active Jews to participation in Bolshevik activities. They served this revolution devotedly. Yes, there were passionate Jews-revolutionists who made the revolution as bloody as it was: Trotsky, Uritsky, a variety of "Shvonders" transformed to CheKists and those who later replaced them: Yagoda, Frinovsky, other NKVD butchers. But there also were Polishes: Dzerzhinski, Menzhinski, Latvians: Peters, Unshliht, Aiduks, Georgians: Beria, Goglidze… Any nation, including the Jewish descendants, has their evildoers who took part in repressions. Nonetheless, haters do not call those crimes Russian or Latvian or Polish; they call them Jewish.

Third, there were two enormous misdeeds performed in the twentieth century: communism and fascism genocides. The carriers of the fascist ideology organized genocide because such was their philosophy to kill Jews and those who resisted. Similarly, the Stalinist regime exterminated those disagreed because assassinations were naturally inherent to the communist creed. Participation of Jews in the communist repressions was because Jews had their butchers as any other nation. However, they did it not because of the Jewish ideology. I even do not rule out that these butchers started as genuine freedom fighters.

By the end of the 1930s, Jewish optimism toward the Soviet rule was replaced with glumness and fear for the children. I will again cite Nikolai Berdyaev, the outstanding Russian philosopher:

"It is wrong that Jews govern Russia. Main governors are not the Jews, prominent part of them executed or jailed. Trotsky is a main subject of hate. Jews played a big role in revolution as a significant part of Russian intelligentsia, which is absolutely natural, and the oppressed status pushed them to do so. I consider a merit that Jews fought for freedom. The fact that Jews used terror and prosecutions is not a specific feature of Jews but a specific and bad feature of revolution at its certain stage" (N.A. Berdyaev. *Christianity and Anti-Semitism. Religious Fate of Jewishness*).

However, Jewish excessive role in the communist revolution turned out to be a painful page in the history of Russian Jewry. After Stalin's death in 1953 up to Gorbachev's Perestroika – the time when my generation was growing up – Jews as if did not exist as a people in the Soviet Union: neither culture, nor education, nor mentions, references, discussions, remarks…. Understandably, many Jewish parents did not bring up their kids with Jewish self-consciousness. As a result, the majority of Russian Jews are ignorant of the Jewish history and Judaism but have much more knowledge on Russian history as a basis nation.

How good (or badly) Jews were treated, I would divide the people of the "host" nation into the following groups:

- ✓ Those who love Jews (I call them *adorers*); for example, I know women who prefer marry Jewish men, respecting them as good family persons, I even know Russian woman who did it a few times: even after divorcing from a Jew, she nonetheless married a Jew again.

- ✓ Those who are neutral to Jews and consider them same way as any other people (*neutrals*). Several times I dated Russian girls at my twenties and on my question, what do you know about Jews and anti-Semitism, they answered, 'nothing'. Their treatment of all Jews had no difference from the Russians or other ethnicities.
- ✓ Those who generally dislike the Jews but recognize the good professional expertise of some of them like medical doctors or lawyers and use their services (*pragmatics*).
- ✓ Those who hate the Jews, and in no way use their services (*haters*).

My observations dictate that *pragmatics* and *neutrals* are the most in number and then *haters* and *adorers*, possibly with the prevalence of *haters*. Sometimes the numbers of haters or pragmatics or neutrals change depending on the internal political situation.

With major emigration from the Soviet Union during the 1970s–1990s, the Jewish issue in Russia became less topical and was diluted with other ethnical problems. According to the Jewish Virtual Library, the number of Jews emigrated from Russia within the last wave up to 1997 was almost three million and according to Russian Census of 2002, the remaining number estimated as two hundred and sixty-five thousand. There has never been so few of them during the two hundred years of the Russian–Jewish coexistence.

Worth noting that in the US, developing anti-Semitic sentiments had the opposite direction compared with the Soviet Union. In the USSR before WWII, anti-Semitism was slight, but after the war, it became intolerable. On the contrary, in the US, as few of my acquaintances American Jews eye-witnessed, it was noticeable before the World War

II, especially in the southeast and in small towns in middle America with the least perceptible in New York City. The situation changed dramatically after many Jewish soldiers within the US Army came back home heroes, and the American anti-Semitism reduced considerably. One of the last open anti-Semitic events my American Jewish friend witnessed occurred in a Long Island restaurant in 1946, where he saw the announcement, "Jews are not served".

For about twenty years, Russia lives with dramatically diminished number of Jews. Two hundred thousand in Russia and seventy thousand in Ukraine is little over 5% of what was a hundred years ago. The Holocaust of 1941–1944 and emigration of 1970–2000 reduced their number eighteen times. Seemingly, the dream of the anti-Semites almost came true – Russia without Jews! Have those dreamers become happier or live wealthier? Hostility is an important motivation in their life. Ethnical migrants from the former Soviet southern republics are now the main object of their hatred. I hope these haters do not represent the core of the Russian people.

After two hundred years together, two peoples, big and small, departed as spouses lived through the long but unhappy life. Small people claimed his desire to go and the big people finally stopped keeping them and let go.

I want to conclude this chapter with the poem of Russian poetess Rimma Kozakova on this topic. The country was saying the last farewell to the certain but not ordinary part of its people who helped this country in the peaceful and warfare times and then was prosecuted by the same country (translated from Russian by LP):

Russian Jews abandon their homeland,
Leave the fatherland for good.
Apocalyptic Exodus -

This is their last resort.
Quit from country and departed
From the soil of their love and sweat.
Ripped connections, boxes fastened.
"Can we stop them?"
"Obviously can't".
Pouring rains in Moscow suburbs,
Fostered room and empty rack.
Label *Zhid** is made by someone
On the signpost Grave of *Pasternak*.
[*Zhid* – offensive name of Jews in Russia and Soviet Union]
[*Pasternak* – Russian poet of Jewish descent].

5
Exodus of the 20th Century

With the last Jew, we will lay to rest the last Russian intelligent

Marina Tsvetaeva,
Russian Poetess

Ancient and recent Jewish history is mostly a history of migration and suffering. Thus, Exodus is a fundamental Jewish concept. Being quick off the mark is one of the features of the common national character. Jews have moved countless times during thousands of years of their civilization.

Jewish migrations from Judea started with the Greek invasion (Ptolemy I, 301 B.C.). The longest Jewish migration known as dissipation continued through the first centuries A.D. with the conquest by the Romans and destruction of the Second Temple. Romans conquered Judea (Pompey, 63 B.C.) and later invaded Jerusalem in response to Jewish riot in 67 A.D. known as Judean War, destroyed the Temple. Thousands of distressed Jews continued to migrate up to the fifth century A.D. to the countries around the Mediterranean Sea and part of them moved further to European areas forming Ashkenazi Jewish communities. Many Jews settled in Spain.

In Medieval Europe, there was a chain of expulsion of Jews: from England (Edward I, 1290), France (Philip IV, 1306), Spain (1492), Portugal (1497), Germany (Saxony, 1536), and other European countries. Those Jews exiled from Spain in 1492 and moved to the Middle East and North Africa became later known as Sephardi. With Western European enlightenment of the seventeen - eighteenth centuries, Jews were not exiled but pre-judgements against them and anti-Semitism widely existed.

The tragic fortune of millions of European Jews in the Holocaust of 1930s–1940s initiated another wave of migration. In 1945–1947, dozens of thousands of the Holocaust survivors emigrated from the post-war devastated Europe: eighty-three thousand to Palestine, forty thousand to the US, seven thousand to the Latin America, and thirty-five hundred to Canada. Merely from Poland, about one hundred thousand Jews immigrated to Palestine instantaneously followed by the pogrom of July 1946 in Kielce.

The reasons for Jewish migration at different times were slavery, massacre, persecution, and for some of them, aspiration to return to the promised land of Israel. The subject of Jewish migration is closely welded with the concept of national loyalty. Russian Jews tired of looking disloyal in the eyes of others and in their own eyes. The change to being loyal towards the Russian Federation after collapsing the USSR is hard – too much frustration with previous bitter experience. These are the facts and numbers:

> "Beginning from 1989, Jewish emigration became so massive that for the first time it played a big role in reduction of Jewish population in Russian Federation. In most of the other post-Soviet states, the number of Jews was reducing even at a greater rate. At some point, this rate was even higher that the one observed during earlier massive emigration from Russian Empire at the end of nineteen-beginning of twentieth centuries. Total, for four decades (1970-2009)

more than 1.9 million Jews together with their non-Jewish relatives left the former USSR. The prevailing number of them -1.6 million – emigrated within 1989-2009. This number exceeded the number of migrants of 1970-1988 in 5.6 times. From all emigrants, of 1989-2009 about 998 thousand people (61%) headed to Israel. The number of Jews and family members moved to the US estimated at 326 thousand. The number of those emigrated to Germany is 224 thousand" (Mark Tolts. *Post-Soviet Jewish Diaspora: Newest Estimation.* Demoscop, #497-498, 6-12 February 2012).

The question of *to go or stay* has always been the Jewish issue. It was relevant for ancient Jews during their presence in Egypt three thousand years ago and after destruction of Second Temple by Romans, then in medieval Europe if not expelled forcefully, which happened more often. In twentieth century, for many of them the return to the historical land was the main reason for leaving. Look where vector of their departure directed (except Israel where different motivations worked): United States, Canada, Australia – countries where population has no main ethnos but the immigrants or their descendants where nationalism do not have ethnical basis. The exclusion is Germany, but Germans carry much afterwar penance from 1945, they want the recovery of Jewish population. Another reason for exodus was disappointment of living in a country where Jews were the "wrong" supplement to the "right" system.

In the Soviet Union few generations of Jews made their lives in the "equal sharing of misery" along with all population. After the atrocious period of persecution in the 1930s–1950s, they brought up specific code of living not to merely survive but strive to live decently. They embraced any form of education and getting an intellectual profession – engineer, medical doctor, scientist, etc. but not faith to the political regime. This social stratum became essential part of the Russian intelligentsia.

The problem of Jewish emigration from the Soviet Union had originated long before hundreds of thousands of Jews went to the South and West. Still in the middle of 1950s that was a tiny trickle of a few dozen people whom the Soviets allowed to go to Israel for good. About that time, one of my distant relatives asked Soviet authorities to allow him to visit his brother in Israel. The authorities responded that if he wants to join his brother, he can go but he would never be able to come back. He did not go. Why he was not allowed just to visit? The answer is simple: after his coming back, he would most likely decide to go for good and furthermore, he would have all his relatives to go with him. That was least wanted by the authorities – Soviet people must be monolithic.

With time, more people applied for emigration, however, the quotas to release stayed the same, and the OVIR (department of visas) did not allow too many of them to leave. To force the Soviet government to release all who wanted to, the US Senate voted for the Jackson–Vanik's amendment that forbade selling some goods to Russia until it let Jewish people go. The exclusion was the wheat and several food products. In exchange for letting the Jews go, the US agreed to sell more wheat so desperately needed to feed Soviet population. In this context, Jews helped nourish three hundred million (at that time) Soviet people and thus, were used as a token money in this game. In 1974, Secretary General Brezhnev agreed to increase the quote at President Ford's request. Some more Jews fled the Soviet Union.

From 1971 to 1979 Jewish emigration increased almost 4 times: from 13 to 51 thousand. Agreement between the Soviet Union and the United States of the time was like a barter: you supply wheat to us, we increase quotation for Jews to emigrate. The exit-visa was given at the condition of formal invitation from an Israeli relative. Also, a person was not supposed to have the Soviet security clearance for the last five years, which was often used as an excuse for not giving the visa to those who were punished by the authorities. A few times the emigration quotes were drastically cut. It was claimed that those who wanted to leave have already left. The last time it occurred in 1981. No one could even think that this interruption would be the last one before the forthcoming breakthrough of wide stream of Jewish migrants gush out from the collapsing country.

Entered Ronald Reagan as a new president of the US, more decisive than Jimmy Carter, the stepped down one. His language towards the USSR was straight forward: The Evil Empire and "Communism is another sad, bizarre chapter in human history whose last pages even now are being written," he said. Eventually Reagan's policy towards the Soviet Union played a critical role in collapsing communism. However, at that point, many people were refused for years from the OVIR in response to their applications to leave. Moreover, the wheat supply to the USSR switched from the US to Canada, so the Jews were no longer a token for the food on tables for Soviet people.

During last thirty-five years, roughly about three-quarters of Jews have left the former Soviet Union. What called them to leave? In my vewpoint, one of the main incentives to leave was their tiredness to live with a *host nation*: too much discontent. Look where most of them moved (other than Israel): US, Canada, Australia – countries of immigrants populated with people of different origins with no *host ethnicity*, where nationalism has no real roots. Germany, with about two hundred thousand Russian Jews, is an exception. Even with a great complex of fault that Germany admits for what it did to Jews and the intention to restore the German Jewish community, it is still hard for many Jews imagine themselves living there. It is a very personal choice. Why so many Jewish migrants from Russia have not repatriated to Israel is a different story. The reason has to do with the question of how much a person feels a Zionist. However, would it be good for Israel if all Jews from all countries moved there? I do not think so: Israel needs support from the outside. We have been providing it.

We now return to the atmosphere that preceded the massive Jewish departure from the USSR. The decision most Russian Jews had to make was the most critical in their lives. Two opposing voices fought in nearly every Jewish soul. The first one persuaded him or her that it is inappropriate even to think about leaving your motherland where you were born. It is the country your fathers spilled their blood fighting Nazis; your grandparents were liberated from the obligatory and humiliating living in the Pale of Settlement; where you had your nice childhood, long-time friends and coworkers; and everything is so familiar and predictable. The competing voice challenged you to think about how you could continue living in a country with nationwide anti-Semitic sentiments; where the government issued secret executive orders for not allowing any promotions for Jews. The country that had a shameful history of anti-Jewish pogroms and campaigns, and grass-root anti-Semitism was traditional and the nastiest; the country that was about to send Jews to Siberia; the country where even a true Jewish appearance or name looked or sounded embarrassing. This dilemma sometimes felt unbearable to live with.

Virtually every one of us had to choose between "to go or not to go" as it has been many times during the last two thousand years of Jewish history. This Hamlet-like question separated people and often ruined families. If parents were divorced and the ex-wife was going to emigrate with a child, she had to get permission from the child's father, her ex-husband. Some husbands used this to extract money from their former wives. On the opposite, some people contracted fake marriages just to get out of the country; other unfortunate spouses agreed not to divorce until they were in the new country, just to make it happen. Since there were many mixed marriages, the famous saying referred to that time was – Jewish spouse is not only a careful partner but also a means of transport (to a well doing country).

The process of making this determination took a long time in every Jewish mind. In the beginning of the 1970s, the number of families who made it was not too big. Yet, the Soviet authorities did not allow many of them to emigrate and therefore, the number of people having the status of traitor increased. Just imagine – you live in a country where all (or almost all) of the residents think of you as a traitor, and it lasts for years. Friends respect you for your courage; others hate you more for the treason.

With very few yet cases of emigration known by the 1970s, for many Russian Jews, the time had come to reassess whether they continued to live in their home country or leave it for a vague but seemingly a better future. The consecrated question was the subject of discussions in any party when two or more Jewish friends got together. There was a well-known saying among the Jews: two people are discussing something and the third one is coming up to them with the words: I do not know what you are talking about, but *we must go*. No one even needed to ask where to go to. It was clear that he meant moving to Israel or America.

Since the whole process took long time, the condition of *going to* America or Israel was like a permanent status, and all surrounding friends and acquaintances were amazed and wondered at the bravery of those who *were going to go*. It was especially notable at the time when the first Jews started to leave, and every case was like an explosion – unexpected, loud, and choking. The emigrants of the 1970s were decisive people, mentally adjusted to big life changes, fed up with the system built up on big and small lies. Those who headed to Israel were courageous and venturous or deeply attached to Zionist ideas.

Most of the Russian Jews had nothing to lose – after Stalin's death the state did not take their lives and freedom unless they actively fought the regime as dissidents. Most of them but not all. Otherwise, how do you explain the fact that some very prominent and famous Jewish actors, writers, military commanders, and culture activists appeared on television at a press conference and blamed those who had emigrated or were willing to do so, and condemned Israel? The answer was the fear as well as the habitude of joining the official doctrine so as not to be oppressed. I do not blame them – they had a lot to lose and obeyed under this threat.

No doubt, the decision to move in the 1970s–1980s was tough when you have a habitual life style, your job, people you work with, your apartment, and especially when you are over forty with little or no knowledge of new language. In the early 1970s, only the most fearless and challenging Jews decided to move; the other (more numerous) part just discussed it. Some people did not get exit visa from the OVIR. Many Jewish seniors, especially those who had gone through WWII criticized the movers. In short, there was a great mess and confusion among many Jews about the opportunity to emigrate. I know some ethnic Russians who made it even harder, saying to their Jewish friends, if you get such a unique opportunity to leave and enter a more civilized society, why not use it?

When people decided to move, their next expected step was solving the job problem. Right before applying to OVIR with the request for the exit visa, the leaving person should have quit their job, because the next day, this information is at human resources. If the person does not quit, he undergoes ostracism and condemnation. Getting the exit visa could take months if not years, so the question of how to live without a job becomes a real issue. If a person is lucky enough, he/she would find a job as a security guard or boiler firefighter where nobody cares who you are and where you are going to go.

This story was typical for people leaving the Soviet Union in the 1970s–1980s. I have two good friends, Gregory and Valentina, a couple. They were my coworkers in Russia and earlier comers to America. They now live half an hour drive from me and when we meet, we often recall the 1981, the time when they were exposed to ostracism because of their intent to leave Russia.

Once Gregory had contacted the OVIR his and Valentina's persecution started: the OVIR informed KGB, which in turn sent notice to the Institute about their "political unreliability" and intention to emigrate. The moment the Institute's First Department (subsidiary of KGB) received the notice, the staff in all departments knew about it. Immediately, as if a transparent wall raised between this couple and others – the wall of fear, indignation, and a secret jealousy. Few people had compassion towards Gregory and Valentina understanding what they were going through. They expressed their feelings to them, secretly fearing that somebody else may report it, and that would be a trouble. Others did not hide their hostility, considering them as traitors. As a punitive action, they were transferred to another department where I worked. It was clear that this could not last long, and that Gregory and Valentina would eventually have to quit.

The resulting point of their history was a common town hall of all employees with the agenda to read them out of… the "best workers" (in former USSR, there was a title "*Udarnik*" – shock worker of communist labor). The head of the department made the first speech. He stigmatized both, saying that being traitors of the Soviet homeland, they do not deserve to be "*Udarnik*". Party and Union bosses gave similar condemning speeches. Then all employees had to vote. Nobody needed troubles for the "improper" vote, and so all employees voted for their exclusion. I can only imagine what this couple felt: coworkers who had befriended with them for so many years, now must condemn them – sincerely or not – but publicly. That looked like an execution.

Ironically, fifteen years later, when I was preparing to make the same move to the US, my coworkers, the same who blamed Gregory and Valentina earlier, organized a party for my departure. Only the downfall of communism could change people's mind so drastically within so short period of time!

The town hall was held in the morning. On the same day at lunchtime, one of our employees brought a birthday cake to the office. She invited everyone but my couple. I asked her not to make their hard life even harsher by not inviting them to share a birthday cake. She said that she was not obligated to invite such bad people. She probably then reported my request to the chief of department. One hour later, the chief called me to his office and warned me for what he called not following the proper attitude towards the people betraying our country. In response, I said, "You know, I divide people for good and bad ones. These people did nothing bad to anyone; they are going to do what they want to do. Why should I hate them?" He looked at me, kept silence for a moment, and told me I could go. I exited his room and thought about what he could do against me. I was a junior staffer, he cannot lower my title because it is the lowest; he cannot fire me for no reason; he cannot prevent my promotion because nobody was going to promote me anyway. I said to myself that there was nothing to worry about and went back to my desk not being upset. It is sometimes good when you have nothing to lose.

For Jewish Communist Party members, there was one additional problem – exiting the party. It was not easy: often, a big meeting of the Party committee was arranged just for one issue to expel a Jew-communist from the party. After multiple convictions and condemnations as a traitor, he/she was out of the Party. Often, all these convictions directed to older WWII veterans who defended the Soviet Union in wars and were now going to leave with the children and grandchildren. The result was sometimes a heart attack. The war veterans' military orders and medals for which they spilled their blood forfeited, as these miserable clerks took them away. This was like a medieval torture for the veterans. Nevertheless, the new exodus had started.

So finally, the permission has been gotten, documents prepared. What is next? Unlike Eastern European Jews getting ready to go to America in the beginning of the twentieth century, a Russian Jew learned English prior to leaving and very little or not at all relied on his relatives who had immigrated some time ago.

In Vienna, which served as a transfer point, some of them choose Land of the Covenant Israel; another part picked Terra Incognita, the US. How did they settle in the new world? I am quoting Joseph Roth an Austrian writer pictured the fortune of the previous wave of Eastern Jewish immigrants in the beginning of twentieth century:

> "Many returned. Many more remain by the wayside. Eastern Jews have no home anywhere, but their graves may be found in every cemetery. Many grow rich. Many

achieved fames. Many make outstanding contributions to foreign cultures. Many lose both themselves and the world. Many remain in the ghetto, and it is only their children who will leave it. Most give the West at least as much as it takes from them. Some give it more than it gives them. The right to live in the West belongs to anyone who sacrifices himself by going to look for it." (*The Wondering Jews*. W.W. Norton & Company, NY – London, 2001, p. 110).

That was written in 1926 but G-d, how relevant it is for the end of the twentieth century! The much bigger stream of emigrants of the 1990s worked in their traces and moved as if answering *yes* to the Shakespearean-like question. Now after more than two decades, I can say their luck and fate make no difference with those of all earlier comers.

For some, the lifetime decision to start a new living with unknown future was painful, for the others easy but it was always grave. Some people had interesting or good paid jobs in science, the arts, or other creative fields, others dreamed of quitting their job and changing anything about the repulsive life.

Reasons for leaving Russia were not too much of a difference in each family: better opportunities for children, unfair treatment of Jews, and the prospective for well-being. All of these were more than burdensome to decide to immigrate. Despite the *"fifth record"*, many in Russia had creative jobs in science or art, which they were supposed to drop and leave without any warranty of getting not even a similar job but the job in general. Going through the challenges of adjustment to a new culture, searching for employment, making a career, rising children and realizing newcomers' dreams – all these laid ahead.

The newcomers faced with big and small obstacles on their way before their life in the new countries became stable – whether the destination was America, Israel, Canada, Australia, or Germany. The prevailing number of immigrants of my community achieved a lot because of their hard work and talents. All these stories are about the opportunities and challenges, success and failures. Whether someone succeeds or fails, it is not about money but integration into a new culture; it varies in everyone's mind. In a new and unaccustomed social environment, everyone sees only the things he/she" wants to see. If someone *wants* to see the good about a new society, he *will* see it but if a person prefers seeing only the negatives, he will only observe the depressing.

Let us be honest: not everyone had to leave his/her country of birth. I have in mind those who cannot accustom to the new life and country, lost self-esteem or does not like the new social and cultural environment. They are not too many and they are unhappy. Some of them who think analytically blame themselves for the wrong move; others blame new country, people – all but themselves.

Immigration is like a marriage; both are challenges. As with marriage, there are few variations: you liked the country (bride) before and like it after moving in (marriage) is a good case scenario. Another variation is you liked it before (had too much expectation) but were disappointed after is the worst case. The third one is if you had no illusion about your life in the new country before and liked it after (marriage of convenience) is the best-case scenario. Thus, whether we are happy, it is all about matching our expectations and the reality. Happy immigration is possible if your expectations are not excessively high and therefore, every little success is seen as a gift, especially if you learned how to live with challenge.

The wife of my friend-engineer told him while making decision to emigrate: when you get ready to work as a street cleaner, then we are good to go. This is the best example of the expected challenges and unexpected successes, which may be achieved later or may not come at all.

Before the departure, some strike a balance. What Russia got more from Jews – good or bad? On one hand, the disproportionable Jewish influence on revolution of 1917, their participation in Bolshevik's terror. On the other hand, a tremendous input in the development of the country, industries, military, outstanding inventions and scientific discoveries, creations in music, arts, literature, and many-many more… Whatever the input was, Jews were traditionally unwelcomed in Russia, and the result followed as their departure from the country when it became possible. The country said its farewell to Jews, the non-ordinary part of their people who used to help this country and were oppressed by this same country.

A modest Jewish family lived in a communal apartment neighboring to any Russian family. Just a regular working family: parents and a kid. At some difficult time, the family emigrated as did many other Jewish families. Many years surpassed, the kid grew up, became a young man, got educated, worked hard and then glorified the new country by creation the global business that changed today's world. That was not a success of the country where that Jewish guy born but another country that gave him an opportunity.

A country is the people rather than the officials. That means that as much Russia lost with last Jewish exodus, so much Russia irreversibly changed.

6
In the Land of Opportunity

JEWS AND AMERICA

I look at the old photos of the immigrants arrived to Ellis Island at the end of 1800s–beginning of 1900s. They looked anxious. The photographs show long lines of people just off the boat waiting for an interview and not knowing a word in English. Through a translator, a churl clerk asks them all the required questions and puts their answers on the arrival sheets. These people fled from pogroms, poverty, limits on settlement, and hope for a better future.

My granduncle immigrated to America in 1914. His brother (my grandfather) stayed in Russia and lived most of his life in a Jewish "shtetl". The two brothers became residents of two opposite worlds. Now, two generations later, their descendants are poles apart culturally as if they represent two different nations. This is the Jewish providence: a few generations of the divided Jews then appear as foreigners.

In less than one hundred years, the next wave of Jewish immigrants flooded America. Again, the anxious and confused new migrants go through the arrival procedures. Everything has changed during this century: America, Russia, and immigrants. Only people's emotions remain the same. Information technology has emerged from the cybernetics fantasy of the 1940s–1950s to leading American industry that has literally changed the world. Airliners instead of ships now bring people to America. The first immigration waves came to the developing country with growth potential where almost everyone was employed. The last wave has come to the most advanced post-industrial superpower with the elusive job market. The historical spiral has come back on a newer level: people of the same tribe came to a drastically changed country.

No more Ellis Island collector, no illiteracy, no Pale of Settlement left behind. New immigrants' appearance is different, they have much better education, and mostly have intellectual professions, basic English and some can even speak. However, the hesitation is the same: would we be fortunate in unknown country; would we be able to find a job or doomed to live helpless life; would our kids succeed anything good in this country. The thoughts everyone feared: would I ever regret dropping my past ordinary life, miserable or comfortable.

America has always been attractive to Jews. Jewish aliens have found equal rights and opportunities so desperately needed for centuries. The Jewish escape to America started from the first twenty-three refugees. They came to New Amsterdam (New York) in 1654 from Brazil. They were descendants of Sephardic Jews (Sephardim) exiled from Spain and Portugal at the end of fifteenth century, then lived somewhere within Ottoman Empire and fled to Brazil with a hope for religious freedom. Unfortunately, the medieval persecution of the Jews came to South America with its colonization by Europeans. Jews had to find other places to live. A few of them chose North America.

At the beginning, most of Jewish aliens were Sephardic, practiced the same Judaic tradition as Ashkenazim (European Jews) but were mentally different and stood closer to the Middle Eastern or North African culture. They brought their culture and business to New York, Rhode Island, Philadelphia, Charleston, South Carolina, and Savannah, Georgia.

By 1700, Jewish population in thirteen colonies estimated two to three hundred. During the eighteenth century, a few bills were issued to legalize rights to Jews living in the colonies: they granted naturalization rights in 1740 (then as citizens of the British Empire). The first Jew was elected to office in South Carolina in 1775. Jews as a people allowed to be part of the federal government in 1788. One of the first important decrees of the government of Rhode Island claimed equality of people regardless of their ethnicity or religion in 1781.

In August 1790, George Washington visited Newport, Rhode Island where he received letter from the local Jewish Community and read:

> "…We desire to send up our thanks to the Ancient of Days, the great preserver of Men- beseeching him, that the Angel who conducted our forefathers through the wilderness into the promised land, may graciously conduct you through all the difficulties and dangers of this mortal life…"

I assume this letter touched Washington so much that his reply was later considered as a manifest of respect and tolerance toward the other ethnicity and religion. A letter from George Washington to American Jews guaranteed them all freedoms and rights, same as other American citizens had:

> "…All possess alike liberty of conscience and immunities of citizenship It is now no more that toleration is spoken of, as if it was by the indulgence of one class of people, that

another enjoyed the exercise of their inherent natural rights. For happily the Government of the United States, which gives to bigotry no sanction, to persecution no assistance requires only that they who live under its protection should demean themselves as good citizens, in giving it on all occasions their effectual support…"

European Jews noticed this letter and believed they could live safely only in America. That was the beginning. Jewish migration from Europe picked up the steam: there were about fifteen thousand Jews in the US by 1840, between two hundred and thirty and two hundred and eighty thousand by 1880 and more than four million by 1927. Before 1880, a few waves of Jewish immigration escaped from Western and Central Europe: Germany, Austria, Bohemia, and other countries. From the beginning to the end of nineteenth century, Ashkenazim from Germany were dominating among other groups of coming Jewish immigrants. Even though they outnumbered Sephardim by the middle of eighteenth century, the latter had prevalence in the American Jewish cultural and religious life up to the early nineteenth century. Then German Jewish liberal religious interpretation took over the conservative interpretation of Sephardic Jews. Eventually German Jews with their literacy and business orientation became an important part of the American establishment.

In the nineteenth century, Western European Jews wanted equal rights with the local people, although there was no imminent threat to their life. In Eastern Europe was different. After assassination of the moderate Russian emperor-reformer Alexander II, large wave of pogroms rolled over the country. That was a deadly threat to the Jewish lives. Massive immigration started from 1881 and lasted about forty years. About two and a half million Jews from Russia, Ukraine, Moldavia, Belorussia, Poland, and Austria-Hungary arrived at the destination of their dream in Ellis Island looking for fairness and freedom. My mind brings me back to the beginning of the twentieth century when millions of Eastern European Jews saved themselves from pogroms fled to America.

Thanks to the Internet, I was able to open the 14th Census of the United States: 1920 – Population. I saw the sheet for the State of New York, County Kings (Brooklyn), Supervisor District No 3, Enumeration District No 1131 results. This was a record of an immigrant Jewish family that happened to be my granduncle, his wife, and their older son (the daughter was not born yet). The column that identified education asked three questions: *"Any school attended any time within September 1919"*, there was no answer for this one; *"whether able to read"* and *"whether able to write"* both answered "yes". Another column with even more interesting question was *"whether able to speak English"*, my granduncle gave the answer "no" and his wife answered "yes."

The granduncle arrived in New York at the age of nineteen. When the Census of 1920 occurred, he was twenty-five years old and he stated he could not speak English! I think he just was shy of his accented language. Of course, he should have spoken enough English to get a citizenship and work as a driver. Anyway, it seems like the present-day immigrants from Russia are far better prepared for setting up a new American life than our ancestors were a century ago.

Those Jews were tailors, artisans, bargainers who fled pogroms in the Pale of Settlement; they were mostly religious and undereducated by today's standard. Their American-born descendants were understandably more successful and now often represent the elite in some areas of intellectual jobs like banking, medicine, justice, and engineering.

How different the first Eastern Jewish immigrants from their modern descendants were, as we can judge by the quote from the 1893 newspaper *Forum* about the Jewish newcomers:

> "Centuries of persecution and oppression tend to develop extreme traits of character, some most commendable, others not so praiseworthy. These people possess all the faults of an oppressed people, but they have also the heroic virtues fostered by their oppression. The Russian Jew seems to possess a dual character: to be the best of men and the worst, to practice the meanest vices and the most exalted virtues. He is suspicious, ungrateful, and often treacherous alike to friend and foe, qualities naturally fostered by centuries of tyranny and repression. On the other hand, he possesses, in large measure, the qualities, which will inevitably make him a notable figure in the social and political evolution of any country of which he becomes a citizen. From an intimate knowledge of these people, I maintain that they are in many important respects among our most desirable immigrants." (No 15, p. 172-182)

The opinion is controversial, but the author was likely to have weighty arguments to think so. Jews, who used to live in the Pale of Settlement and survived the hardship, were suspicious when they communicated with ethnical Russians – both sides as if lived on different planets. Jews brought these feelings to American soil. Based on this evaluation, I see differences in the character of a Jew from Russia then and now. In my viewpoint, this distinction is the result of education. Higher education has become a hope in the Jewish families of the Soviet epoch.

Millions of Jews originated from different countries and of different background and culture found themselves in America in twentieth century. As always, firstcomers looked down to the fresh ones. The German American Jews considered Eastern European Jews at the beginning as not desirable. This is common among the immigrants: having achieved more for a longer time, the earlier comers are arrogant toward the newcomers, especially if the beginners lived in the Russian or Polish provinces and had a backwards' pattern of life. The Russian tsarist government restricted their access to education, and they lost out to more settled Germans. Nowadays, the difference between descendants of any Jewish immigration waves is invisible.

American Jews are an influential part of the society. The Jewish effect on the American economy, politics, culture, medicine, science, and education is substantial. Surprising but it took just one generation for most of the Jewish newcomers not just to integrate but succeed and thrive. C. Silberman examines:

> "Who are these people, Christians wonder, who have moved so rapidly from obscurity to positions of prominence, even influence, in American society – people who so closely resemble other Americans in some ways and who are so stubbornly different others?" (C. Silberman. *A Certain People. American Jews and Their Lives Today*. Summit Books, New York, 1985, p. 22).

The number of answers to this question is as many as the number of Jewish successful stories. Still there is something distinctive in common, which makes the Jews go where they may realize their attainment. Furthermore, it does not matter whether they self-identify Jewish or non-Jewish. There might be a genetic or a cultural property behind this state of mind.

The religious component in Jewish life has played various roles in different epochs. For thousands of years, religious and ethnical components were inseparably associated with the condition of being a Jew. Over time, it has largely narrowed from the universal holy power (ancient and Medieval Jews, modern Orthodox Jews) to a spiritual lifestyle (European Jews of eighteenth and nineteenth centuries, inhabitants of the Pale of Settlement, and modern Conservative Jews) and then to holiday observances (modern secular and Reformist American, Israeli, and European Jews). For the time being, religious and ethnical components may exist independently in any Jewish soul. From the nineteenth century on, and especially in the twentieth century, the number of secular Jews increased substantially. According to Gallup, nowadays, over 50% of Israeli Jews do not consider religion as an important part of their everyday life. In 2005, the proportions of Jewish denomination among all American Jews were as follows: Orthodox – 13% (20% raised Orthodox in the childhood); Conservative – 26%; Reform – 34%; Reconstructionist – 3%; and Just Jewish (secular) – 25% (20% raised Just Jewish) (Jonathon Ament. *American Jewish Religious Denominations*. National Jewish Population Survey 2000-2001, February 2005, Report 10, p. 9). We can see that the level of Jewish Orthodoxy decreases in favor of secularism.

For secular Jews, their Jewish identity is merely recognition of ethnical but not religious affiliation. Jerry Klinger of the Jewish American Society for Jewish Preservation brought up his opinion:

"Jewish American survival is facing its greatest crisis in over three hundred years. Contemporary American Jews do not consciously worry about getting along anymore until they are shocked back into historical reality by anti-Semitism or Jew bating and hating around the world... The majority of American Jews does not know why, and cannot express why, they should choose to be Jewish. Gefilte fish, matzo ball soup, bagels, Yiddish language expressions in English, is not enough reason to choose to be Jewish… The majority of American Jews are Jews primarily through the memory of cultural affiliations. Gastronomic Judaism or attending Jewish film festival is considered being Jewish by some." (*The Meaning of American Jewish History*, http://jewishmag.com).

In this statement, I see the homesickness for Jewish traditions, which the American Jews have not preserved. Having a different cultural background, I have a different viewpoint on the issue. Attending Jewish film festivals, loving gefilte fish, and keeping memory of cultural affiliation is not too little to save the Jewish identity. To be a Jew is not necessarily so much about the sense of duty of attending a synagogue and strictly obeying religious rules but having a feeling of belonging to the tribe, loving its history, and understanding the suffering your people went through. In the Soviet Union, it was as if the Jewish history did not exist: the Holocaust tragedy was hushed up and the anti-Semitic policy flourished.

The American Jewish population increased at the end of twentieth century with respect to the Soviet Jewish immigrants. Russian Jews residing in the US differ from the American Jews now and at least for the next thirty to forty years to come until our descendants assimilate and become part of the American Jewry. According to their preferences, Jewish immigrants from the Soviet Union split into two flows: American and Israeli. Russia and Ukraine have been the biggest suppliers of Jews to America during last one hundred thirty years and to Israel for the last forty years. People of these two flows remain very close to each other culturally and politically as indigenous from the country with deep anti-Semitic traditions.

The uniqueness of America is that it is a nation of immigrants. No one, excluding the real native Indians, can say we are the original owners of this land. This national spirit creates tolerance and prevents this country from ethnical nationalism. This is unusual and attractive to Jews from Russia. In the gas station where I worked during my first year in America, an auto mechanic worked at the bordering repair shop. He was an American born Italian descent and much annoyed by my accent. He did not like me and not hide his sentiment. If I said a word or name incorrect, he often mocked my accent and then repeated "oh, f-n place!" Finally, as I felt overwhelmed with his hostility, I asked him, "What do you want from me?" He said, "You are supposed to be in Russia, not here." "And your grandparents were supposed to be in Italy", I responded. He shut up and did not make it an issue anymore because he had no line of reasoning. Once naturalized, an immigrant has equality with the natives. Any American's ancestors were also immigrants. Therefore, multiculturalism is an innate part of the American life apart from the European countries. Therefore, I think America handles the new realities of the multiculturalism better than Europe does.

Immigrants play important role in developing the US. I call it the "syndrome of a provincial" (or newcomer): to match the level with people of the mainstream, an alien should study more, work harder, and achieve higher marks that later lead to greater accomplishment.

Beginning from the 1990s, millions of ethnical Russians, Ukrainians, Jews, Georgians left the collapsed empire. About half of the Jewish flow from Russia directed to America and Canada; another big part moved to Israel, and smaller numbers of Jews moved to Germany, Australia and other civilized countries. According to different sources, about seven hundred thousand American citizens and residents have Russian as a first language and at the same time, Jewish ethnicity. Few of the community members emigrated in 1970s and the majority moved in at the end of the 1980s, beginning of the 1990s. During 1989–2000, Israel, US and other western countries received a few hundreds of thousand new immigrants from Russia… a huge human flow. Even though the newcomers had the same cultural background as the previous group, they differed. First, by the number – at the end of the 1970s, there were little over 173,000 native Russian speakers in the US and by the year two thousand, 700,000 people spoke the Russian language at home. Second, there were fewer official obstacles and grass-root offences for those who intended to leave, making leaving easier. Third, from the 1990s, Americans no longer expressed as much interest in the large flows of people from Russia as they did to aliens from Russia in the 1970s. In addition, there was a possibility of return that made immigration conceptually reversible, although still hard mentally.

The bigger part of the Russian immigrants in America was of Jewish descent. They formed a new community with most of population concentrated in greater New York, Los Angeles, Chicago, Philadelphia, and a few other areas of the large cities.

The language of this community is Russian, not Yiddish as it was with immigrants from the czarist Russia just a hundred years ago. All in all, this is a noticeable stratum of immigrants in modern America and one of the most successful ones. Immigrants from the former Soviet Union are mainly well educated, used to overcoming obstacles and difficulties, and are gradually becoming more influential in the US.

I think about all Soviet and Russian immigrants of the 1970s and 1990s as members of one wave because they have the same common history and culture – we all went through a miserable life (or commonwealth for those wistful) in our former country of residence. However, there are differences in taking on the new life in a new country for those who left the Soviet Union of the 1970s, the powerful super-country with the KGB on watch. The earlier immigrants, condemned by most of their compatriots, felt dismal. Arriving in America, they became people of destiny with no right to return. They left their habituated world and entered one where the impoverish life in a small but non-communal apartment, state aid, and food stamps was thought by them to be quite wealthy. Americans treated them as if they had fled from a war theater.

Immigrants from Russia are successful in many aspects and in general, they are the ideal immigrants. Less in number than Asians and the Latino Americans, they are less noticeable by the mainstream. However, they have rapidly adjusted to a new job market, work ethics, and social environment. Their ambitious children have been attending the best American universities and become a prominent part of the US intellectual workforce. But before it came about, their parents had gone through the difficult way.

Every immigrant must go through challenges of the first years settling in a new country. My next story is remarkable rather than ordinary but may give a better representation about the ways the nowadays wanderers settle.

THE IDEAL IMMIGRANT

The story of my friend's Eddie life is exceptional as much as the life of a brilliant individual could be. His entrepreneur talents and natural ability to bring people together provided his success in America. The secret of his achievement was his personality. We know happy stories about the newcomers. Eddie's story is indicative because it shows that a great success is still possible in modern America for any active and talented person.

When we landed in New York JFK airport, our friends Eddie and Svetlana met us. At the time they lived in the US for sixteen years, were long-time American citizens, and self-confident about the local life, taking to it like a duck in water. Your beginning goes much smoother if you have a friend sharing a shot of vodka with you in your early days in a strange new land.

I cannot think of my youth without my friends with whom we had so much fun getting together. Eddie was always a leader in our group of peers. He is late but seared in his friend's soul. This friendship shaped my youth. I met Eddie when we were sixteen while studying at an evening school. These schools were for people who worked in the mornings and continued their school studies at nights. We worked as metalworkers and then went to school by 6 pm. Eddie was social and had many friends. We always had something to discuss, whether it was business or social life, girls, future life, or money. We spoke about anything that teens might be interested in anywhere and anytime. He brought me into the round of his friends who became my friends too.

He was neither handsome, nor well built; nonetheless, he was fantastically popular with the girls. Further, he did not parlor-snake after them; instead, they chased him and called him all the time. The secret of his charisma was in his sharpness; he also was quick-witted and ingenious and could find precisely the relevant words that touched everyone with whom he communicated – so exact and witty his phrases were.

At first, when he showed up in a new group of people, nobody paid much attention to him but once he said his first short expressions, he won their attention and then gradually caught everyone's interest. He then became the gravitational center of a group, so when people met him next time, he was already everybody's good friend.

He had a talent to attract different people. His short wording shaped in jokes hit the point that someone had in their mind. That was compelling, and nobody could stay aloof to him. This wonderful ability to charm people with a sense of humor, smartness, and his great entrepreneurial talents were the reasons for his impressive success in business many years later. In all his enterprises, he always kept in mind alternate ways of doing business in case the primary one failed.

When we graduated from high school, each of us went his own way. He entered the Polytechnic Institute and I found myself in the Engineering Maritime School. We often met, and it was even more motivating when we had two girlfriends who befriended to each other. These parties of four were cheerful.

My parents loved him because of his attention to them: every time I went to sea for several months he used to visit them, and his care of them was touching. Vera, my younger sister, I suspected, was secretly in love with him and much later, she confessed to me about it. He was a leader. He always had some fresh ideas like where to spend time, whom to visit, and how to make money. He had different cohorts of people with whom he communicated. Once a year, we visited Leningrad Synagogue (while not being religious) for the Simchat Torah celebration, where we met many young Jewish boys and girls our age.

These connections were so strong that even now we keep up our friendship with a few of them. As always, he was in the center of any of these groups, talking, joking, and helping with something they needed. He was open but at the same time, he never shared more information than he thought people might need to know. I never knew what deeds bonded him with so many people. I think he had the natural ability to attract people that Dale Carnegie described in his book *How to Influence People.*

We continued keeping up with our friendship after we both married and became family husbands. Our wives did not object to our traditional getting together unlike many other Russian wives due to men's inclination to drinking. We kept up with our visits steam room with few other friends. We spoke a lot about the Jewish emigration that had just begun in the early 1970s. To me, it was far from my realities at that point. Yes, we suffered anti-Semitism in one way or the other, but we knew where the bad stuff comes from and what to expect. The anti-Semitism supported by the state was as predictable as any other ideological dogmas. We had to live with it (thanks God, no pogroms) and perceived it as an imminence. Such was my view on emigration when I learned that Eddie and his family were going to emigrate. I knew Eddie was a freethinking person and could have expected this decision. Yet, when in 1979 he told me about his plan to leave, I was shocked. I clearly remember that day in March 1980 when I saw him off at Leningrad airport. I was sure I had seen him for the last time. He had a family of four by that time: wife and two little kids. I could not even imagine how they would live in a foreign country with no language, no friends, no money, and no job. Finally, the plane took off, headed to an intermediate point in Vienna.

Our communication finished I thought forever. I could not have correspondence with him because it may have affected my job sustainability through the mail interception by KGB. I only heard about him from his retired father. I thought how hard it must have been for oneself to integrate into a new society culturally and psychologically. It was problematic to imagine myself in his shoes.

In about 1983 we, a few friends, wrote letter to him and sent it with somebody who was going to go to America for good. Months later, we received response from Eddie with his gifts. He sent me a scientific calculator with many functions that was unbelievably luxurious for the reality we lived in. I fondly thought if such a sophisticated stuff was now affordable for him, then he must have been doing well.

Sometime in the mid-1980s, Eddie worked in Canton, Ohio. One of his friends brought him to a local Jewish Club where Eddie became acquainted with the US House Representative Ralph Regula. Whether the Rep had a meeting or something else in the Jewish Club but he was there at the time Eddie and his friend arrived. I do not know what the circumstances of their meeting were. They talked about the situation with the Jews no longer allowed to emigrate from the Soviet Union amid the stronger-minded President Reagan came to the White House. Eddie wanted his father who was living in Leningrad to join him in America, but the father was not given an exit visa.

The Congressman took the problem seriously and generalized it to all Soviet Jews who desperately wanted to leave Russia. He was very active in solving this problem: wrote a letter to the Soviet Ambassador Dobrynin asking to recommence Jewish emigration from Soviet Union, dropped in on Moscow, then Leningrad, visited Eddie's father in his apartment, and then invited him to come to Canton. His help worked out. Sometime later, in 1987, Eddie's father arrived in Canton. In the press conference organized by Rep. Regular, Eddie's father spoke on the existing Jewish problem in Russia and called for letting the Jews go and resume emigration. Eddie translated his father's speech.

I am far from thinking that the press conference alone solved the big problem but there was Eddie's input in it. Anyway, starting from 1988 the immigration resumed until it faded out by the end of 1990s. As an appreciation of Eddie's input to Jewish immigration as part of a human rights problem, he received the official US flag with certificate from the White House.

In spring of 1987, Gorbachev's Perestroika and Glasnost were just deepening and one of the first relaxations was the permission to visit the Soviet Union to all former emigrants. Eddie was one of the first to visit. He stayed at his father's apartment and called me to come. In one hour, I came in and we met seven years after his departure. His appearance was tidy and well groomed, the look had changed just a little but soon this impression left me. We took a shot of vodka and then talked.

He told me he started in Dallas, TX because his relatives lived there. For the first several weeks, he got some help from them and then managed to find a job as a drafter in a small company. In some time, he was laid off, and the next work he found through a job shop. He then signed a contract agreement as a consultant, went to Canton, and then he went to Kansas for half a year. His family still lived in Dallas. I knew his relations with his wife were far from ideal. Eventually, they separated in 1986. In the same year, I divorced from my first wife, so when we met after seven years in 1987 in Leningrad, we were free men as long ago.

Next day the old friends, Eddie, Anatoly, Mike, and I, got together in a steam room as we used to do decade previously. After the steaming and some beer, we went out to street. Eddie was surprised how many changes in post-Brezhnev's Soviet Union had occurred since he left. I did not suspect his business thoughts occupied his mind.

We spent a few good days visiting old friends, walking, discussing the life, work, politics, and our failed marriages. In a few days, I saw him off at the airport and he flew back to New York where he settled after quitting his consulting work in Canton.

Eddie made several more trips back and forth during 1987–1988, looking narrowly at the new environment, business, and social life in Russia. After these trips, he decided to look for business opportunities thanks to legislatorial relaxations for freedom of import-export by the Soviet factories. In one of his visits, he told me that he and Svetlana – then Eddie's girlfriend – agreed on his quitting work in New York and attempting to make business in Russia for a one-year period. In case he failed, he would go back to the US. Knowing Eddie, I was sure he would succeed.

I was right. From 1989 to 1995, he managed to build up a serious and successful business that if not for the take on against him would have become a business to a worldwide scale. Using his open mind, natural intellect, common sense, and abilities to influence people, he started making new acquaintances among the presidents of Russian manufacturing facilities, earning their trust. He learned and analyzed the American and worldwide markets and demands for different products, as well as the Russian export market; he traveled throughout Russian cities visiting many factories. He was moving into the Russian business not even rejecting any small opportunity for trading.

One time in 1988, we met in Moscow (I was there for my business trip) at an international exhibition where he represented American business community offering to establish trade with the Soviet Union. I had no idea why he was among the American representatives in the international business exhibition. I just knew that seven years ago, he started in this country with no English and no money but with great human and entrepreneurial talents.

His energy and creativity were restless. On another time, he organized a few tours for a group of mayors of big Soviet cities with stopovers in the American cities and nationwide businesses.

Three friends - three fathers: Anatoly (left), Eddie (right), and I (center) with sons. Leningrad, October 1977

The Fifth Record

At the end of the 1980s in Moscow, Leningrad, and other cities, many new business centers had started and active young men (recent leaders of young communist organization – *Comsomol*) attempted to organize manufacturing, trades, and set up business contacts. Later, many of them became prominent entrepreneurs and leaders of the Russian business. These centers played important role in creating and promoting business environment in the country at the early time of decentralization of the economy. One time I watched how Eddie explained the American way of doing business to these young men. I just thought how in the world has he so much comprehension about it. I asked him this question after the meeting. "Well, I thought about and learned it all these ten years in America," he replied. He was a business-gifted person. Eddie arranged meetings with different people who interested him. Every time he met with a group of people, he spoke about anything that was interesting to them and was able to find the best approach to what they were interested in.

Eddie's honest, open, and aggressive way of starting business turned out to be fruitful and began bringing in commercial contracts in about one year. He supplied medical and dental equipment for Russian hospitals and clinics, selling precious metals like ferro-titanium but most of his time, he devoted to the pulp. He fixed connections with directors of different Russian pulp manufacturing factories. Eddie's qualities as a fair and captivating person helped him earn trust from the pulp manufacturers. The business picked up steam. He usually spent more than half of his time in St. Petersburg and the rest of time in New York. Several people he hired helped him in Russia.

His business in Russia was not just like "buy cheap-sell high". He always remembered where he was born and what his first language was. I will give you just a few examples of his alms-deed for Russian kids. He could not see people's sufferings… such was his character.

In about 1988, a horrible railroad catastrophe happened near Ufa, Bashkiria. A gas pipeline was situated nearby the rails. As it was later determined, there was a gas leak from the line. Possibly the leak had formed long time previously because the gas accumulation was huge. It is difficult to understand why the gas leak had not been detected earlier. On that unfortunate day, two trains were moving towards each other on different tracks. At the very moment they were passing each other, a huge explosion of the amassed natural gas occurred, and then a huge fire grasped the entire area. It was like the end of the world. Because of this tragedy, over seven hundred people died in the explosion and fire and over a thousand were burned and injured in the two trains. A girl of fifteen was coming back home on the train to her native town of Yekaterinburg (East of the Ural Mountains) from the children's camp of Artek in Crimea on the Black Sea. Badly burned, her face, arms, and neck received skin burns. I do not know how Eddie learned about this poor girl. In short, he brought her to New York and found a sponsor who agreed to pay for the hospital and operations. When the girl was not in a hospital, she lived in Eddie mother's Brooklyn apartment. During the four months of her treatment in New York, she underwent two plastic surgeries and came back home in a much better shape than she was before the treatment.

Another of Eddie's charity deed involved a Russian girl from Krasnodar who was knocked down and overrun by a truck and paralyzed. She could not move her arms or do simple things. Eddie brought her to Canton and placed her into Timken Hospital. She spent about six months there for intensive curing. At the end, she could even comb her hair. The hospital presented her with an electrical scooter thus, making it possible for her to move without any help. Before the boarding to aircraft, the Aeroflot flight crew did not want to take the scooter in the plane. The Eddie paid and then they agreed. The following fortune of that girl was interesting and romantic. Still in Canton's hospital, she befriended with the paralyzed young American guy. They liked each other. In some time, the guy accompanied by his father flew in Krasnodar to see the girl and ask her to marry him. As he got her agreement, he took her to America. After the story had such a happy end, the girl's father wrote letter to Eddie saying that God will bless him for his good deeds.

Eddie also arranged Russian children's art exhibitions in several American cities. He did many good deeds for Russia at the time when most of the newly emerged Russian businessmen wanted just to grab, swipe and steal. His idea of helping people who needed help became his creed. He treated people's pain and problems like his own and was always responsive to them. If someone who was in his eyeshot needed help, he or she did not even have to ask for it, Eddie understood the need and helped.

The first signs of Eddie's deadly disease were felt in 1992 in St. Petersburg. He was hoping it was not cancer. He visited different American and Russian doctors. The diagnosis was like a gun shot: bladder cancer. He was not even forty-seven; he had just taken off so high with his business and become a recognized person in the international pulp industry. The surgery was performed in the New York hospital. The result was promising, and Eddie got a chance to become a cancer survivor. Three weeks after the surgery, he returned to St. Petersburg and then flew a business trip to Yekaterinburg. Svetlana accompanied him; he needed some help since he was still weak. He got back to his business and was busy again.

The new problem showed up unexpectedly. In the morning of March 1995, Eddie was going to go to his office when he saw a luxury car from the window of his

St. Petersburg apartment. He had already seen this car for several days and had a feeling that somebody was watching him. His intuition prompted him that they were going to be intercepted. Eddie's driver, who was waiting for him in his car, also suspected something was wrong. He got out from the car and called Eddie from the street phone to report a surveillance. Eddie told him to keep sitting in the car and be ready to flee. Svetlana and Eddie left the apartment and ran to their car. Once in the car, they quickly took off. The luxury car followed them, caught up with them, and they heard shooting. The driver made a turn, then another turn, and managed to get away. Eddie told him to go to the American Consulate on Furshtadskaya Street.

On coming to the Consulate, they rung the bell and were welcomed by the Consulate staff. Eddie asked the General Consul for admission. The Deputy Consul invited them to his office. Eddie told him what happened to them minutes ago and asked him to allow them to stay just one night. The Deputy Consul helped them with a room and advised Eddie to shut down his business in Russia if it became dangerous.

The next morning Eddie secretly went to Finland. In a few weeks, they again secretly came back to St. Petersburg for couple of days just to wrap up the business. Right before his leaving, he called me and asked if I want to see him before leaving Russia. Within an hour, we met in the railway station at the train to Finland. We had some time before the departure of train. He told me he figured out that his partner ordered the assault on him. The plan was to get rid of Eddie as a partner. As all the connections were set up and the uninterrupted pulp supply was put on the right tracks, he was no longer needed. Eddie later got evidence of that.

That time around, we saw each other for the last time in Russia. We hugged and said goodbye to each other. Eddie and Svetlana got into the St. Petersburg–Helsinki train.

Eddie's Russian business was over. I had already known that we are going to meet in America.

Eddie lasted another three years after we met up in New York. The disease caught him again. He insisted that the doctor tell him how much time he had before dying, as he needed to know. The doctor did not want to tell him but then finally said, "two weeks." In one of his last days when we were alone, I asked him what he felt. What I heard struck me. "I have nothing to regret about my life, all I wanted to do, I did," he said. "I had my own business that made me independent. I have two children, I secured their future, and I have the wife who takes much care of me. I am going away happy." He passed away at the end of October and did not live the three months to meet the new millennia and the new world challenges associated with its coming. I said my last farewell to my friend.

Eddie's nature of course was not the moral fiber of all Jewish people but his own. However, if we talk about the best of Jewish character: humaneness, readiness to help, intellect, compassion, business insight – it was all about him.

He was my friend. The Russian mind allows calling somebody a friend only if he is close to you, shares something that you would have not told anybody else, and knows that he would never betray you but always protect and help. The real friendship involves readiness of sacrificing for the sake of friendship. In American culture, the word 'friend' is anyone who treats you friendly. Of course, you may communicate and share mutual business with a friend but to a certain point; beyond the point is a private life and nobody can interfere. For Russians it is more difficult to get close to each other and Americans are friendlier and easier make friends. It is not better or worse, just differently.

SOVIET BRIGHTON BEACH

Brighton Beach! It is a synonym of Russian America, the symbolic and real name of the immigrant community densely populated this magnificent oceanic area. I take a walk on the Brighton Beach boardwalk where all residents are my compatriots from the former superpower. Brighton's life is electrifying, and local people are so accustomed to a new lifestyle that they look like they have never lived anywhere else except this heavenly place.

It is a quiet September evening, and the ocean breeze makes it even more pleasant. The boardwalk is crowded with dapperly dressed people walking along the beach. I look at their faces and catch pieces of Russian phrases when draw up with them. Everything reminds me of some south Russian resort-town on the Black Sea. I would not believe I was in America if it were not for seeing rare policemen in the New York City uniform.

Brighton is a brand for Russians. It is sometimes called "Little Odessa" for its likeness with the mild maritime breeze and salt air of the famous Black Sea Russian/Ukrainian city. Great varieties of different people from the former Soviet Union are mixed by similar cultures and south Russian spirits. Just come by the Russian deli and grocery store and you will not hear any English.

The first Soviet Jews started residing here in the beginning of the 1970s and gradually replaced American Jews, Italians, and all other residents. I always hear south Russian or Ukrainian dialects, no English whatsoever. The inhabitants of this neighborhood are my compatriots – former citizens of the former superpower. The intimidated image of that superpower made America spend so much time and stamina to gain a foothold as a winner in the notorious Cold War. That weird and enigmatic war is in the past and now floats away. Nonetheless, the odd past of the residents is still with their well-fed present, and the combination makes up the essence of this community.

Most of the immigrants live in the neighborhoods with a high concentration of the community members. Brighton Beach is one of them. Once you are here, you are in a unique social environment, a different and wonderful world where the acting Constitution and laws are American but the culture, outlook, and language are Russian.

Brighton motions me with its relaxation and glare, pretentious manner and glamour, peculiarity, and our common destiny. Women dressed in fur just for shopping; men having businesses within the community without any need for speaking English. All these features create an atmosphere of the cash luxury and domination of the specific crony business that used to flourish in the Soviet Union. Brighton is a philosophy of the life style: we used to live a harsh life in the former Soviet Union and now we want to relax at the ocean, have any food, dress, and furniture we like, and preserve our language, habits, and thinking.

My acquaintance told me an episode that happened to her on Brighton Beach when she had just come to New York from Ukraine. She asked a woman in the street how to get to a subway station in English. A woman paid attention to her hard accent and asked if she could speak Russian. "Yes," my acquaintance answered. "Then why are you f-cking off speaking English?" the woman exclaimed in Russian. Typical local style: Russian culture dominates here by default, and if a Russian speaker tries talking to residents in English, she or he shows off.

God forefend me from looking down at these people. I am one of them. My depiction of the Brighton Beach community is a take on to watch it from inside, as I am part of it and have friends there.

Some of the Russia-town residents are only comfortable with ethnical food, television, radio, and newspapers, and evade communication, reading books, newspapers, or listening to the radio of the American mainstream. A few of them are not too interested in better understanding of another culture of the country they came to for good; others find it difficult or useless, thus making a cultural ghetto for themselves.

Is this like the way it was always with Eastern European Jewish immigrants? This is what Austrian journalist Joseph Roth observed in the beginning of the twentieth century,

> "The Jew who intends to go to America doesn't start learning English, as you might have supposed. He already knows how he's going to get along in the new country. He speaks Yiddish, the most widely used language in the world – in terms of geography, not the number of those who speak it. He will make himself understood. He does not need to understand English. There are Jews who have lived in the Jewish quarter of New York for thirty years, and they still speak Yiddish and can't understand their own grandchildren."

Now, almost one hundred years later, we can see it is similar with another "Jewish" language – Russian.

Brighton Beach is now an appellative name. I think people in Russia have heard its name even more often than Americans do because of the Russian movie (comedy) that has Brighton Beach in its name. When I am at the Brighton streets, I feel like I got off a long-distance train to a small south Russian or Ukrainian township. Everything here is so familiar to me: language and frame of mind, appearance, habits, and food. Some people from the poor empire were lucky enough to get a golden key to a door leading to a paradise. They opened that door and moved across the ocean, where they started a new life on a fertile soil. It is like a continuation of the loved fairytale

Golden Key by Alexei Tolstoy that stops exactly at the door entrance. The paradise, however, is not without problems but who said that the easy life is necessarily a good life?

It makes no difference what country in the post-Soviet area they had lived in before coming here. No matter whom they are – Georgian, Mountain Jew, a Jew from Moscow, Belorussian, Uzbek, Russian, Ukrainian, or Siberian – they all are from the USSR. Envy, Russia! What you want to forcefully reestablish as a reincarnation of the Soviet Union is here in America! The difference is however, in the concepts of life, politics, economics, everything... Thanks God, Azerbaijani, and Armenian do not fight here for Nagorny Karabakh, Russian and Georgian do not fight for Ossetia, Russian and a Moldavian do not struggle for the Pri-Dnestrovie, and Russian and Ukrainian do not kill one another for Crimea and Donbass.

All social classes of the former Soviet society meet in this wonderland. They sell, buy, trade, eat, drink, lie on the beach, sit in restaurants, talk, play domino or chess, work hard, or stay on welfare. Old men sitting on the boardwalk bench recall what big bosses and how powerful they were in the past. They are unclaimed here and that is something they miss. Life is full and satisfying when you are in demand.

You stay in line for hot and delicious Russian *piroshkies* (patties) with potato and mushrooms inside. Isn't its Russia? The difference is you are wealthier, securer, breath-in better quality air, and are better respected by the state. From there, Brightoneans enjoy the habitual food and style of their native land, as well as all the advantages provided by the Constitution and laws of the step-motherland.

To complete the picture of Brighton Beach, a few words about my visit to a Brighton restaurant. I once stopped by one of those on the shore with my relatives. Rich food and drinks are inherent features of Russian-style restaurant service. My niece Masha and her husband Garrett joined us.

The Fifth Record

Pictures of Brighton Beach

They just recently graduated from the University of Washington and moved from Seattle to New York for good. Garrett did not speak any Russian, so six of us at the table spoke English. To make the picture complete, I need to say the restaurant had many visitors that spoke Russian loudly. There were two men at the table next to ours. They were drinking and eating so much that the full bottle of vodka they started an hour or so previously was empty and they ordered one more. Garrett watched this with genuine interest and we paid attention not to those two drinking men (we used to see pictures like this from the childhood) but rather to Garrett's reaction: he looked shocked. Then Roman, my stepdaughter's husband, who was with us, pointing to Garrett, said, "America is a wonderful country, I must say. It is only possible here that a man native to this country sits in a New York City restaurant and feels like a foreigner."

Yes, this is Brighton Beach –the preserved Soviet culture on the American territory.

Every time when I come by Brighton Beach, I look at the local community people with sorrow. I understand that in some time, the whole community will dissolve and disappear as a cultural unity. Immigration from the former Soviet republics, once blown up from 1989–1996 and then gradually reduced, had faded by 2000. Our generation of the heavily accented people is aging. In twenty-five to thirty years from now, the human landscape in the Brooklyn neighborhoods of Brighton Beach, Sheepshead Bay, and Bensonhurst will be different. Eventually, there will not be a community of Russian speaking Jews, just Americans with Russian Jewish roots. The distinctive community will evolve into an indistinctive part of the mainstream. Our children will still remember their country of origin and be appreciative to us for bringing them to this country. Our US-born grandkids will barely know our story and fortune. I do not want this to happen. This is the reason I wrote this book.

CHALLENGES OF THE NEW AMERICAN

Whereas my destiny in the Soviet Union had mostly depended upon the situation in the country and little upon myself, in the US, everything in my career and life depended on me. It is difficult, however, to write about the American social and political principles without running into clichés. Therefore, the story of my settlement will include only the actions, not the reasoning.

This is not a chronicle of failure or success but the story of the cultural adjustment to a different world.

May 1996, Brooklyn, New York

My first year in Brooklyn, New York is remembered by the tiny one-bedroom apartment where my family of four fought the roaches left after previous tenants. I never thought there could be so many of them. We all struggled with any possible means, and when we finally won the battle, a few months later a better apartment was made available, and we moved there.

I sent out my resume to the companies associated with the marine engineering industry – the industry I had been dedicated to for many years back in Russia. Some of the companies politely promised to put my resume on file, which meant forget about them; others did not respond at all. By September, I figured that my Russian experience was not worth much. My enthusiasm was fading and the obscurity started disturbing me more often. I had no job and I was in the dark about my future.

I had never been in the US before I came here for good. I thought my modest English would be enough for the plain talk. I thought once you found any job, you would live as an average American does. I thought I would get an opportunity in the marine industry, but never thought it would not be possible at all. None of my thoughts came true; the reality turned out to be different. American marine industry turned me down with my Russian experience, and later I understood the real reason for that. For the level I applied, the reason was cultural – having no experience of working in a Western type of company meant that I had to go through a long way of adjusting myself to different approaches to high profile work, language and work ethics issues. Again, this refers only to a certain high level position I thought I would have applied for. Understanding of my miscalculation came in later with grasping American experience.

July 1996-April 1997, Brooklyn, New York

My first temporary and part-time American job was at a gas station in Brooklyn. The job is my first real contact with locals. People of different cultures populated the neighborhood; the gas station was located between Bensonhurst and Borough Park. Hasidic Jews in station wagons with dozens of kids on the back seats, loudly speaking Italians, emotional Puerto-Ricans, jigging up and down Afro-Americans, and even recently arrived modest Russians – they all filled up their cars there. That was a place where I got invaluable local life and language experience.

I had never seen Hasidic Jews back in the Soviet Union; it is sad and ironic at the same time. It is sad because the Soviet ideology forbade being an open religious observant even more to Hasidic. It is ironic because a person of Jewish ethnicity, I nonetheless, knew little about the religious Jews. This little came only from the novels of Sholom Aleichem and my father's stories.

I looked at the Borough Park residents, their habits, and lifestyle with a great interest heated up with thoughts about the nature of my ancestors. I just imagined my presence among them if born a hundred years ago.

I once had an issue with money. Normally gas attendant collects cash from the customers, then puts it in bundles of $150–250 each and locks them in a safe box. Then manager comes and takes all the money. On that day, I collected several bundles and put them into safe box. The last bundle was for $330, which was too much. I clearly remembered that I put it in the safe box. On that evening, after my shift was over, I went home and got a telephone call from the owner. She told me that the manager had informed her that $330 was missing. Then she said that I had to come in tomorrow to find out where the money is.

After I hung up the phone, I felt smeared with something stinky. For the first time in my life, I was under suspicion. I did not sleep all night and tried to re-run the time and visualize it again. No, it could not be that I left this money on top of the safe box or a table and somebody stole it; if I had plenty of money, I would never have left it like that. Then what was it? Did somebody set me up? Who? The manager? The owner did not admit that the manager had lost the money; she did not even discuss that possibility. She would rather not trust me. Anyway, I clearly remembered putting the money into the safe box! The owner finished the story decently; she did not fire me but ordered that in the future I had to make the bundles of not more than $120 each. I still feel bitter fact that I was under the suspicion while being innocent.

In a month, I accustomed to my new work, and the people of the neighborhood got used to my accent and me. One episode I remember was associated precisely with my English. A customer ordered me to gas his car. He said, "Full", which meant fill the tank. I finished pumping, and the meter showed about $20. He gives me $4. Looking at my face, he added, "I ordered you to gas my car for four dollars." "How could you order four dollars, if you said full?" I asked. "You better learn English if you don't understand what I am saying," was his answer. That was too much for me. "My modest English is enough to understand the difference between "four" and "full" but if you do not want to pay, okay, I will pay for you, but next time don't gas your car when I am here," I told him. "I don't like it," he just said and took off.

November 1996, Boston, MA

Soon I acquainted with a man who was also from St. Petersburg. He worked in a company founded by the followers of Professor Altshuller (Russia) who developed a general method for creating any invention. He described the basics in his book *The Algorithm of Invention*. I had read the book while still in Russia and liked it. Roughly, the idea was that in order to make any technical invention, the inventor had to use the special algorithm to come with the solution. After the problem with functionality identified, the inventor should select the known physical or chemical principle or phenomena from the listed ones which could best solve the technical problem and apply it to that specific device. So, the process of making an invention becomes more like a routine process.

My new friend suggested that I send my resume to that company, and I did. In a couple of weeks, I got a call from them - they invited me to attend a typical presentation given by one of the engineers. Of course, I agreed, and in a few days, I came over to Hilton hotel in the center of Philadelphia. The presentation sound good and after it finished, I spoke with the lecturer and discussed it. I thought it may be a good job for me doing similar presentations if I was accepted. Returned home, I called the company and expressed my favorable opinion about the presentation. They invited me to come to an interview. I thought how lucky I was – just a few months passed since we had come here and I was going to get a decent job.

In a few days as assigned, I arrived in the company's headquarters in Boston with the morning bus. A person, he was the VP in charge met me in the office, and we greeted each other. At the very second, when his and my eyes met I understood we do not like each other. It was on a subconscious level: something in his appearance was repulsive, and I think as it usually occurs, he likely felt similar about me. I wanted to get this thought out. He brought me to a conference room where several other people were sitting around a large table. I told them about my background, my former engineering and scientific experience, and answered the questions. I said that I hoped it would not be too difficult to learn the technical aspects of their business.

The interview finished. I walked out; there was some time before the departure of my bus. Several people interviewed me, but I knew the last word would come from the VP who I had met first. I was almost certain he would not hire me. Therefore, I was not surprised when in few days, I got a telephone call to hear they could not give me a position because I had no American experience but that in a couple of years I would be welcomed for the interview again. I answered 'Thank you' and hung up the phone. They knew from my resume that I had no American experience, so there was no reason to setup the interview at all! I had no desire to speculate about this failure. I just needed to move on fast, or my train would arrive to nowhere.

February 1997, Long Island, New York

I scheduled my next job interview for a mechanical engineering position at the diesel-electrical station in Long Island. The manager-interviewer gave me a tour through the engine room, and showed me the big engine, the old slow-speed Fiat diesel. He said they had a problem using low sulfur fuel that resulted on deposits forming on the piston crown. I was familiar with the problem – the combination of low-sulfur fuel and high-alkalinity lubricant is a potential danger for the engine. Then he brought me to another engine room. We had to ride there. I sat into his car. At that point, I made a mistake that probably cost me this job – I did not buckle up. Going backward, I understood what he might have thought: since the person does not obey even basic rules, he does not deserve this job. It was my fault.

It is in a human's nature to have good dreams and expectations. The higher the education, the more expectations, and if it is not fulfilled, one feels frustrated.

April 1997, New York, New York.

I finally finished my environmental course studies, got the necessary licenses, and found a job in a midsize environmental company with headquarters in midtown Manhattan. I was glad to get a job, even an on-call one. The company gave me a beeper, and I always had to have it on. I clearly remember the first call I got was to perform project monitoring in one of the schools in Queens. I met a coworker who was supposed to give on-site training, so that later I would be able to work independently. He was friendly, and we got along well. By the end of this two-week project, I felt more confident with work.

My projects were located throughout all five New York boroughs and to find them sometimes took much effort and time. The job was to collect air samples and oversee contractor's work during asbestos abatement. There were night and day-time shifts, so not enough sleep at times but nothing could compare with the feeling of independence and the ability to provide a living for my family in the several months after our coming. It was an environmental work: generations who built America made it a great country, but they paid little attention to the environment and spoiled it. Time to gather stones had come.

Thinking about the actual career I have had in America, I do not stop surprising that I switched seven jobs within the first eight years! In Russia, a person who jumps from one job to another too often called a job-hopper. It is a new game in America. This starting time was critical for my following life.

I had to climb up on the steep stair of my brand new career as fast as I could as not too much time laid ahead.

September 1997 – May 1999, All Five Boroughs, New York.

In 1997, a new problem with banking and financial business loomed unexpectedly on the horizon: year 2000 difficulty (anyone doubted the year 2000 was coming?) The trick was in mainframe computer programs, the year number was pre-programmed as two last digits: 97 meant 1997. This minimal and easy-to-correct setback turned out to be a huge problem. To make corrections in decades of thousands of programs running in banks, financial and government institutions, hundreds and even thousands more mainframe programmers needed. So, many computer-programming positions were expected to be in demand.

I do not say I wanted to become a computer programmer, but two feelings struggled inside me. One was like what do you need, you are coming to senior years, just live modestly, and enjoy the life as much as you possibly can in your circumstances. Another one pushed me to move ahead not to lose probably the last chance to earn more and live better. The second sentiment won and I enrolled in the computer programming courses, one of many that started up quickly in response to the Year 2000 problem. For half a year I studied new-to-me mainframe-programming languages and worked at the same time on my regular job. Sometimes coming back from work to Brooklyn at 2–3 AM, I had to looking for parking for thirty to forty minutes, and after a desperate search would eventually drop my car at the side of street that was supposed to cleaned at 7 AM. Then I had to get up before 7 AM to move my car to another side of the street as not to get a ticket and by 9 AM enter the class, and then go back to work. These were difficult months but the decent and good paying job of a computer programmer lay ahead!

On finishing my classes, I took some private lessons to get more experience and finally by fall of 1998, I was on the programmer's job market. A series of telephone and face-to-face interviews and job fare visits followed. One of the telephone interviews lasted four hours, another one over two and a half hours, and every time I had to keep the drive. It seemed like all potential employers were satisfied with my answers during the job interviews, but so far there were no offers. This condition lasted until May 1999, the time I attended my last interview. Suddenly after that point, the interviews, invitations, phone calls stopped. It was as if all activities have been cut by someone's hand. Reading the press and watching television I understood that a bad thing just happened to the information industry. It was a great stock crush as the market bubble burst in the high-tech industry.

This burst happened to coincide with finishing the Year 2000 Project, and thousands of computer programmers losing their jobs. With their high paying jobs, they lost good income and some of them would never get back to programming. What I lost was one year of my time, four-digit money for studying, and pain to complete it. However, I took my chance and turned this page enriched with a comprehension that any Klondike that seemed unbreakable yesterday, may rest in ruins today.

After the epic experience with computer programming, understanding has come to look for advancement in my environmental field. I freed myself from my computer programming dreams and started sending out my resume as an environmental specialist.

February 1998, Clinton Township, New Jersey

Just after I lost my hope for the marine engineering work, one advertisement came up in Lubrication Engineering Magazine. Exxon was looking for a specialist for their engine lubricant research laboratory. I routinely sent my resume. In about a week I got a call from Exxon and scheduled an interview in their Corporate Research in Central New Jersey. They requested me to prepare a presentation for my previous research in this field to consider me as a candidate. Wow! They wanted my presentation!

I took three days off from my job to prepare the presentation. On the assigned day and hour, the limousine sent by the company was waiting for me. I dressed formally, got down, and we took off.

Two associates, a lady and a gentleman, both Exxon employees met me. They showed me where to check-in to hotel (it was pre-paid) and took me to Italian restaurant for dinner – it was part of the protocol. Our conversation was pleasant: I told them about my professional history, something about my research and dissertation, and they told me about the Corporate Research. I understood that they evaluated me by the standards unknown to me.

Next morning, lady-associate – the one I had a dinner with – picked me up from the hotel and we rode to the Corporate Research building. She brought me to Human Resources and presented me to the manager. We sat down and the manager told me about the company, how good the benefits are and so on. I was listening to her thinking just take me onboard, whatever your benefits are. Nevertheless, it was part of the procedure, and I spent about half an hour there.

The next room was the testing laboratory where I saw test machines and engines so familiar to me from the American technical articles I had read in Russia. The testing equipment impressed me: all test engines that I knew from the publications were here and running. I wanted so much to work here!

At 10 AM, my presentation started. When I finished in about half an hour, people even applauded, and it was unclear whether they liked the topic or just appreciated it as a performance in a second language. I answered all questions and it took another fifteen minutes. Then I had to go through the interview process. Overall, I passed from one associate to another ten times with thirty minutes lunch with two associates, which was part of the procedure too. The last stop was in the big boss's office, and then again, I went down to HR. I was sure they would hire me.

On my coming home, Marina, Eddy, and Svetlana met me like a hero. We all expected good news. I could not wait for the call from Exxon. Two weeks passed with no phone calls, and then I decided to call. The answer sounded like a court sentence: they had found somebody else for this position.

That was the end of my illusion about the work I dreamed about and devoted myself to for so many years. I had to come down to earth to start from scratch, but I could not admit that each failure discouraged me so much. The loss of enthusiasm was just not affordable, and I finally had to resolve there was no job for me with the background I had. More exactly, there might be positions somewhere but the incumbent should have been born and educated here and gone through all career steps to be able to get an offer.

In core, I was still a marine engineer but the devotion to one and only profession was over.

July 1999, Orlando, FL

In 1999, it turned three years since I had left Russia. These were three stressful years of adapting to new environment, re-estimating values, and adjusting to new job market. That was like entering a new civilization on a higher level. By the extensity, strain, new experience, and absorption, I can compare them to twenty other customary years. For an active newcomer, if the yearly increment of your annual income continues to be significant, the process of settlement is not finished. Once it stabilizes, the adaptation does too. We were right in the middle of this process.

After years of settling and job-related emotions, my family and I went on our first vacation to Florida. We landed in Fort Lauderdale, rented a big Cadillac, and drove to Orlando, to Disney World. Everything was fabulous for all of us. The modest hotel room was viewed as a luxury apartment. Cheap restaurants were like fancy ones, and of course, the wonderful Disney World that we could not imagine even in our dreams. Our last three days we spent at the ocean beach resort. I visited Florida many times later but did not experience such feelings of happiness.

At moments of exuberance, we mentally come back to our past. In my thoughts, I return to my childhood, to Soviet values and brainwashing, to the source where common Russian people's characters and their way of thinking come from. My Florida vacation, for some reason, was the time and place that got me thinking about our destiny, about the second chance that we took. Some say when you think of your past, you part from it. That is correct.

January 2000, Brooklyn, New York.

Everything is for sale in America. However, nothing is more difficult than selling your invention. Some inventors are trying to sell the original ideas because manufacturing the invented device may be too difficult for the individualist-inventor. Nonetheless, companies do not want to buy the ideas, they need an acting device that has proved its efficiency. I tried selling the onsite engine oil analyzer. The analyzer had to perform some engine diagnostic function and evaluate the remaining service life of the oil-in-use.

Here I have to say some words about a man with whom I had kept in touch with for many years until his passing away. He morally supported me even before I landed in this country. I met Gaylord Hold in 1991 (before the collapse of the USSR) in the Black Sea port of Novorossiysk at the presentation Chevron conducted for the Soviet Steamship Companies. We then met few more times at the international meetings. He was with Chevron for over thirty years. For about twenty years, he traveled all over the world presenting Chevron products as an expert in marine and railroad engine lubricants and additives.

By that time, he had already retired. I discussed technical things with Gaylord. Our relationship were so trustful that I disclosed to him one of my technical ideas and offered him to be a coauthor in patent application. He liked the idea and was willing to help promote it but said it was my invention and I would have to be the only author.

We spent several months exchanging emails and discussing the implementation, possible areas of use, and market. Gaylord, as an expert in American diesel engine and oil products, gave me valuable advice. I wrote a draft of the proposal and sent it to Gaylord. He said it was well written but he wrote a new one. He did a marvelous job not only correcting but also on overwriting the full text of the proposal. He was so delicate that in his letter to me, he explained that it was not because my text was written poorly but it was just easier for him to re-write it all over. Surely, the proposal now looked much more persuasive.

I sent my proposal to the company of my choice. The Sales Manager responded me in his email that he thought that I was probably on my way to something big. After that, there were several weeks of correspondence. Finally, I had a telephone conversation with the General Manager; he asked me what royalty I was looking for. I gave him an evasive answer, and then we agreed that I would send him an agreement to sign. I compiled the text using a standard confidentiality agreement form and sent it to them. I was encouraged!

After a few weeks of no response, I understood that they would never get back to me. I did a similar try with another company, and the result was the same. Happily, I am not an inventor who is obsessed that his idea would save the world. The good thing I learned out of it was that I tested how this system works. Unless someone have an invention that a company needs so badly that they are willing to take a financial risk, inventor would fail to sell it.

August 2000, New York.

The learning curve of gaining a new experience has the fastest increment at the beginning and then gradually comes to the exponent. At some point, I wrongly understood my current timeline position on the curve. I had yet to approach to the exponent but mistook it for the final step in my adjustment course. My priority at that point was fast advancing. I had yet to know what a true challenge would mean. It came to me soon.

In a new company (number four), everything went smoothly until it came to a report submission to a client. Here, I must say that I took over a few uncompleted projects. The engineer who worked on the projects and whom I never saw quit the company right before my joining. He had not completed portions of work that I considered as already finished. It was my mistake that I did not go after all his results to double check them. There were omissions and shortages, and the demanding client scrutinized my deliverables for the project. Several months of troubles followed these submissions.

The hardship made my life hellish: I could not sleep, was distressed and discouraged. At the end, the president broke down, her patience snapped, and she called me and said that she was cutting my salary. I knew she was upset but I was saddened. Although it affected me economically, it impacted me even more mentally. In depth, I understood she has the right to do that, but the nettled ambition could not leave me. I started looking for another job; I needed to restore my self-esteem. When I finally found a new job after five long months of search and announced that I was leaving, it was the president's turn to surprise.

I joined a new company after going through sore trials in the preceding company but acquired an invaluable experience. Per the Russian saying: one beaten man is equal to two unbeaten ones. I felt much better.

March 2001, Manhattan

The next company hired me specifically to complete the environmental consulting part of the big construction project. I was busy with this project for about two years with some interruptions. When my work ended, I realized that I might leave with no work. Marina had been laid off about a month ago, we had to pay the mortgage, and I was the only one in my family who worked. Worst comes to worst and soon after my portion of the project finished, the president called me to his office. "We are getting slow. Can you stay home for some time?" he asked me. "Peter, I know we have a few projects for which I am not qualified but can I get some training and do a job?" I asked in my turn. He kept silent. Then I brought up my last weighty argument: it is a bad time for me to be laid off because my wife has been laid off too. He said that he did not know this, and I felt his mind was puzzled. "Okay, I will think what I can do," he said.

Next day, he came up to my cubicle and said that I could stay and get some training for a new project. My job was secured! I kept in mind the decency of the president, the quality that I always respect in people. Next week I started working on a new project and this became my second specialty earned in America. When the opportunity for my normal work was back, I resumed it.

I have done many building surveys throughout the years and now can literally say I have seen New York City from the inside. The capital of the world looks different from the outside. One survey was at a manufacturing facility. A bulletin on the wall announced, "A new theft has recently happened, resulting in the enforcement of security…" I felt that the security department was number one in the facility. Once we came in, I reported to reception the purpose of our visit. The receptionist called the security department and told us to wait.

In about half an hour, a tall, handsome man of about forty years old, the Chief of Security, showed up. He warned us, "No photos allowed in the facility," then called another security person appeared, who accompanied us throughout all areas. What was in the huge shop area surprised me. I saw the run-down interior with hundreds of women assembling products at the tables and conveyers. They looked focused on what they were doing. All these women were immigrants. I unmistakably determined it by the eyes: obedient and fated. It is an alternative to outsourcing: cheap hand labor and minimal spending for repair and maintenance. I intuitively recalled *The Modern Times,* familiar to me from my childhood, Charlie Chaplin movie of the 1930s. The picture I saw was like a hundred-year-old wind of a modern slavery.

Meanwhile, the security chief told me the owner wanted to see us. He took us to a conference hall where we sat on the soft armchairs around the big table. I expected to see a dressed-up gentleman with a million-dollar appearance. In a few minutes, I saw a cheerfully busy bold man talking on his phone while entering the hall. "Are you guys working for the … (company name)?" he said, on finishing his conversation. "No, we work for a different company and do a different type of survey," I told him, "Can we take photographs of the locations of our interest?" "You can take any pictures you want, just don't take photos of the operations." He appeared to be very communicable and smiley.

When we were going to say goodbye, I noted he looked at my business card with my last name and then he said, "zeit gezund" ("Be healthy" in Yiddish). We looked at each other, the invisible bonds tie us. It did not matter whether we belong to different cultures. It was on a sub-conscious level.

SEPTEMBER 11, 2001, NEW YORK

I remember that fine morning, sun, cloudless sky. Summer heat dropped, and nice fall came to New York City. This time of year, the city is especially nice: morning rays illuminate the serene capital of the world and people rush to come to their work offices, somebody carry coffee with croissant, others did their breakfast at home. The day started as always quiet and not promising to be different, finished with the unbelievably big tragedy to planetary scale, which broke the normal course of history.

At the time, I worked on 10th floor of the building at the north side of the Union Square. On my way to work on that day as usual, I took the F Subway line from Avenue P in Brooklyn and in forty-five minutes, I got off from train at 14th Street Station and 6th Avenue in Manhattan at 8:45 AM. In ten minutes, I was approaching the northwest of Union Square where my office was located on the tenth floor. Suddenly, I saw a crowd of people in front of me. They were all looking south. I came up and saw a big fire at the North Tower. I just thought that it was too big for a regular fire. I asked somebody what had happened. He said it was probably a missile. Missile? Why? Suddenly, the passenger airplane hit the South Tower from the center and a huge explosion followed. That was an attack! Now both towers were in flames. In a few minutes, I heard fire engine and ambulance alarms heading to the WTC.

I went up to my office on tenth floor; we turned on the television and saw all channels showing the same picture: The Twin Towers were in fire. Nobody could work, we watched in despair. In about an hour, both towers collapsed with an interval of few minutes. A woman-employee sobbed. I tried to call Marina – she was working at 7th Avenue in midtown – the telephone service was shut off.

About noon, I got down to the street: there was no public transport in-service. Crowds of confused and lost people were walking. I joined one of the flows heading south. I needed to get home somehow. From the WTC site, huge clouds of smoke were coming up and going east to Brooklyn. They were of light gray color and although it was a sunny day, it seemed like evening, as so much smoke was coming up.

Thousands of people continued to walk south towards the WTC. All streets were closed to transportation, except for fire, police, and ambulance. In about an hour, I went out to Delancey Street and from there to Williamsburg Bridge.

That was closest walking way to Brooklyn. At Williamsburg Bridge, two flows of people met: one coming from the north – our flow going from the relatively safe areas of lower Midtown – and another flow coming from the south, the WTC and surrounding areas. The appearances were different: people from the north were tired but clean; those coming from the south looked exhausted and covered with grey ash: dress, hair, hands. Their faces reflected the horrible shock that they were seconds from death. Young women looked like old ones. Men from the Downtown and Wall Street, captains of world finances, wore messy and gray covered business suits and dark gray shirts, instead of white. Apart from those who perished in the rumble just two hours ago, they were alive. They will understand their luck later but for now, they were just shocked.

On the other side of Williamsburg Bridge, the Orthodox Jews offering free water, juices, and snacks met us. I could hardly stop the tears. This is what you call mitzvah. To me, that moment was like unification. A horrible disaster pulled together the American nation.

Next day, thousands of cars put American flags on them. Seeing them was a grief of the huge loss and the hope that people will unite when faced with deadly danger.

A worldwide extremist terrorist group attacked America. This was the beginning of a new era of fight with the world evil. It sprouted as cancer metastases unexpectedly for the rest of the world accumulated a huge stock of hatred to those who do not follow their obscurant statements or live not in accordance with their dogmas on the world order. So much was crucial to be done to surrender that evil!

September 2004, Manhattan, New York.

Three years passed from the day of the national tragedy that changed America forever. That day will be in the souls and hearts of New-Yorkers' as one of the most tragic in modern history.

One of my projects was especially notable. It was the former Douche Bank on Liberty Street in Lower Manhattan to the south of the World Trade Center. I am going to tell you one episode connected to 9/11 that occurred 3 years later in one of my projects. The building was partially damaged when the Northern Tower collapsed. It remained unoccupied from that day, its corridors, rooms, halls kept silenced witnesses of that horrible day. People left it expecting the next aircraft-missile… It was even more stressful to be inside as the building inside kept mute evidences of the terrorist attack. Windows were covered layer of dust. On one of the windows I managed to distinct the words written by a finger where dust did not settle for some reason: *"Help me, I see dead people!"* Probably a person who wrote this observed the happening catastrophe about 300 feet from him or her and desperately made the inscription – may be somebody would read it. In a few minutes, the South Tower collapsed, touched and partially destroyed Douche Bank building from 11th to 24th floor making a gush area. The fortune of the person who wrote on window is unknown, hope he or she survived.

I do not think anybody was able to see these words on one of the windows 42-story building – written three years ago on the glass, it was seen only at the specific angle. It is likely, I was the only one who read it and remembered, therefore, I believe it was addressed to me. Now I address it to you, reader, as one more evidence of the tectonic shift came with new millennia: conflict of the world civilizations. I was a witness of its first stunning strike.

FORMER RUSSIANS, NOT YET AMERICANS

Let's now see how Russian speaking community has formed after a few decades of immigrant years. Speaking about the community I do not mean an organization – people from Russia and former Soviet republics are pretty much disunited. Also, I do not mean just Russians or Russian Jews, the ethnical division here simply impossible. My observations are about all Soviet natives in America.

The acquired values of the Western world through years of immigration experience mixed with Soviet cultural past formed a distinct community of the people associated by only two attributes – native Russian language and the common past. All other qualities are different: from education to attitude towards America and Russia. It is difficult to explain who is typical "Russian" and we will not even attempt to do that. We are going to discuss a few traits of a character of one immigrant community remarkable for their big progress made during just two-three decades after they got "off the boat".

When part of the former Soviet people found themselves in America, I thought all of them, at least first generation, would never reach the level of the American-born people in terms of social status, wealth and other aspects of comfort life. This is understandable: immigration to different world with so dissimilar ethics, aesthetics, traditions, not to say about the language – what social and psychological comfort we can talk? I made a mistake. Russian community faster than other immigrant groups earned decent place under the American sun.

Russian community in the US is as diversified as it was in the Soviet Union. Speaking the same language, people used to live in different regions of the huge country that made them culturally disparate. This especially applies to different attitude of people from Russian provinces and the big cities, or northern and southern areas. Those born and grown up far away from the capital and few other big cities carry a seal of unsophistication: more hard-nosed, down to earth, and heavy footed. Certainly, a place of origin does not guarantee level of civilization but as a rule of thumb, it is more likely that high people's refinement could be observed in the northwestern regions of Russia. Even though the immigration has leveled different natives here in the US, people make friends easier among the compatriots originated from the same areas with an identical subculture.

Another thing I wanted to point out are the surprising sentiments of distancing of many Russian community members toward their compatriots, not someone specifically but as a culture (although, they pal around with their nationals). I think the reason for this phenomenon of dislike comes from the Russian fundamental tradition of giving less respect to the insiders and more to the foreigners. I previously thought this problem was pure Russian but it is not.

Once I had two coworkers in my car – one of Chinese descent and another one who was Pakistani. Suddenly, a small truck cut me off and I had to apply the brakes strongly. My colleague of Chinese descent looked at the truck driver's Asian face and said, "Chinese people are the worst." I was surprised and then asked the Pakistani how he evaluates people from his country. What he said was another surprise for me: "Pakistanis are the nastiest," he told me. *Well, then we are not too bad*, I thought to myself.

It is interesting to analyze the differences between Soviet-Russian immigrants with respect to the political epoch of their arrival. Those who turned up in the 1970s and those in the 1990s have the same history, language, and culture. They all endured the Soviet lie, chronic shortage of food, and a communal misery. Therefore, I think of all Soviet and Russian immigrants of 1970–2000 as a one big wave.

However, there are differences in taking on the new life for those who left Soviet Union in the 1970s – the powerful super-country with the KGB on watch – and those who immigrated in the 1990s. Soviet officials and the public condemned the earlier emigrants at the time they departed. Arriving in America, they felt like people of destiny with no right to return. They left a habituated world and entered a remarkable one, where the modest life in a non-communal apartment, state aid, and food stamps was thought by them to be well off. Sense of the acquired freedom was special. Americans treated them as if they fled from a war theater. The break in immigration from the USSR in the 1980s just underlined the distinction between these two sub-waves.

During the 1990s, few hundreds of thousand immigrants from Russia arrived. Even though the newcomers had the same cultural background with the first group, they nevertheless, differed. First, by the number – at the end of the 1970s, there were little over 170 thousand native Russian speakers in the US and by 2000; over 700 thousand people spoke Russian language at home. Second, Russian officials were not humiliating Jews with the intention for them to leave anymore. Third, at the beginning of the 1990s, Americans were no longer expressing such a strong interest in Russian aliens.

At the time, the huge immigration flow from the impoverished Russia brought many educated and intellectual people, as well as number of the corrupted felons. As opposed to people of the first sub-wave, members of the second one had the possibility of returning home. It made the emigration conceptually reversible. The potential opportunity of going back, although not easy mentally, was a very new game rule.

The relations inside the immigrants, depending upon the time of arrival to America, are also notable. Some of the earlier immigrants of the 1970s look down on their compatriots that entered in the 1990s, calling them the *"sausage immigration"*. The delusion is that whereas the first ones ostensibly immigrated for political reasons, those who immigrated after collapse of the Soviet Union did so for a pure practical reason – *looking for a wealthier life*.

In contrast, Americans look at this differently. Thus, my friend Gaylord, a retired expert from Chevron, wrote in his letter of recommendation about me "... he came here for a better life... with full support of his family." The attitude that stays behind these words is the opposite of what some of my nationals exercise. Generations of immigrants looked for a better life. They left their countries for America for different reasons: political, religious, ethnical, economical, and eventually built this country, as well as a wealthier life for themselves. We have come for the same reasons. Considering the hope for a better life as something shameful is a typical Soviet envious approach. Quality of life in this country was not given to most of us as a grant; instead, we build it up from zero. The equal opportunity was the only granted thing.

I said it was granted to most but not to all of us. Senior-newcomers over fifty-five - sixty years old have minimal chances to start working other than as stock workers, home attendants, or babysitters. They may be in a good physical and mental shape but due to their limited ability to learn and communicate, they have little opportunity to find a job as professionals. The rare exclusions are those with leading positions in science – a few lucky ones continue with the same research work they did in their former country. I sympathize with the people who are only fifty-five to sixty years old, still healthy but unemployed. All their professional motion has been in the past.

I heard this story from my friends, a couple of Russian immigrants. Once upon a time, there lived twin sisters: Russian Jewish girls Ann and Clara. They both were eighteen and just about to enter real life. It is necessary to mention they lived in the USSR and it was 1935. As many Soviet Jews, they had a relative in the US. In the early 1930s, when the Soviet government claimed an extensive course for industrialization, many American engineers and managers came to work in the Soviet industrial objects. Their uncle (let's call him Uncle Samuel) was one of them. He lived and worked temporarily in Moscow with his family and had the pleasure to meet with his relatives.

The year 1935 was the time before the big purge of 1937–38 repressions and NKVD (Stalin's secret police) had become even more suspicious of all foreigners and people who kept contact with them. Therefore, Samuel was going to leave the country as soon as possible. As a good relative, he wanted to take these twin sisters with him to the US. It is not possible to retell all the details of his departure but it turned out that he could take only one of his nieces, Ann, not both. Given the condition to leave urgently, he could not hold onto the second twin Clara. Thus, Ann found herself in the US, and she studied and then occupied administrative positions in different companies while Clara remained in the Soviet Union, studied, and worked as a teacher at school. They grew up in opposite political and social systems. They did not see each other over 50 years until 1991. The family of the "Soviet" sister finally immigrated to the US. The sisters were over seventy when they finally met. They both were retirees. Each one had her own different life experience.

Life carried out a unique social experiment: two genetically similar individuals lived their whole lives in different environments over half of century and then after fifty-six years, they rejoined. I am sure their meeting was touching. The sisters had much to talk about. The American sister helped her Soviet twin to accustom to her new life. However, what the American twin did not understand was why her benefits was lower after she finished her almost fifty years' career than all the government aid her sister obtained on entering the country. The question has no answer.

Notwithstanding the benefits senior people obtain, the old men playing cards or chess on the Brighton benches or women whose communication skills are now useless undergo a cultural crisis. They praise America but feel inferior outside the community. Going through the crisis may last for decades and even for the entire life for seniors.

R. Cohn emphasizes that in general, Russian immigrants comprise the best-educated group in the U.S. immigration history. Some 75% of them completed higher education, whereas only 23% of all other groups of immigrants in 1991–1998 had occupations that required the higher education, such as professionals, technical managers, and officials that reflected certain education. That provided success in the highest-paying professions and a high-level of overall satisfaction. (R. Cohn. *Immigration to the United States.* Illinois State University, posted 2010-02-01, http://eh.net/enciclopedia/article/cohn.immigration.us).

The "secret" is simple: Jewish and Russian immigrants mostly belong to the intelligentsia with clear ambition to education, intellectual work, and professional advancement.

Incorporation into a job market is still not cultural integration, and the latter is the most difficult. No wonder people prefer to live within the communities that are the model of civilizations.

The Russian Jewish community is especially anti-socialist. They all had been vaccinated by the real Soviet socialism, which affected the political views of generations born before 1970s and who lived in this distorting mirror kingdom. Therefore, the community is politicized.

This is where most of the Russian-speaking immigrants' political standpoints come from. For a substantial portion of their life, they had lived in a society where regular people had no rights: no real election, no freedom of meetings, press, or opinions. I do not say everyone suffered it much: if a child was born behind the bar, he does not realize there might be another life. A few dissidents protested. Other people just complied with the system, even against their will. The real choice for political preferences has come only in America, a few years after settling in this country. It came through the paradox that I am going to discuss.

The political preferences of the immigrants from Russia are based on their past Soviet experience. Many of them are drifting to right. Many make out as conservative and are more inclined to vote for Republican candidates because of their stronger support of Israel, tough position against terrorism, and less dependency on the government aid. However, in such humankind areas as adherence to religion or women's right for abortions, stem cells research, or possession of guns, even the senior community members prefer a liberal approach. Political partiality is often generation related: many young people support the Democrats, whereas the older ones are more inclined to the Republicans. As young people get older and wealthier, they often gradually become more conservative.

To continue the subject with political affiliation, I did my evaluation through communication with many of my tribal friends, acquaintances, and social contacts on political topics like the role of the US, Russia, or Israel in modern world. This is what my non-scientific observations show within the Russian community:

On the US politics in modern world – most of Russian Jews are pro-American,

On Russia's politics in modern world – only a few of them evaluate it positively; the majority thinks of it negatively,

On Israeli politics in modern world – the majority are pro-Israeli,

On the Democratic and Republican Parties agenda – the majority is pro-Republican and only some are pro-Democratic (does not refer to the young members, mostly liberals).

People of the community are inclined to vote pro-American and pro-Israeli, and this is not a surprise for me. Russian Jews living in America vote in favor of the US not just because it is now a home country for them. Living here, they gained something they never had in the past: respect to human dignity, life, and property. The Russian government and population have traditionally neglected these values. This cause has made Russian immigrants love America. Pro-Israeli feelings are because of the ethnical adherence and the Israeli devotion to democratic values as the only democracy in the Middle East. In addition, many of them have relatives living in Israel.

On Russia's role in the modern world, the country has not been considered a democracy but rather an authoritarian state oligarchy, and its foreign policy is the standoff against the US. Russia's policy towards the former Soviet republics resulted in spoiled relations with nearly all of them. Bad remembrances from our past seem even more intolerable looking back from across the ocean.

For Russian immigrants of any ethnic origin, visiting their country is an adventure but the returning for good… not discussing! What an anti-shot did the state give to its children that almost none of them out of millions wish to go back!

Support of the Republican Party's agenda by the community members (especially from the people over forty) needs to be understood. Further, there is an opinion within the immigrant communities (other than Russians), that if you are an immigrant, you are Democrat by default. It might be correct for any but the Russian street residents.

Several reasons put so many Russian Americans to the right side of the US political specter. The *first obvious reason* is since we suffered the radical left Soviet socialism, we do not like any lefts, including Democrats and their agenda. The impartial evidence in favor of this reason: Cuban Americans in Florida who used to suffer the leftist dictatorship of Fidel Castro are also inclined to conservatism and voted predominantly for Trump in 2016 and the Republican nominee Mitt Romney in 2012 presidential elections. However, the trend is not always right for the young Russian immigrants who did not experience the Soviet regime and may have various, sometimes leftist political inclinations.

The *second reason* is a concept of political correctness as one of the important issues of the Democratic agenda. What I mean is the extreme form of political correctness may lead from securing the rights of minorities to damaging the rights of the majority. Not having exercised political tolerance, many Russian immigrants hate "political correctness". That is understandable because often this correctness becomes ugly and creates conditions that provoke hiding the truth and unequal opportunities for everyone. We will come back to it little later.

Having seen these two marginal approaches to the relationship between majority and minorities – suppressing the minority in the Soviet past and giving legal preferences to them in the American present – most of the Russia-town residents do not support either of them. That eventually leads them to certain choice of not supporting the political correctness, a movement that is now tightly associated with the lefts. That is possibly the reason why they look like hard liners in the eyes of many Americans.

The *third reason* for the conservative political preferences of the immigrants from Russia is their... successfulness. It is because of their ability to work hard, have good career advancements, and achieve relatively high living standards for themselves and their families. In just a short time, the majority of them have become fully independent of government help and take personal responsibility for themselves.

Let me make it clear. Financial crises have originated from the crash of the real estate market. We can blame banks for giving out the unfounded credits for homes, but I doubt people who borrow to buy unaffordable dwellings and then could not pay their mortgage used much common sense. Those who bought it for their residency had to calculate the affordability within the considerations of the lifestyle they wanted to maintain. Those who bought it for business purposes and then failed with selling or giving for rent should have realized all the possible risks. Anyway, this is all about the responsibility of people for their families, not about fairness or helping poor people.

In the former Soviet Union, government assistance did not exist, so everybody counted on himself or herself. Russians brought this philosophy of economic independency from the government to the US and it helped them to build their well-being.

The *fourth reason* is in the traditionally better American relations with Israel during the Republican administration compared with the Democratic one. We can more easily find Republican Party supporters among the Christian religious conservatives. American Jews traditionally vote for Democrats because they believe the Democratic platform is closer to the concept of Judaism than the Republican one. On the other hand, Republicans call for more support to Israel. The paradox with the American Jews predominantly supporting Democrats, in my view is possibly in the specifically interpreted Judaic tradition of cooperation and communality. American Jews understand it as more donations and support coming from the wealthy to the poor people, which is consistent with the Democratic platform. As opposed to them, for many Russian Jews, the Republican individualistic tradition takes precedence, although religious values do not play an important role for Russians. That is what makes this community politically unique as being both secular and conservative.

The other reason of this paradox is that some of American Jews do not associate themselves with Israel. A few even consider it as "a non-legitimate state." I personally know a Jewish American man who thinks this way. To have opposite views on the plain matters is also in the Jewish tradition. Some even incline to perform harm to selves to appease others. Otherwise, how do you explain the fact that few American Jews joined the anti-Israeli flotilla to support Gazans. That is not the Russian Jewish case in America and in Israel. Most of the Russian Jews root for the Jewish state not only because of relatives living there but also through a comprehension of what it means to be a Jew. Such is the outlook of many of the community members and a source of political preference.

Russian Jews in America have gained new experience and integrated to a mutative job market. They are Russians in America but Jews in Russia. They left Russia but keep a Russian mind. They never practiced the Jewish tradition but identify selves as Jews. They have yet to assimilate into the American mainstream but formally considered as a majority. What a thought-provoking destiny!

THE COUNTRY I DO NOT WANT TO LOSE

The United States as a country has been originated on political, social, economic experience for which Europe spent over a thousand years to acquire. Adjective *the most* is still often heard in America. Impressive scientific achievements, number one world economy the most powerful military, widely known and watched movies, novels of the great American writers, arts, the most advanced information technology and many-many more – all these built its unique image.

Even though western civilization and culture came from Europe, everyone knows that the bastion of this civilization is the United States. The cultural environment does not stay the same. During a few decades, America is gradually becoming a country where the diversity of cultures now starts to dominate over the mainstream culture, especially in the big cities. It is not a good or bad change, it is just given by the provision that this is a country of immigrants. It has been especially notable during the last decades. Few grounds change the American culture.

The first reason is that a greater number of people are now coming from different continents, whereas a century ago, Europe was the land of origin for most immigrants whose culture had much more in common with the American one.

The immigration statistics of 1991–1998 show that 31% of new immigrants are from Asia, 25% from Mexico, 24% from another America, and only 9% are from Central and Eastern Europe with almost zero from Western Europe. The US is not mainly white and black anymore as it was forty to fifty years ago. The average yearly number of legal newcomers is now over one million. With decades of millions of newcomers during last two centuries, the country has changed its ethnical division drastically. Cultural differences between the mainstream and newcomers is becoming more distinctive.

The second reason is the means of communication and transport. A hundred years ago, once a family crossed the ocean and found itself in America, the communication with relatives and friends living in the country of origin was problematic: letters waited for months, not to say about visits. Now relatively frequent visits to former countries of residency, communication by electronic mail, Skype, Facebook, and technical ability to watch other countries' national television programs, make it much easier to adhere to the original culture.

The third reason is globalization, especially during the last decades. Before the collapse of the close-minded communism and globalization era, the differences in consumers' markets in the Western and Third World countries were drastic. However, during the last fifteen to twenty years, the regional economies have integrated to the Western means of communication, transport, and trade. This resulted in an enormous filling of the world market with state-of-the-art technology and goods like automobiles, computer and electronic and gadgets, and clothes. Globalization and open markets are changing the world.

There is one more reason, the *fourth one*: people now love personal distinctiveness more than ever. Just fifty years ago, the American style was a role model for many nations; millions of people were attracted by the American free elegance of behavior, its music, or literature – recall *stilyagi* (hipsters in the USSR of the 1950s and 1960s). Nowadays it is different: not many immigrants change their original names to sound more American. On the contrary, most of them feel proud to be born in another country and still adhere to their culture.

The early cultural principles in the US developed on the moral beliefs of Anglo-Saxon Protestantism. S. Huntington pointed out that most of the carriers of this culture were seen as prudish, law-abiding, straightforward, and individualistic people, polite and friendly, with a clear understanding of what is right and wrong. (Samuel P. Huntington. *Who Are We? The Challenges to America's National Identity*, Simon & Shuster, New York-London-Toronto-Sydney. p.69).

This culture was being absorbed by the peoples coming to America from other continents carrying other cultures, and it eventually became a culture of the American mainstream. Within this culture, the individual's rights are essential. Greater respect to an individual affects other spheres of human activities. In engineering, it is more human- oriented design; in public offices, it is a better-organized order to serve visitors faster; in business, it is more honesty and respect to a partner and friendly environment.

In the past, as S. Huntington noted, immigrants generally wanted to be Americans. The state of affairs changed substantially in modern time. Now we can see the opposite trend: some of the immigrants, while trying to preserve their culture, are not willing to assimilate into the American mainstream. That makes America less homogeneous about cultural identity than fifty years ago.

Cultural disparities on different continents are vast. What considered to be normal in one society, may not be acceptable in another. At times, the American culture appear to be incomprehensible for the Russian mentality. For instance, I used to be surprised seeing a young American guy sitting in the overcrowded subway train not yielding his seat to an old or woman with a kid. In Russian culture, that would have considered impolite. This is an example of extreme individualism. On the other hand, sometimes Russian culture shows the experience, which is incomprehensive for the American people. Take for example, the Moscow or St. Petersburg entraining into a subway train during rush hour when crowds of people enter a train and compare this with the same rush hour in New York City subway. Just for comparison, let us imagine a sluggish person enters a train with crowd of other people and he or she does not rush to move deeper inside a train. In the Russian train, a high-voltage crowd pushes so extensively that there is little chance to stay intact. In the American train, I have not seen people pushing the sluggish person to advance inside the train. The result is the same: both trains move to the next stop taking all passengers. The respect is different. Americans respect the individual's right not to be physically pushed, all it takes just extra ten seconds of entraining. These are only two illustrations showing how different Russian and American cultures are. Any culture understands respect in its own way.

At the time of my arrival in the mid-1990s, America was a country-winner of the longtime Cold War and short but effective Gulf War. The longtime "cold enemy" Soviet Union was prostrated, and the first Russian government was busy with its own major problems on how to feed their people. The world merchant and super competitor in the face of China had yet to emerge on its full scale. For the US, China of the 1990s was still a developing country, where no real economic or political threat was coming from. Still many goods had a label *Made in USA* and the American job market was as huge as never before. There was little or no national debt and no financial deficit.

From time to time, some annoying signals came out from the rogue countries like North Korea, Iraq, and few African countries but no global threats seemed to exist in world regions. Iran, just a third-rate country, was not known yet as the country aspiring to become a nuclear power. America did not lead any foreign war, and the world was truly one-polar with the US domination in any area: politics, economy, ideology, and security. Terrorism was not among the first five concerns. I remember the popular hit of the time having the words, *I don't care who you are, where you from as long as you love me.* The wording is indicative and reflects the atmosphere of mollification in people's mind. The Western world thought this idyllic picture would last forever.

America did not consider seriously any terrorist threat even with the USS Cole explosion, the bombing of the American Embassy in Zambia, and the first WTC terror campaign having already happened. The government and people believed they were safe. They believed in what they wanted to believe: we are the richest, strongest, fairest, most prosperous, safest, and least vulnerable country. This serene feeling created a complex of superiority and the immunity of any threat.

A seismic change occurred after the 9/11 tragedy. Religious fanatic and terrorists attempted American lives, values, and the way of thinking. The epoch of complacency ended. It was as if the American society sobered up after decades of carelessness based on the feeling that we are safe since we were divided by the ocean from the violent world. The big announcement at the runway entrance to JFK Airport: *Welcome to JFK Airport where America Greets the World* soon after the terrorist attack was replaced with something like *JFK Airport is the Gate to America*. Taken separately without connection to 9/11, it might be considered as a normal change of greeting for the different one. However, in the light of the increased suspicion, the change was meaningful: America is no longer greets anyone.

After 9/11, other terrorist attacks – in Boston marathon, in military base Fort Hood, killings in San-Bernardino, Orlando, etc. – trust and openness from common Americans got undermined. Instinctively, many began suspecting the people of certain faith in possible preparation for illegal activity. "If you see something say something" is now posted anywhere in railway stations, subway, roadways, and public offices. You could conjure all day long that just some bad people do bad things, but it would not come closer to truth in terms of who is responsible for terrorist acts in the name of the faith. Blaming all Muslims is not fair but switching it to some abstract haters is an extreme grade of political correctness, which is between hypocrisy and absurd. To rid of metastases of terrorism, people of Muslim culture should play more important role in rooting out of that infamous activities initiated by some fundamentalists within their culture. Radical Islamism must be condemned by Muslims. Even if terrorists are destroyed from drones and aircrafts, these remedies are powerless of terrorist-loners.

By 2010s, a few other countries like economically powerful China and re-militarized Russia showed up as powers claiming as new world poles of influence representing political challenge to American leadership. These new poles want more significant role for themselves than before. From one side this is understandable: in the regions where these big countries located, they care about their interests. The question is what political vector may be imposed by the new poles of influence to smaller countries in the regions? The multi-polar world adds much of uncertainties to the world order these center of influence countries would always balance on the edge of big or small military conflict as having too opposite political interests. Would a single-polar world with one country as a gendarme to others be better? Good if it is a responsible democracy but what if it is autocracy and all solutions are up to one man? Then the world order might be adjusted to this one-man justice.

In the variety of cultures and races, United States represent the ethnical world model. In one of the companies I worked, fifty people represented natives from 18 countries from all continents. A role model for all countries! The company was successful, all people had good business and personal relations. Few times a year all got together: in summer we had picnic and for Christmas we had party at a restaurant. On the day before Thanksgiving, all made potluck. That is an example of the real "melting pot" in this country when people of different cultural background cooperate. This was possible because having a huge cultural difference, people integrated under the cohesive and attractive American culture, i.e. Anglo-Saxon's culture with its certain work ethics and welcoming relations between individuals.

As a country of immigrants, America is more tolerant than other countries to aliens. Not always was like this. The Protestant culture no doubt was foundational in forming the American nation. In nineteenth century, American Anglo-Saxons were wary towards Irish immigrants and then to originals from Italy, Germany, European Jews but by the end of that century all these comprised backbone of US population. Starting from 1970s a growing rate of immigrants from Latin America, China, India and Africa have been coming. Political correctness is not always biased, it often helps alleviate inter-racial and inter-cultural nuisances. It just does not have to go too far.

Racism and its counterweight political correctness is a difficult subject. Superficially, if racism is bad, then political correctness is good. Yes, but that is not the whole story. White racism is disgusting and, it has been so much condemned during last decades. While it still exists mostly as an implicit prejudice, it is not an open hostility as it was long ago. Shelby Steele, a black conservative columnist, film maker and lecturer at Stanford University noted that it is not white racism killed four thousand people in 2017 in Chicago. America has repented, recoiled, and has now zero tolerance for white racism but still there are many accusers. Police is easy prey for these accusers because its job related to compulsion, protection and self-defense. Any clash between a white cop and a black man tends to be considered as having a racial background. This theme is closely associated with an issue of political correctness.

The term "political correctness" was adopted by the New Lefts (in contrast with the "Old" Lefts, whose ideas were close to Marxists) in the 1970s and then widely spread in Western usage by the 1990s.

Defined by Wikipedia, political correctness

> "… is a term, which denotes language, ideas, policies, and behavior seen as seeking to minimize social and institutional offense in occupational, gender, racial, cultural, sexual orientation, certain other religions, beliefs or ideologies, disability, and age-related contexts."

In other words, no one who differs by any identity from any mainstream should be offended based on his or her difference. After 1917, the suppressed minorities were noblemen, Jews (again in the 1940s and on), religious believers, intelligentsia, dissidents, homosexuals, etc. What we have seen in the US of the last decades is another extremity: the minorities have legal advantages over the majority. The political correctness often goes far beyond the common sense and evolves to its contrary. The divergence is so confounding that it calls upon a protest. No, I never come back to the ideas of suppressing the minorities, nor do I accept giving advantages to them on the account of others; I just support equal opportunity for everyone.

Had I known while living in Soviet Union about such a notion as a political correctness, which aims to protect different minorities from persecution by a majority, I would have applauded it. Jews were unwanted minority over there and they would have been happy under any protection from their civil rights pinching. Through centuries, minorities in Russia persecuted. Before 1917, the old believers, Jews, non-conformists, revolutionaries; after 1917, former noble men and women, merchants, all former owners, Jews (from 1940s), believers, dissidents, homosexuals were maltreated and oppressed. What we see in the US last decades is the opposite extreme: the minorities have legal advantages over the rest. Justified movement for political correctness turned out to be a contrary – pinching of a majority for their non-existing fault. Hey, this is anti-Americanism in America! Can we provide just equal starting opportunities without all these excesses?

Nonetheless, political correctness is necessary within reasonable limits. Non-politically correct truth for a few representatives of one minority group can be lie for all people of this minority. For example, it is truth that all radical Islamic terrorists are Muslims, but it is lie that all Muslims are terrorists. Telling the truth about a few, we unjustifiably spread it to all minority. Just because of this, political correctness is necessary. However, it should not hide the real things behind a sweet lie and have blind eyes to any unethical or criminal behavior of people from any minority. We can see it too often.

We got used to traditional political inclinations on one side for less dependency on the government and less taxes, and on the other side, for more government help and collection more taxes from wealthy people. Those are everlasting political priorities of each side. During the time of the US existence, free entrepreneurship opened the unrestricted and great opportunities for business, which made America great. However, when I hear from the ultra-lefts that these taxes should be increased to 60-70% from the rich, I am thinking of possible transforming the United States to a South American type of country seduced by the socialism and then suffered from its consequences.

America is getting more polarized on the political spectrum: the lefts become leftists, and the rights become ultra-conservatives. From the initial groups of citizens with some philosophical differences, Republican and Democratic parties have transformed to two hostile and fundamentally unreconciled camps. For old America it was incredible: the left socialist Bernie Sanders during a few months of 2016 campaign had evolved from the unknown senator to a high-rated presidential candidate. Listened to progressive democrats, an unbiased someone may think the oppressed people speak out against the oppressors, i.e. the Republicans. On the other hand, previously, it was also impossible that someone denying political correctness and claiming isolationism, becomes the President of the US. Opposite parties come to be enemies. Why is that happening? This is my subjective view:

First, too many people on the conservative side have accumulated anger during the past presidential terms: for recession of 2008-2010, for loss of millions of jobs, for indecisiveness and weakness in the international politics, for treason of loyal to America regimes in the Middle East, for the not affordable for middle class "Affordable Care Act" (medical insurance reform), etc. These people made Trump president in 1916 and supported him later.

On the other hand, many people on the liberal side simply hate President Trump. No matter what he speaks or does, all is wrong for them. They just cannot take his personality. Trump's position to the right from traditional Republicans has changed the Republican Party: the majority moved to the right and only a few senators and House Representatives show disagreements with his actions. So, good or bad but personal rather than political qualities of the President made input into this political polarization.

Second, many fresh and young left activists including elected officials on the local, state and federal levels do not like traditional American values: least dependence from any government, reliefs of entrepreneurship including fiscal, reliance on your own abilities and competences, personal responsibility for someone's quality of life, etc. They bring up a defensive ideology of the "oppressed" people, which are only able to demand for themselves but not provide to others. That kind of culture did not characterize American values before. Furthermore, America is still great just because American people have never embraced socialism, which is so loved by these progressive lefts. Their proletarian fight and hatred towards conservatives, traditional principles, rich people, as well as to Israel and Jews is so aggressive that now also becomes a concern for the moderate Democrats.

Third, the progressively increasing immigration from different countries including those where anti-American culture has been explicitly expressed and supported by the grassroots. Some categories of immigrants predominantly support left activists with their "take away from the rich and give out to poor" agenda. As the far-left New York City Mayor DeBlasio once noted, there are plenty of money in the country, they are just in wrong hands! Was it a call to take this money away and share? I have seen this in my country of origin – the way to nowhere! Regretfully, but I see fewer of the *moderate* Democrats and Republicans. The borderline between them increases transforming a once united nation to hating each other groups.

Two milestone concepts concurrently made the modern America: the robust protestant culture and ethics inherited from the first Anglo-Saxon settlers and further represented by the founders and the constitution they created, let's call it the umbrella; and the variety of cultures represented by immigrants from all over the world, let's call it the diversity. Taken separately, these models, the umbrella (mono-culture) and the diversity (multi-culture) show two extremes. Together, this is a combination provided boosted development of the country through the right work ethics, entrepreneurship, aspirations of newcomers and enormous opportunities for anyone. This fusion has made America great. If either of the extreme takes over, America may lose its exceptionalism and stop being great.

I hope that most of Americans will realize potential threat of political hostility bringing aloofness to our society that may put it at the edge of civil standoff. I am very concerned about the inclination to the socialist ideas in America especially among many of the millennials. We had left it behind in the collapsed Soviet Union and do not want it to happen again – too much grief and distress! I also do not want to lose the uniqueness, greatness and exceptionality of America, the country I love. The country, which is adored by some and hated by others for the same qualities.

7
Jewish Identity and Loyalty

The key is not in the origin, not in blood, not in genes but what pain is closer to your heart: Jewish or the dominating nation's you grew up with.

Alexander Solzhenitsyn

Identity is the most powerful, though susceptible factor in human's mind, which controls the motivations. It determines adherence to a certain group, for example football fans possess identity of a certain football club followers. The stronger perception of identity, the more expressive human's spiritual activity. Just think about the Russians and Ukrainians, two brotherly peoples of similar culture with sense of different national belongings. The firsts say: join us, be like us. The seconds say we do not want to be like you, nor do we want to join you. The argue resulted in the factual identity war with thousands of victims. Same grave problems occurred with Britons – Northern Irelanders, Serbs – Kosovans, Spaniards – Basks, Spaniards – Catalonians, and many other neighboring peoples through the history. Depending on which side you are, those wars were named either the war for independence or the separatist war.

Identity in the immigrant's communities is a different game: you are the novice and you need to adjust yourself to the new environment, otherwise you are isolated and excluded from the normal social life. The problem comes if someone's mind cannot integrate into the mainstream culture.

IDENTITY CRISIS

It is up to everyone to self-identify – you are who you feel you are. I cannot think of a normal person who has never asked self who I am. This sensitive sphere of the cultural identity is in core of everyone's mind. Ordinarily, *national* and *cultural* identities go along with one another. But what if they do not? That was the case for the Soviet Jews. This controversy was specifically Jewish problem in that country.

As you are a newcomer in a new country, after a few weeks of surprises and charms, difficult times come. It is not a disappointment, but rather sobering and feeling that your native culture and habits at times come to disharmony with the local ones. It is hard to find your place, your job and get used to new order. In these circumstances you become a philosopher, ask yourself difficult questions to which you cannot not find answers: why I am here? How would my life come about? Well, years go after years, you are established, understood and accepted new game rules but philosophical quest on the self-identity is still not clear. After decades in Soviet realities as a Jew, then after decades in America as a Russian immigrant, it becomes a puzzle to identify yourself: who am I now? Russian? Jewish? American? A combination of different cultures in one person causes identity confusion. The question is what is my identity if I alienated from all these mainstreams? My mind splits my cultural identity between three great civilizations: Eastern, Judaic, and Western but links them at the same time. Reflections on this matter have been keeping me on the hop.

Previously, the identity issue interested Russian Jews only as an ethnical pain as objects for anti-Semitism. Their identity is now trifurcated. They are Russians as the carriers of culture and language, Jews by the blood, ancestry, and mind, and Americans by the country where they live and to which they keep loyalty. These three identities compete for precedence. Some people have room for all three I's in the character; other ones just pick one or two that is closer to their heart. Anyway, immigrants of the last wave feel perplexed about their identity.

All previous immigrants wanted to liberate from their past and desired to become Americans sooner. The last wave is different, and I attempt to understand the essence and character of the recent (and not so recent) immigrants from Russia, and figure how their dissimilar past and present affect them culturally. Not only the country influences immigrants but they also affect the country.

At this point, many immigrants do not want to assimilate. Besides, the assimilation expects partial or full losing of the original identity. To preserve it fully or partially, another choice will be integration to a new society without sacrificing cultural and habitual features. This is also correct in terms of the Jewish self-consciousness. The author of *Judaism as a Civilization* Mordecai Kaplan argues,

> "As soon as a people lose its distinctive customs and folkways, its civilization begins to disintegrate. Customs, by their very nature, tend to retain their form long after the original meaning is outlived, and as long as they can bear new interpretation, it is proper that they should be retained.... Thus, also have the Jewish people maintained its historical continuity."

In the Soviet Union, the ethnicity was scripted in the passport, and the state evaluated people based on this record. Came to the US, Russian Jews were surprised how differently they are identified by the local people. In the eyes of Americans, their affiliation is now Russian because of the first language spoken. The American Jews, both religious and secular are far from them culturally even though their great-grandparents possibly lived in the same Pale of Settlement.

Russian Jews had a troubled identity in Russia and brought it to America. A Jew in Russia has the ethnical notion rather than religious or cultural one. Having distanced from the religion during decades and adhered to Russian culture, Jews nonetheless, remained Jews by their record in the Soviet passport and street opinion. We all try to understand who we are at some point, and the answer depends on the circumstances. If a Russian Jew is suppressed, suffers restrictions, or persecuted as a cosmopolitan, or limited in the acceptance to universities, or rejected for job promotion, he/she feels miserable as a second-rate person. If not suppressed, he takes the lead as a lawyer, moneymaker, engineer, medical doctor, politician, or a scientist. Culturally, he has a double affiliation: Russian and Jewish. On one hand, his language, mind, and habits are Russian. On the other hand, something barely visible in his appearance and mind but clearly distinguished is Jewish. The normal practice among Soviet Jews was not to highlight their Jewishness to avoid possible outpouring of anti-Semitism.

As opposed to this, American Jews have never hidden their ethnical belonging. Russian Jews found in the US a good feeling of not shy to be Jewish. Besides, after years spent in the US, they get their third affiliation: the Americans. At that, the third identity does not rupture their souls as the first two did in Russia. Their ethnical association here in America is now neither visible, nor distinguished but normally respected.

In the US, if you say I am a Jew, everyone thinks you practice Jewish traditions. In a country where the Jews live (other than Israel), their consciousness splits. They simultaneously carry the culture of the society where they born, where they now live, and the Jewish culture. The ratio between these three parts varies depending on the scale of absorption – from full assimilation to cultural isolation. For the people with more than one cultural background, self-identification is an intimate process, for which an individual answer a few questions of self.

    I see two ways of thinking. The first way is based on the *mind and qualities* of the person. For example, born and lived for decades in the Soviet Union, the country where all Jewish related attributes suppressed, I grew up with divided state of mind. Externally, the Russian attitude prevailed but internally, I felt my Jewishness. It was not because I had to show my loyalty to the dominant culture but because of a call from my mind. Even though I am pleased to be among Jewish people, I speak neither Yiddish, nor Hebrew, and I am secular. In addition, I read Russian writers, learned Russian history and arts in school as mandatory subjects, and had Russian coworkers and friends. That means that my Russian part still dominates in my state of mind even after so many active years in America. In short, this way of self-identification assumes the honest answer the question of *who you are*.

    The second way of thinking is based on the *attractiveness*. If the qualities of one culture – history, traditions, and way of life – are more attractive to someone than the qualities of another culture, there is a better chance that this person would self-associate with the more desirable culture. The ordinary behavior and people's state of mind reveals the attractiveness or unattractiveness and motivates someone to make a choice to which culture he/she personally prefers to adhere. For example, a first time-met person is good, unless he has proved he is bad is a typical American style – communicable and gentle – which makes the American cultural approach attractive to many people. In Russian cultural tradition, there has been unfriendliness towards the unknown individual. Both behaviors have historical roots. This way of self-identification assumes answers the question of *who you want to be* rather than *who you are*.

Those are the rational features of attractiveness; however, there may be irrationality in our likings. It is when you stick to the country or society not for the certain objective reasons but despite them. One cannot explain it logically, just emotionally.

Famous Russian filmmaker Andrey Konchalovsky once said, "I love Russia; I just do not like her." This statement is not controversial but explains what many Russians think about their country. They love it as a motherland, love the nature, great literature, music, and hospitality – anything exposed to the external world. At the same time, they do not like it because of the way people treat one another, for the boorishness, for blaming others for the low quality of life, for the low merit of human life.

My early thoughts upon coming to America were how to assimilate into the mainstream as soon as possible. To make it happen, I insisted that all in my family spoke English with one another. The idea failed because Marina and I felt limited in the expression of what wife and husband needed to say to each other. Our children were interested in talking English to their peers rather than to their parents. We went back to the Russian and dropped the idea of the accelerated absorption.

By the ability to integrate immigrants of the middle age can be divided by three types (I am not considering people of the younger age because they easily adjust and integrate to any new environment as well as the seniors who do not integrate due to age constrains):

First type is the people who keep up all their views, habits and the way of life intact. They tend to self-isolate within their cultural ghetto. They are possibly disappointed with their new being due to different reasons – unsatisfied with a job or no job, new family problems came with immigration: for instance, wife became a bread-winner and husband feels miserable. They live with their past having nostalgic memories on how successful and respected they were and how despondent they are now. Years passing by, and the bad feelings just getting stronger. They just overestimated their expectations.

Second type is the immigrants struggling to get rid of anything related to their former country. They want to unnaturally accentuate that their American basis has nothing to do with the former culture. They try to change the old practices and stances in favor of dominant new ones. The faster they make this change, the more difficult for them to stay in their own shoes and, furthermore, the more ridiculous their conduct.

Others, the majority, comprise the *third type* that occupies the rest of the immigrants' spectrum. They may agree or disagree on different aspects of new culture and feel bifurcated in terms of national affiliation. This is a crisis that almost all immigrants go through their first years.

Cultural assimilation is a process of buildup from the culture of minority to the culture of majority that eventually affects the identity. I do not believe assimilation can happen in the brain and soul of the middle age newcomers even after twenty or thirty years from the arrival. One can acquire some habits, behavior, work ethics, and accented language but not the way of thinking. Then the next generation slides into the culture of majority. It does not matter who your parents were, you are an insider if you fluently speak and behave as most Americans.

It is very natural that humans are interested to know how their ethnicity, nation, and community are interrelated in the mind. That gives an idea of how tight different upbringings can bind up in one person. Self-identification has something to do with the place of birth and race, and everything to do with the culture and mind. I had a coworker in Russia who was a Jew and had Jewish name. However, he did not think about himself as a Jew, nor did he appreciate anything related to Jewish. He just self-identified as an ethnical Russian. "You are not Russian in the eyes of the Russian guys and will never be because your last name Rosenblum would never be considered Russian. However, you cannot be a real Jew since you do not see yourself a Jew. Hence, you are going to suffer not feeling the reason", I responded to him when we discussed the issue.

Some art activists of Jewish descent in Russia nowadays have accepted Russian Orthodoxy and attended church services. They did it for the same reason that my former coworker did. This is strictly a personal choice. Identity switch does not mean anything in terms of people's treatment, except that people of different ethnical or racial identity must always keep in mind not to emphasize the differences in humans of another identity because it may sound offensive. That must be the one and only point of political correctness.

Ethnical belonging is unchangeable because it has to do with parentage and ancestry. The national identifier is changeable. If someone moves and then naturalizes in another country, he may change his national adherence if he wills to do so. Whether the cultural identifier is changeable is a subject with a big question mark.

Every teen asks him or herself *who I am* and how *can I identify myself*. These questions are not just for curiosity but demonstrate normal interest in understanding what group of people he belongs to. Language, family, and friends, as well as traditions, outlook, and life style, are all items that frame the culture that affects the young people's choice of identity.

Psychologist Erik Erikson developed theory of the personal identity (*Identity: Youth and Crisis*. W.W. Norton & Company, New York, 1968). He studied human development extending over the entire lifespan. According to Erikson, there are eight stages of psychological conflicts inside the personality. The fifth stage Erikson named "fidelity" is *identity versus role confusion.* Questions arise at the adolescent period, when a teen asks self who am I, how do I fit in, and where am I going in life? Erikson believes that if a teenager does not feel pressure from his parents, he would think independently, explore, and find his/her own identity. New immigrants if they do not isolate themselves within ghetto may feel like the teens looking for their new role in the society. *The identity crisis comes up when you are confused of what culture is more closely associated with you.*

To learn what other people of my circle think on their identity, I did my own little social experiment. At the end of every December, our relatives and friends get together in my New Jersey house to celebrate X-nukah, as we call it (mixed abbreviation of Christmas and Hanukah). At the time, about two dozen people came over, and I thought it was a good chance for me to ask how everybody self-identifies. I gave everyone (except little kids) an anonymous written question: *Who do you think you are: Russian ____%; Jewish____%; American____%. Please note it has nothing to do with your blood. You are who you feel you are.* Everyone, depending on what he/she feels, was free to pick or split his/her identity.

The answers to this question showed that half of my relatives self-identify for 50% or more Russians; 27% see themselves for 50% or more Jewish, and only 14% identify themselves Americans for 50% and over. On average, my relatives identify themselves as Russians for 52%, Jewish for 27%, and Americans for 21%.

The answers of my relatives surprised me. Although it is not a scientifically representative questionnaire and reveals the cultural identity of only these people, it is about the core of middle and senior age immigrants. It is indicative. There may be a variety of reasons for this conclusion. Just to say we are different from the people of the American mainstream means not much. It is indicative that about 30% of this group do not see themselves Americans, while being American citizens. For some of them, it may reflect dissatisfaction with the new life or inability to communicate on an equal footing, which is common for immigrants. For others, lack of mental flexibility plays a role. People identify themselves differently, and it has to do with their perplexed identity. In another poll, the scientific one, the Jewish constituent in self-identity prevailed. S. Kliger studied self-identification of modern Russian Jews in America:

> "60% of those living in New York identify themselves as "definitely Jewish" (70% in Philadelphia); 20% as "somewhat Jewish" (15% in Philadelphia); 15% as non-Jewish, and for the rest 5% it is "hard to say". (*Russian Jews in America: Status, Identity and Integration Challenges. Russian-speaking Jewry in Global Perspective.* Bar Ilan University, Israel, 14–16 June 2004)

Whether a person feels his identity confusion depends on the degree of his cultural integration. The degree of the integration, in turn, depends on the age when a person comes in, how long he lives in a new society, his ability to absorb a new culture, language, and habits, as well as his desire to integrate. Reconsideration of a person's identity in the migrant's mind may take place if one feels that something has changed in his views on self and the surrounding world.

American and Israeli psychiatrists, based on the statistical data, determined that Russian Jewish immigrants were significantly more demoralized in the US than their compatriots in Israel. Different moral status in these two countries makes me think of Israel as a country where Jewish newcomers (repatriates) easier self-identify with the Israeli mainstream than their compatriots do in America.

These Jewish newcomers *who become Israelis* come in to the land of ancient ancestors. There is a connection and unifying idea between them and the locals – nationality, they all descend from the Abraham's tribe, which alleviate them to self-identify.

The other newcomers *who later become Americans*, come in to the lands that historically did not belong to most of the local population. The neophytes are supposed to join this society where the only unifying idea is freedom for all and everyone.

Both uniting factors, the nationality in Israel and the creed in America are important but national factor remains stronger, hence, Jewish integration into the Israeli's society occurs more naturally and with less confusion. One could say even more categorically: Jews-repatriates to Israel do not have identity crisis – they returned to their land after two thousand years of dissipation, and that land belongs to them.

Jews of the modern-day emigrated from the Soviet Union, dissipated throughout as it was two thousand years ago. Anywhere we are, we found our place under the sun. However, there is just one country to which I feel like the unfulfilled debt. It is because I do not live there due to my own choice. Easy to understand that I mean Israel. Every time I am there, I see the ambiance of home and it makes difficult to me to answer the question of why I am not there.

The cultural self-identification of person forms with the family influence. With respect to this, it seems interesting to understand self-identification in mixed families, including Jewish and non-Jewish parents. It is very common in the Russian Jewish community. If only one of the parents is religious, then a child would be closer to the ethnicity of the religious parent. It is simply because the child would be interested to follow procedures, initially taking it as a game and then getting used to it. In the case of both parents being non-religious, which was more likely in the Soviet Union, a child or teen would consider the personal attitude each of the parents or grandparents. In addition, many other circumstances affect child's self-identification: the influence of the peers, reading books, social environment, national politics, etc. Even though both parents are non-religious, still each one may have inclination to the history or traditions of his or her ethnicity. That might develop a tense relationship between them, especially about the way they bring up their kids.

I have a friend who grew up in a family that exactly fits the case above: Russian mother and Jewish father. He recalls his maternal grandmother, a Russian Orthodox believer, calling him (the grandson) anti-Christ. His father passed away before his mother did but when it came to his mother's last will, she signed not to bury herself with her late Jewish husband. This is unusual, but it may and does happen.

Growing up in the mixed families, some people remain divided between two ethnicities during their lifespan; others take one side with no hesitation. In the former Soviet Union, it had always been a challenge to have one Jewish parent. Having both Jewish parents, at least you knew why you suffered.

The adult immigrants have a bigger confusion than the kids because of their accented language and lost courage when faced with challenges they did not expect, especially during the first years of immigration. Immigrants from Russia look like regular Americans, and first time met, people of the mainstream expect the smooth language, but hear a discernible accent.

The new cultural experience overlaps with the existing background, and we get a mix of cultures. I call it 'crisis' because if a cultural identity trifurcates, and he or she does not know which one prevails, that is a mess in the soul. If somebody emigrated at the age over thirty says he has no mixture of cultural identities, I will not believe him. We all are more or less experience the identity crisis. There are also some paradoxes of the new national identity that I would like to discuss.

Soviet Jewish writer and journalist, Ilya Ehrenburg disclosed the crisis of the undetermined identity in one of his poems (translated from Russian by LP):

> I cannot live with Jews,
> I part myself from them,
> But when the time has come,
> I am with you again.
> I am surprised by you,
> Your energy, your grit.
> And your nomadic fate.
> I poisoned with your blood
> And deeply in my soul,
> I love you as a troubled son
> Who is despondent and dismay,
> I'm feeling Jewish anyway!

The poet could not say better about the bifurcation of consciousness felt by very many Jews all over the world.

ON PARADOXES OF THE NEW NATIONAL IDENTITY

Russian-speaking Jews are basically not Russians – how could they be if they were oppressed there? nor are they classical Jews – where is Torah, prayer, Synagogue on

Saturdays? and not the Americans (Canadians, Australians, Germans). Their identity combines Russian culture and Jewish heritage intertwined with American experience. These three components do not stay constant: Russian culture fades out with every new generation and the western culture occupies more. As to the Jewish heritage, it is different and depends on the family tradition. Ratio between the three parts ranges from complete assimilation to complete cultural isolation. Comprehension of identity crisis of the new Wandering Jews shows a few paradoxes which go along with that crisis:

First Paradox - Americans verify nationality by the country of origin, whereas Russians establish it by the ethnicity. Russian Jews came to America already partially confused with ethnical and cultural identities. Adhered to the Russian culture, they are nonetheless, considered to be Jews in Russia. On coming to America, they became Russians in the eyes of Americans.

Second Paradox - as immigrants, Russian newcomers join other groups of immigrants: Africans, Asians, or Latino Americans commonly considered to be minorities. This status gives the latter some official privileges over the people of mainstream. These privileges however, do not apply to the newcomers from Europe, which automatically makes them members of the mainstream. As any Russian immigrant lands in America, he/she formally becomes part of the mainstream Americans because there is no other racial affiliation for them except for the *White Caucasians*. Thus, they become part of the American mainstream by default. One may not know even a word in English stepping on the American soil but officially, he is not a minority. However, there is something positive in it. Having fewer privileges than other minorities make this group more enduring through actively working forward and seeking advancement. Russian-speaking Americans are not legally a minority group. At the same time, in the people's minds, they are the *minority* because of a different culture and first language spoken. So, if they belong to both a *mainstream and a minority*, then who are they finally? The truth is: the community of Russian Jews is a *minority* in the cultural expression. When it comes to benefits normally credited to minorities – affirmative action or advantages for college admission or favorable status of minority business enterprise for small businesses – the benefits which they are not eligible – they are the *mainstream*.

Third Paradox – it is known that most of the Russian immigrants, especially those over 40, lean the Republican Party rather than Democratic, i.e. keep more conservative views in politics than the average American on the East and West coasts. This has to do with their past life experience in the country of totalitarian dictatorship. They do not want to have even the moderate lefts at power, not to say about the ultra-lefts and therefore, the prevailing number vote for conservatives. Paradoxically, apart from the classical conservatives, who embrace the religion and where the faith takes important place on the scale of values, Russian-speaking immigrants are mostly secular, and many do not object the abortions. The atheistic conservatism?

Fourth Paradox – comes from the contradiction between what Russian Jews are willing to be and what they really are. They left Russia many years ago but keep Russian outlook; they are ignorant of Judaism but consider themselves Jewish; they scarcely integrated into American society, but integration and success have not caused them a notable part of the American society as it has been in Israel. This is not only because of the different proportions of Russian Jews within the populations in these two countries but also due to different psychological comfort of self-identification of Jews in Israel and in the United States. Due to the national character of the State of Israel, self-identification of repatriates is natural and psychological comfort is better than in the US. Even the immigration is called repatriation over there and that is not a paradox.

Fifth Paradox - If we try to apply classical definitions of the nation to Russian Jewish immigrants, the definitions turns out to be inapplicable: these Jews do belong to Jewish ethnos but do not belong to Jewish nation.

JEWISH LOYALTY

We finally, came to the main question of Jewish coexistence with other peoples and the answer may give us a key to understanding Exodus as a historical conception. "A person who deserves my loyalty receives it", said American writer Joyce Maynard. That is the shortest answer.

It is true that the argument of Jewish disloyalty has always been a cornerstone in the treatment of Jews by the aborigine nations. It was often claimed as justification and one of the reasons for anti-Jewish sentiments. Solzhenitsyn wrote about the "Jewish sense of *not full belonging* to the country of residence." This is so logical and explainable – get the deserved people's dislike – for your *not full belonging* to the country! However, there is some stretch with this "logical" picture of the people's dislike. Why the Koreans, Greeks or other peoples who lived in Russia and had another national country were not questioned about their *not full belonging* to Russia? Why the Jews only?

And one more question: did the Jews who die defending the USSR in the war against fascism fully belong to the country? The number of Jews died in the Great Patriotic War (WW II) not including Holocaust was 140 thousand – 4.7% of the total Soviet Jewish population in 1939, fourth place after the Russians, Ukrainians and Byelorussians. The answer is obvious: Jews who died defending the Soviet Union fully belonged to that country!

How about the alive Jews? The truth is: many Soviet Jews in fact felt *not full belonging* and it was caused by the state's oppression and some people's negative treatment of them. What would you expect – *they can be oppressed but must fully belong?* So, is A. Solzhenitsyn correct? Yes, but with the clause that his statement should have been accompanied by the reason of *not full belonging*. The use of that statement as justification of the reason for anti-Semitism is wrong because it switches the cause and consequence.

The American Petition for Naturalization of the beginning of twentieth century shows the sensitivity of issue with the aliens' loyalty at granting the citizenship. Every immigrant was required by law to

> "…*renounce absolutely and forever all allegiance and fidelity to any foreign prince, potentate, or sovereignty, and particularly to RUSSIA, or any Independent State within the bound of the former, of whom at this time I am a subject*…"

(Russia is mentioned in this context because the petition customized for the person who emigrated from that country and accepted his US citizenship).

In other words, an immigrant had to drop his loyalty to the former country and pledge his faith to the new country. Nowadays, the application for citizenship does not contain such words as *renounce absolutely and forever all allegiance to foreign sovereignty*. However, the fundamental question of keeping loyalty to two countries simultaneously remains a problem for some.

Webster's Dictionary explains the word *loyal* as faithful to one's sovereign, government, or state. Faith to only one nation implies no faith to any other nation. Jewish loyalty has always been divided between the country of living and Jewish unanimity as much as their identity. There were divergences from this judgment for some people, but it is true.

Can anyone be loyal to two or more countries? This is not only the Russian question but international. We specify Americans of different descends as Italian Americans, Latino Americans, Greek Americans and many other Americans. Jewish Americans have the same prerogative to hold the twofold loyalty as Americans of any other origins. If you do not do anything unlawful that may jeopardize state's security, there is nothing wrong with the dual loyalty. In my opinion, the quality of being loyal is violated if person's action brings damage to the country of citizenship. The case of the US Navy officer Jonathan Pollard who spied for Israel and got life in prison (recently released) is an example. To me, the sentence is too harsh, and I think he has atoned for his guilt after spending over a quarter of a century in jail. However, this is what could happen if someone violates his loyalty to the country of residence in the sensitive subject of national interests.

The way America treated Japanese Americans after Pearl Harbor and Russia treated ethnical Germans (lived in Russia since the reign of Ekaterina II) after Germany's invasion in 1941 is now seen as cruel and inhuman. The world is different now from seventy years ago. Whether an immigrants roots from the friendly or hostile country, it should not matter. No one in the civilized society who originated from a hostile country should be blamed unless he does something unlawful to the country where he lives.

I am thinking about the changes in Jewish loyalty to Russia as a response to a bad treatment of Jewish citizens.

It was deeply in the Russian tradition that all citizens had to love the establishments, otherwise they were bad citizens. In the 1970s, all Jews were considered disloyal because of their potential opportunity to emigrate even though only a non-significant part of them had decided to leave the country at the time. Due to restrictions to occupy many positions or acceptance to universities, Jews felt their inferiority and started to leave in bigger numbers. Soviet officials considered their emigration as betrayal and this was used as a legal excuse for even more controls. With that, Russia, as a state, had always assumed to be loved by all her citizens, including Jews. However, since Jews did not expose the wanted love and continued to emigrate, Russia felt offended by them. Such was the relationship of Jews and the Soviet authorities until the end of Perestroika.

The official behavior towards Jews improved after the Soviet collapse but it was too late: about 80% of them had already left for Israel, America, Canada, Germany, and other countries. The remaining 20% are not limited to occupy any position or study in any prestigious universities, and Jewish emigration has drastically lessened. Moreover, I have a feeling (I would be disappointed if wrong) that numerous Russians now regret that so many clever, capable, decent, and even some cunning Jews left Russia.

Jewish stance on Russia depended on their treatment by Russians, and it affected Jewish loyalty to the country. The state of Jewish feeling towards Russia varied at different periods. Treatment of Jews by Russian emperors depended on the personal anti-Semitism of an emperor. Russian empress Ekaterina I in 1727 and later her (and Peter's the Great) daughter Elizaveta in 1742 issued orders on the expelling the Jews from Russia. Probably the Jewish expulsion from Russia was not enforced, and the next order issued by the Emperor Alexander I in 1804 was little more liberal. The list of prohibitions was not too long: Jews had to register; they were banned from holding any wine stores, restaurants, or inns. Discrimination of Russian Jews strengthened by the Emperor Nicolai I, Alexander's successor. The rules of his decrees *On Jews* (1828 and 1835) forbade them changing their names and living outside the Pales of Settlement.

    The emperor Alexander II treated Jews relatively better. I said relatively better because Jews were still required to live within the Pale of Settlement in small townships in the central or western Russia and did not have equal rights with Christians. Just some little relaxations like normal education allowance or privileges for the craftspeople were permitted to them. Nevertheless, Jews were not used to good treatment by any government and were grateful to Alexander II during his visit to Vilno (Lithuania). They organized an impressive meeting, which A. Kovner described in his *From the Notes of a Jew* at the end of the 1890s.

    At the time of difficult Russian transition from feudalism to capitalism, Russian authorities under Alexander III became harsher, and Jewish pogroms started at his reign with conniving authority. That triggered the first massive wave of Jewish migration to America and Palestine. A consequence of the pogroms, it continued during the reign of the last Russian Emperor Nikolai II, who was especially anti-Semitic. Cruel pogroms occurred in different parts of Russia, Ukraine, and Moldavia. Most of the Jewish immigrants of that time (1880–1920) came to America from Russian regions. The census of 1910 stated that the number of foreign-born immigrants whose "mother tongue" was Yiddish or Hebrew was 838,193 from Russia as country of origin; 124,588 from Austria; 41,342 from Romania, and 13,699 from Hungary. Many of them and their descendants later brought fame to America: Yul Brinner, Leonard Bernstein, Kirk Douglas, Benny Goodman, and many, many more.

The Bolshevik October Revolution of 1917 came and during the civil war of 1918–1920 over twelve hundred pogroms took place just in Ukraine. Many Jews took the communists' side as a better alternative to pogroms and stagnation in the Pale of Settlement. The white armies of the czar's Generals Denikin, Wrangel, Kolchak, and others massacred Jews for their support of Bolsheviks but sometimes the Red Army terrorized Jews too, although not systematically. The Ukrainian national army under Ataman Petlyura carried out the greatest massacre of Jews; tens of thousands of Jews were raped, beaten, maimed, and killed. The total number of Jews killed was thirty thousand, and with those died of wounds or illnesses because of pogroms, the estimated real total was one hundred and fifty thousand.

Since termination of the Pale of Settlement after the February Democratic Revolution of 1917, Jews were no longer restricted to live wherever they wanted. In the 1920s, hundreds of thousands of them moved from small Jewish settlements to big cities like Moscow, Leningrad, Kiev, Odessa, and Kishinev in hope for a better life. After decades of humiliation and pogroms of the 1880s–1910s, Soviet Jews could choose places where to they wanted to live freely. Jewish youth went to schools and universities and by the end of the 1920s to beginning of the 1930s, a significant number of the educated Jews had prominent positions as Soviet industry leaders, heads of scientific laboratories, in political institutions and Communist Party committees. Thus, they became members of the newly formed social class called the intelligentsia. The communist regime was cannibalistic, no question about it, but the terror of at least 1920s-1930s was not aimed against the Jews as the ethnos (that began later, in 1940s).

Solzhenitsyn, referred to Concise Jewish Encyclopedia, marked that in 1936, there were 13.6% Jews among university and doctorate students while the relative population of Jews in the Soviet Union was 1.8% then. For the first time in Russian–Jewish joint history, the Jews enjoyed equal rights with all other peoples. They returned their favor with interest. Jews devotedly served the new socialist society and many of them played outstanding roles in Soviet industries, arts, diplomacy, education, as well as in the notorious NKVD and KGB.

As mentioned, treatment of Soviet Jews equally to other ethnicities lasted until the end of 1940s with the "anti-cosmopolitanism campaign" against the prominent Jewish activists and doctors, and Soviet Jews started to feel an out-of-body experience then. That was not a disloyalty yet – it came later – but a fear for their own lives and fortunes. The disloyalty to Soviets came with the next generation, whose teen age fell on 1960s-1970s.

A few more words about those Jews who have been staying in Russia due to their reasons. They answered *no* to the question *to go or not to go*, though almost all of them had a confusion in the soul. I respect their choice and do not discuss the reasons. I would tentatively divide all of them by three groups:

First group I would name "former" Jews – those who deeply associated with Russian life, ways of thinking and self-identified as Russians, some even accepted the Orthodox Christianity. They are not many but that is their choice and it is very personal.

Second group, numerous, does not forget who they are, does not hide it any longer but not advertise their origin. They are active and feel inclusive contributors to Russian life.

Third group practice official Russian Jewish activities. They are influential, authorities speak with them, they connected with international Jewish organizations. They never criticize the supreme leadership but express moderate support. In any case, they may not be concerned about their future: even the most notorious anti-Semite would not blame or attack them not to be ashamed by international organizations.

The question is how long this equilibrium would last. Every people deserve its government, in other words, what is the people, that is the leadership. For Russia, due to historical and cultural reasons, the opposite association is also relevant: what is the leader, that is the people. The current Russian governance is Orthodox-Autocratic but strangely, it is not anti-Semitic, at least explicitly. If sooner or later the Orthodox-Autocratic anti-Semites come to power, the situation easy to conceive, then the first two groups of Russian Jews would become the hostages or in the best-case scenario, leave the country. I do not worry about the third group, they are protected: the showcase Jews have always been desirable even in the rogue countries. The first two groups are the concern.

The loyalty of the *host* ethnos to its ethnical country is naturally bound. The Jewish case is different. Since Jews, as a people, did not have their own country from the beginning of the first millennia until 1948 and had to live within other ethnic groups, their constancy directly depended on the relation between them and the *host* ethnic or religious groups.

Historically Jewish loyalty to Russia and other countries shifted with the altering of their treatment by officials and peoples: *the better stance on Jews, the finer the Jewish loyalty.* Here are the examples:

- During Arabic domination in Spain (Cordova Califate in tenth Century), Jews in Spain were under protection of the enlightened Calif Abdurrahman III. *Jewish scientists and thinkers were promoted to ministers and counselors,* and Spain achieved prosperity;

- Reign of Pole King Kazimir the Great in fourteenth century was a distinct in his *good treatment of Jews: they allowed to own lands and rent it*. During the time, Poland enhanced its political and economic status at Jewish participation;
- Emperor Alexander II treated them well and *Jews adored him;*
- Alexander III and Nicolai II admitted Jewish cruel pogroms and were anti-Semitic, and *Jews started massively emigrating from Russia*;
- Early Bolsheviks condemned anti-Semitism and allowed Jews to occupy prominent positions in the 1920s–1930s and *Jews sincerely served these authorities and believed in their equality with other ethnicities*;
- Stalin and later communist leaders persecuted and oppressed Jews within the campaign of *rootless cosmopolitans* in the 1940s–1950s and later limited their access to education and job promotions, and Jews *lost their loyalty to Soviet government and again massively emigrated when it became possible;*
- The new Russia does not oppress Jews, they have started redeveloping their national culture and have no limits in occupying any position, and *Jewish emigration nearly fades out.*
- The US has been welcoming Jews all the time, and *Jews did so much for this country that it is hard to spell out.*

Was Jewish exodus from the Soviet Union and its republics inevitable? Objectively – yes, because the *fifth record,* which apparently meant anti-Semitism was part of the state policy. On another hand, not all Jews wanted to use the opportunity to leave due to different reasons. After collapsing of the Soviet Union, prerequisites to the exodus diminished, and continued up to 2000s emigration was due to economic and social factors rather than political ones.

What we see from the history is practical Jewish approach to the country of residence: *loyalty in exchange of the equal opportunity and no persecution.*

Fair enough?

In Place of the Epilogue

Someday, in hundreds of years from now, the eternity would condense big historical profiles to small magnitudes in text-books. The history of Russian Jews of the twentieth century, for us long and dramatic, full of tectonic consequences, would likely fit in just a few lines. How these lines would look like? May be like this?

Limited to reside in special areas and restricted with rights… Underwent pogroms… Helped Russian revolutions to materialize… Participated in Bolshevik's dictatorship and terror… Helped building political regime turned out to be the worst… Glorified Russia by great achievements in arts, literature, scientific discoveries, inventions… Exposed to killings, burnings, gas poisonings by butchers of Holocaust… Prosecuted for "disloyalty, cosmopolitanism, Jewish nationalism" by Stalin's regime… Accused in betrayal of communist ideas and leaders… Accused in creation of communist ideas after collapse of communism… Suffered government supported and grassroot anti-Semitism… Most of them left Russia to the recreated State of Israel or dissipated throughout other countries by end of the 20th century…

Destiny of one people within one century!

www.ingramcontent.com/pod-product-compliance
Lightning Source LLC
LaVergne TN
LVHW011801060526
838200LV00053B/3649